Reader's Guide
to
LEWIS CARROLL

Reader's Guide to LEWIS CARROLL

Dr. Matt Bacak

CENTRUM PRESS
NEW DELHI-110002 (INDIA)

CENTRUM PRESS
H.O.: 4360/4, Ansari Road, Daryaganj,
New Delhi-110 002 (India)
Ph.: 23278000, 23261597

B.O.: No. 1015, Ist Main Road, BSK IIIrd Stage
IIIrd Phase, IIIrd Block,
Bangalore - 560 085 (India)
Tel.: 080-41723429
Visit us at: www.centrumpress.com

Reader's Guide to Lewis Carroll

First Edition, 2009

ISBN 978-93-80106-92-2

PRINTED IN INDIA

Printed at Balaji Offset, Delhi.

Contents

Preface

Either the well was very deep, or she fell very slowly, for she had plenty of time as she went down to look about her and to wonder what was going to happen next....then she looked at the sides of the well, and noticed that they were filled with cupboards and book-shelves; here and there she saw maps and pictures hung upon pegs. And thus begins Alice's fantastical adventures that have endured in their popularity for over a century, influencing contemporary authors, artists, musicians and inspiring adaptations to the stage and screen. Carroll's particular mix of creativity, fantasy, word play, satire, nonsense, and dry wit have gained him iconic status in popular culture with such memorable characters as Alice herself, the March Hare, the wise Dodo, a mad Hatter, the hookah smoking Blue Caterpillar, and the Cheshire Cat.

Lewis Carroll guarded his privacy while alive and after his death much of his personal papers were destroyed; nine of his thirteen personal journals survive although some pages are cut out. Thus suspicions have been raised and many myths and misunderstandings about the man, as well as critiques and speculative psychoanalyses into what kind of man he was including drug abuser, socially inept and an unhealthy interest in children. His stories for children remain the most popular, but not only was Carroll a prolific author of highly original fiction he also wrote essays, political pamphlets, short stories, poetry, and mathematical textbooks. He was a gifted mathematician and a natural teacher and created many cipher and word and logic games.

An avid photographer, he captured hundreds of images of still life, landscapes, and his favourite subject, people. Regardless of the controversy surrounding his life, his works have been translated to dozens of languages, many still in print in the twenty-first century, and Lewis Carroll remains one of the most popular writers read by young and old alike.

He also loved literature and studied such authors as John Bunyan, William Shakespeare and John Ruskin and went on to appreciate many others like Charles Dickens, George Eliot, Samuel Taylor Coleridge, Elizabeth Gaskell, and Lord Alfred Tennyson, who also became a friend. He expressed his creativity in writing poetry and short stories for his own magazines including *The Rectory Umbrella* which his siblings read to great amusement. The year after he matriculated to Christ Church College (the same as his father's) and moved to Oxford University (1851) his mother Frances died—her sister Lucy Lutwidge (1805-1880) then moved in to the Rectory to help care for Charles' younger siblings.

In 1867 Carroll travelled through Europe and Russia with preacher and friend from Oxford, Henry Parry Liddon (1829-1890). The same year his father died, 1868, his siblings moved to 'The Chestnuts' in Guildford, Surrey. With over ten years' worth of poems Carroll published his first major collection as *Phantasmagoria* in 1869. His epic nonsense poem "The Hunting of the Snark" was published in 1876. In 1871 Carroll's sequel to *Alice, Through the Looking Glass and What Alice Found There* appeared, including another famous poem "Jabberwocky". Carroll's humorous play *Euclid and his modern rivals* was published in 1879.

Author

Chapter 1

Introduction

Charles Lutwidge Dodgson (27 January 1832 – 14 January 1898), better known by the pen name Lewis Carroll, was an English author, mathematician, logician, Anglican deacon and photographer. His most famous writings are *Alice's Adventures in Wonderland* and its sequel *Through the Looking-Glass* as well as the poems "The Hunting of the Snark" and "Jabberwocky", all considered to be within the genre of literary nonsense.

His facility at word play, logic, and fantasy has delighted audiences ranging from children to the literary elite, and beyond this his work has become embedded deeply in modern culture, directly influencing many artists.

There are societies dedicated to the enjoyment and promotion of his works and the investigation of his life in many parts of the world including United States, Japan, the United Kingdom, and New Zealand. Dodgson's family was predominantly northern English, with Irish connections. Conservative and High Church Anglican, most of Dodgson's ancestors were army officers or Church of England clergymen.

His great-grandfather, also Charles Dodgson, had risen through the ranks of the church to become a bishop. His grandfather, another Charles, had been an army captain, killed in action in 1803 when his two sons were hardly more than babies. His mother's name was Frances Jane Lutwidge.

The elder of these sons — yet another Charles — was Carroll's father. He reverted to the other family business and took holy orders. He went to Rugby School, and thence to Christ Church, Oxford. He was mathematically gifted and won a double first degree, which could have been the prelude to a brilliant academic career. Instead he married his first cousin in 1827 and became a country parson. Young Charles' father was an active and highly conservative clergyman of the Anglican church who involved himself, sometimes influentially, in the intense religious disputes that were dividing the Anglican church. He was High Church, inclining to Anglo-Catholicism, an admirer of Newman and the Tractarian movement, and he did his best to instill such views in his children. Young Charles, however, was to develop an ambiguous relationship with his father's values and with the Anglican Church as a whole.

YOUNG CHARLES

Dodgson was born in the little parsonage of Daresbury in Cheshire, the oldest boy but already the third child of the four-and-a-half year old marriage. Eight more were to follow. When Charles was 11, his father was given the living of Croft-on-Tees in north Yorkshire, and the whole family moved to the spacious Rectory. This remained their home for the next twenty-five years. During the earlier times in his life, young Dodgson was educated at home. His "reading lists" preserved in the family testify to a precocious intellect: at the age of seven the child was reading *The Pilgrim's Progress*.

He also suffered from a stammer — a condition shared by his siblings — that often influenced his social life throughout his years. At twelve he was sent away to a small private school at nearby Richmond, where he appears to have been happy and settled. But in 1846, young Dodgson moved on to Rugby School, where he was evidently less happy, for as he wrote some years after leaving the place:

I cannot say ... that any earthly considerations would induce me to go through my three years again ... I can honestly say that if I could have been ... secure from annoyance at night, the hardships of the daily life would have been comparative trifles to bear.

Scholastically, though, he excelled with apparent ease. "I have not had a more promising boy his age since I came to Rugby" observed R.B. Mayor, the Mathematics master.

He left Rugby at the end of 1849 and, after an interval

that remains unexplained, went on in January 1851 to Oxford, attending his father's old college, Christ Church. He had only been at Oxford two days when he received a summons home. His mother had died of "inflammation of the brain" – perhaps meningitis or a stroke – at the age of forty-seven.

His early academic career veered between high-octane promise and irresistible distraction. He may not always have worked hard, but he was exceptionally gifted and achievement came easily to him.

In 1852 he received a First in Honour Moderations and was shortly thereafter nominated to a Studentship, by his father's old friend Canon Edward Pusey.

However, a little later he failed an important scholarship through his self-confessed inability to apply himself to study. Even so, his talent as a mathematician won him the Christ Church Mathematical Lectureship, which he continued to hold for the next twenty-six years. The income was good, but the work bored him. Many of his pupils were older and richer than he was, and almost all of them were uninterested. However, despite early unhappiness, Dodgson was to remain at Christ Church, in various capacities, until his death.

CHARACTER AND APPEARANCE

PHYSICAL APPEARANCE

The young adult Charles Dodgson was about six feet tall, slender and deemed attractive, with curling brown hair and blue or grey eyes (depending on the account). He was described in later life as somewhat asymmetrical, and as carrying himself rather stiffly and awkwardly, though this may be on account of a knee injury sustained in middle age. As a very young child, he suffered a fever that left him deaf in one ear. At the age of seventeen, he suffered a severe attack of whooping cough, which was probably responsible for his chronically weak chest in later life. Another defect he carried into adulthood was what he referred to as his "hesitation", a stammer he acquired in early childhood and which plagued him throughout his life.

STAMMER

The stammer has always been a potent part of the conceptions of Dodgson; it is part of the belief that he stammered only in adult company and was free and fluent with children, but there is no evidence to support this idea. Many children of his acquaintance remembered the stammer while many adults failed to notice it.

Dodgson himself seems to have been far more acutely aware of it than most people he met; it is said he caricatured himself as the Dodo in *Alice's Adventures in Wonderland*, referring to his difficulty in pronouncing his last name, but this is one of the many "facts" often-repeated, for which no firsthand evidence remains. He did indeed refer to himself as the dodo, but that this was a reference to his stammer is simply speculation.

PERSONALITY

Although Dodgson's stammer troubled him, it was never so debilitating that it prevented him from applying his other personal qualities to do well in society. At a time when people commonly devised their own amusements and when singing and recitation were required social skills, the young Dodgson was well-equipped to be an engaging entertainer.

He could sing tolerably well and was not afraid to do so before an audience. He was adept at mimicry and storytelling, and was, reputedly, quite good at charades. Dodgson was also quite socially ambitious and anxious to make his mark on the world as a writer or an artist. In the interim between his early published writing and the success of the *Alice* books, he began to move in the Pre-Raphaelite social circle.

His scholastic career may well have been intended as something of a stop-gap on the way to other more exciting achievements. He first met John Ruskin in 1857 and became friendly with him. He developed a close relationship with Dante Gabriel Rossetti and his family, and also knew William Holman Hunt, John Everett Millais, and Arthur Hughes among other artists. He also knew the fairy-tale author George MacDonald well — it was the enthusiastic reception of *Alice* by the young MacDonald children that convinced him to submit the work for publication.

DODGSON THE ARTIST

From a young age, Dodgson wrote poetry and short stories, both contributing heavily to the family magazine Mischmasch and later sending them to various magazines, enjoying moderate success. Between 1854 and 1856, his work appeared in the national publications, *The Comic Times* and *The Train*, as well as smaller magazines like the *Whitby Gazette* and the *Oxford Critic*. Most of this output was humorous, sometimes satirical, but his standards and ambitions were exacting. "I do not think I have yet written anything worthy of real publication (in which I do not include the *Whitby Gazette* or the *Oxonian Advertiser*), but I do not despair of doing so some day", he wrote in July 1855.

In 1856 he published his first piece of work under the name that would make him famous. A romantic poem called "Solitude" appeared in *The Train* under the authorship of "Lewis Carroll". This pseudonym was a play on his real name; *Lewis* was the anglicised form of *Ludovicus*, which was the Latin for *Lutwidge*, and *Carroll* being an anglicised version of *Carolus*, the Latin for *Charles*.

ALICE

In the same year, 1856, a new Dean, Henry Liddell, arrived at Christ Church, bringing with him his young family, all of whom would figure largely in Dodgson's life and, over the following years, greatly influence his writing career. Dodgson became close friends with Liddell's wife, Lorina, and their children, particularly the three sisters: Lorina, Edith and Alice Liddell. He was for many years widely assumed to have derived his own "Alice" from Alice Liddell. This was given some apparent substance by the fact the acrostic poem at the end of *Through the Looking Glass* spells out her name, and that there are many superficial references to her hidden in the text of both books.

Dodgson himself, however, repeatedly denied in later life

that his "little heroine" was based on any real child, and frequently dedicated his works to girls of his acquaintance, adding their names in acrostic poems at the beginning of the text. Gertrude Chataway's name appears in this form at the beginning of The Hunting of the Snark, and no one has ever suggested this means any of the characters in the narrative are based on her. Though information is scarce (Dodgson's diaries for the years 1858–1862 are missing), it does seem clear that his friendship with the Liddell family was an important part of his life in the late 1850s, and he grew into the habit of taking the children (first the boy, Harry, and later the three girls) on rowing trips to nearby Nuneham Courtenay or Godstow.

It was on one such expedition, on 4 July 1862, that Dodgson invented the outline of the story that eventually became his first and largest commercial success. Having told the story and been begged by Alice Liddell to write it down, Dodgson eventually (after much delay) presented her with a handwritten, illustrated manuscript entitled *Alice's Adventures Under Ground* in November 1864. Before this, the family of friend and mentor George MacDonald read Dodgson's incomplete manuscript, and the enthusiasm of the MacDonald children encouraged Dodgson to seek publication.

In 1863, he had taken the unfinished manuscript to Macmillan the publisher, who liked it immediately. After the possible alternative titles *Alice Among the Fairies* and *Alice's Golden Hour* were rejected, the work was finally published as *Alice's Adventures in Wonderland* in 1865 under the Lewis Carroll pen name, which Dodgson had first used some nine years earlier. The illustrations this time were by Sir John Tenniel; Dodgson evidently thought that a published book would need the skills of a professional artist.

The overwhelming commercial success of the first Alice book changed Dodgson's life in many ways. The fame of his alter ego "Lewis Carroll" soon spread around the world. He was inundated with fan mail and with sometimes unwanted attention. Indeed, according to one popular story that Dodgson denied decades later, Queen Victoria herself enjoyed *Alice In Wonderland* so much that she suggested he dedicate his next book to her, and was accordingly presented with his next work, a scholarly volume entitled *An Elementary Treatise on Determinants*.

He also began earning quite substantial sums of money. However, he didn't use this income as a means of abandoning his seemingly disliked post at Christ Church. In 1872, a sequel — *Through the Looking-Glass And What Alice Found There* — was published. Its somewhat darker mood possibly reflects the changes in Dodgson's life. His father had recently died (1868), plunging him into a depression that would last some years.

THE HUNTING OF THE SNARK

In 1876, Dodgson produced his last great work, *The Hunting of the Snark*, a fantastical "nonsense" poem, exploring the adventures of a bizarre crew of variously inadequate beings, and one beaver, who set off to find the eponymous creature. The painter Dante Gabriel Rossetti reputedly became convinced the poem was about him.

THE PHOTOGRAPHER

In 1856, Dodgson took up the new art form of photography, first under the influence of his uncle Skeffington Lutwidge, and later his Oxford friend Reginald Southey. He soon excelled at the art and became a well-known gentleman-photographer, and he seems even to have toyed with the idea of making a living out of it in his very early years.

A recent study by Roger Taylor and Edward Wakeling exhaustively lists every surviving print, and Taylor calculates that just over fifty percent of his surviving work depicts young girls, though this may be a highly distorted figure as approximately 60% of his original photographic portfolio is now missing, so any firm conclusions are difficult. Dodgson also made many studies of men, women, male children and landscapes; his subjects also include skeletons, dolls, dogs, statues and paintings, and trees. His 'controversial' studies of nude children were long presumed lost, but six have since surfaced, five of which have been published.

He also found photography to be a useful entrée into

higher social circles. During the most productive part of his career, he made portraits of notable sitters such as John Everett Millais, Ellen Terry, Dante Gabriel Rossetti, Julia Margaret Cameron, Michael Faraday and Alfred, Lord Tennyson. Dodgson abruptly ceased photography in 1880. Over 24 years, he had completely mastered the medium, set up his own studio on the roof of Tom Quad, and created around 3,000 images.

Fewer than 1,000 have survived time and deliberate destruction. His reasons for abandoning photography remain uncertain. With the advent of Modernism tastes changed, and his photography was forgotten from around 1920 until the 1960s. He is now considered by many to be one of the very best Victorian photographers, and is certainly the one who has had the most influence on modern art photographers.

THE INVENTOR

To promote letter writing, Dodgson invented *The Wonderland Postage-Stamp Case* in 1889. This was a cloth-backed folder with twelve slots, two marked for inserting the then most commonly used 1d stamp, and one each for the other current denominations to 1s. The folder was then put into a slip case decorated with a picture of Alice on the front and the Cheshire Cat on the back. All could be conveniently carried in a pocket or purse. When issued it also included a copy of Carroll's pamphletted lecture, *Eight or Nine Wise Words About Letter-Writing*.

Another invention is a writing tablet called the *Nyctograph* for use at night that allowed for note-taking in the dark; thus eliminating the trouble of getting out of bed and striking a light when one wakes with an idea. The device consisted of a gridded card with sixteen squares and system of symbols representing an alphabet of Dodgson's design.

Among the games he devised outside of logic, croquet, billiards and those played on a chess board, there are a number of word games, including an early version of what today is known as Scrabble. He also appears to have invented, or at least certainly popularised, the Word Ladder (or "doublet" as it was known at first); a form of brain-teaser that is still popular today: the game of changing one word into another by altering one letter at a time, each successive change always resulting in a genuine word. For instance, CAT is transformed into DOG by the following steps: CAT, COT, DOT, DOG.

Other items include a rule for finding the day of the week for any date; a means for justifying right margins on a typewriter; a steering device for a velociam (a type of tricycle); new systems of parliamentary representation; more nearly fair elimination rules for tennis tournaments; a new sort of postal money order; rules for reckoning postage; rules for a win in betting; rules for dividing a number by various divisors; a cardboard scale for the college common room he worked in later in life, which, held next to a glass, insured the right amount of liqueur for the price paid; a double sided adhesive strip for things like the fastening of envelopes or mounting things in books; a device for helping a bedridden invalid to read from a book placed sideways; and at least two ciphers.

THE LATER YEARS

Over the remaining twenty years of his life, throughout his growing wealth and fame, his existence remained little changed.

He continued to teach at Christ Church until 1881, and remained in residence there until his death. His last novel, the two-volume *Sylvie and Bruno*, was published in 1889 and 1893 respectively. Its extraordinary convolutions and apparent confusion baffled most readers and it achieved little success. It does contain an extremely concise account of three-valued logic when Bruno counts "about a thousand and four" pigs because he is certain about the four but estimates the remainder. In three-valued logic, unknown plus four = unknown).

The only occasion on which (as far as is known) he travelled abroad was a trip to Russia in 1867, which he recounts in his "Russian Journal" which was first commercially published in 1935. He died on 14 January 1898 at his sisters' home, "The Chestnuts" in Guildford, of pneumonia following influenza. He was 2 weeks away from turning 66 years old. He is buried in Guildford at the Mount Cemetery.

CONTROVERSIES AND MYSTERIES

THE PRIESTHOOD

Dodgson had been groomed for the ordained ministry in the Anglican Church from a very early age and was expected, as a condition of his residency at Christ Church, to take holy orders within four years of obtaining his master's degree. However, he evidently became reluctant to do this. He delayed the process for some time but eventually took deacon's orders on 22 December 1861. But when the time came a year later to progress to priestly orders, Dodgson appealed to the dean for permission not to proceed. This was against college rules, and initially Dean Liddell told him he would have to consult the college ruling body, which would almost undoubtedly have resulted in his being expelled. However, for unknown reasons, Dean Liddell changed his mind overnight and permitted Dodgson to remain at the college, in defiance of the rules. Uniquely amongst Senior Students of his time Dodgson never became a priest.

There is currently no conclusive evidence about why Dodgson rejected the priesthood. Some have suggested his stammer made him reluctant to take the step, because he was afraid of having to preach. Wilson quotes letters by Dodgson describing difficulty in reading lessons and prayers rather than preaching in his own words. But Dodgson did indeed preach in later life, even though not in priests orders, so it seems unlikely his impediment was a major factor affecting his choice. Wilson also points out that the then Bishop of Oxford, Samuel Wilberforce, who ordained Dodgson, had strong views against members of the clergy going to the theatre, one of Dodgson's great interests. Others have suggested that he was having serious doubts about the Anglican church. It is known that he was interested in minority forms of Christianity (he was an admirer of FD Maurice) and "alternative" religions (theosophy).

Dodgson became deeply troubled by an unexplained sense of sin and guilt at this time (the early 1860s), and frequently expressed the view in his diaries that he was a "vile and worthless" sinner, unworthy of the priesthood., and this sense of sin and unworthiness may well have had an impact on his decision to abandon the priesthood. There is currently no certain explanation of why he rejected the priesthood, or why he was, at this time in his life, assailed by a sense of guilt and sin.

THE MISSING DIARIES

At least four complete volumes and around seven pages of text are missing from Dodgson's 13 diaries. The loss of the volumes remains unexplained; the pages have been deliberately removed by an unknown hand. Most scholars assume the diary material was removed by family members in the interests of preserving the family name, but this has not been proven. All of the missing material, with the exception of a single page, is believed to date from the period between 1853 (when Dodgson was 22) and 1863 (when he was 32).

Many theories have been put forward to explain the missing material. A popular explanation for one particular missing page (27 June 1863) is that it might have been torn out to conceal the belief that Dodgson had proposed marriage on that day to the 11-year old Alice Liddell. However, there has never been any evidence to suggest this was so, and a paper that came to light in the Dodgson family archive in 1996 alleges some evidence to the contrary.

THE "CUT PAGES IN DIARY" DOCUMENT

This paper, known as the "cut pages in diary document", was compiled by various members of Carroll's family after his death. Part of it may have been written at the time the pages were destroyed, though this is unclear. The document offers a brief summary of two diary pages that are now missing, including the one for 27 June 1863. The summary for this page states that Mrs. Liddell told Dodgson there was gossip circulating about him and the Liddell family's governess, as well as about his relationship with "Ina", presumably Alice's older sister, Lorina Liddell. The "break" with the Liddell family that occurred soon after was presumably in response to this gossip. An alternate interpretation has been made regarding Carroll's rumored involvement with "Ina": Lorina was also the name of Alice Liddell's mother. What is deemed most crucial and surprising is that the document seems to imply Dodgson's break with the family was not connected with Alice at all. However, until a primary source is discovered, the events of 27 June 1863 remain inconclusive.

MIGRAINE AND EPILEPSY

In his diary for the year 1880 Dodgson recorded experiencing his first episode of migraine with aura, describing very accurately the process of 'moving fortifications' that are a manifestation of the aura stage of the syndrome. Several people have suggested the odd experiences Alice undergoes in the stories may have been inspired by migraine-like symptoms. Indeed a condition, Alice in Wonderland Syndrome, has been named after it. Also known as micropsia and macropsia, it is a brain condition affecting the way objects are perceived by the mind. For example, an afflicted person may look at a larger object, like a basketball, and perceive it as if it were the size of a mouse.

Dodgson also suffered two attacks in which he lost consciousness. He was diagnosed by three different doctors; a Dr. Morshead, Dr. Brooks, and Dr. Stedman, believed the attack and a consequent attack to be an "epileptiform" seizure (initially thought to be fainting, but Brooks changed his mind). Some have concluded from this he was a lifetime sufferer from this condition, but there is no evidence of this in his diaries beyond the diagnosis of the two attacks already mentioned. Some authors, in particular Sadi Ranson, have suggested Carroll may have suffered from temporal lobe epilepsy in which consciousness is not always completely lost, but altered, and in which the symptoms mimic many of the same experiences as Alice in Wonderland.

Note that Carroll had at least one incidence in which he

suffered full loss of consciousness and awoke with a bloody nose, which he recorded in his diary and noted that the episode left him not feeling himself for "quite sometime afterward". This attack was diagnosed as possibly "epileptiform" and Carroll himself later wrote of his "seizures" in the same diary. It's worth noting that epilepsy runs in families, and Carroll had at least one other family member with epilepsy (also recorded in his diaries), and that speech hesitations, facial asymmetry, as well as some deafness are not uncommon in certain epilepsies. It is also recorded that several of Dodgson's siblings suffered from a speech hesitation, suggesting again that any existing neurological condition was within the family as reported in Interviews & Recollections, editor Morton N. Cohen.

SUGGESTIONS OF PAEDOPHILIA

Dodgson's friendships with young girls, together with his perceived lack of interest in romantic attachments to adult women, and psychological readings of his work—especially his photographs of nude or semi-nude girls—have all led to speculation that he was, in modern parlance, a paedophile. This possibility has underpinned numerous modern interpretations of his life and work, particularly Dennis Potter's play *Alice* and his screenplay for the motion picture, *Dreamchild*, and a number of recent biographies, including Michael Bakewell's *Lewis Carroll: A Biography* (1996), Donald Thomas's *Lewis Carroll: A Portrait with Background* (1996) and Morton N. Cohen's *Lewis Carroll: A Biography* (1995). All of these works more or less unequivocally assume that Dodgson was a paedophile, albeit a repressed and celibate one.

Cohen claims Dodgson's "sexual energies sought unconventional outlets", and further writes:

We cannot know to what extent sexual urges lay behind Charles's preference for drawing and photographing children in the nude. He contended the preference was entirely aesthetic. But given his emotional attachment to children as well as his aesthetic appreciation of their forms, his assertion that his interest was strictly artistic is naive. He probably felt more than he dared acknowledge, even to himself. Cohen notes that Dodgson "apparently convinced many of his friends that his attachment to the nude female child form was free of any eroticism", but adds that "later generations look beneath the surface".

Cohen and other biographers argue that Dodgson may have wanted to marry the 11-year old Alice Liddell and that this was the cause of the unexplained "break" with the family in June 1863. But there has never been significant evidence to support the idea, and the 1996 discovery of the "cut pages in diary document" might imply that the 1863 "break" had less to do with Alice, but was perhaps connected with rumors involving her older sister Lorina, or possibly their governess. Some writers, e.g., Derek Hudson and Roger Lancelyn Green, who have fallen short of accepting Dodgson as a paedophile, have tended to concur that he had a passion for small female children and next to no interest in the adult world.

"THE CARROLL MYTH"

The accepted view of Dodgson's biography has been challenged recently by a group of scholars led by Hugues Lebailly and Karoline Leach and others who argue that Dodgson's diaries and letters reveal him to have been very different in many key aspects from the traditional image. Leach's book, In the Shadow of the Dreamchild, in particular has raised a considerable amount of controversy.

Lebailly has endeavoured to set Dodgson's child-photography within the "Victorian Child Cult", which perceived child-nudity as essentially an expression of innocence. Lebailly claims that studies of child nudes were mainstream and fashionable in Dodgson's time and that most photographers, including Oscar Gustave Rejlander and Julia Margaret Cameron, made them as a matter of course.

Lebailly continues that child nudes even appeared on Victorian Christmas cards—implying a very different social and aesthetic assessment of such material. Lebailly concludes that it has been an error of Dodgson's biographers to view his child-photography with 20th or 21st century eyes, and to have presented it as some form of personal idiosyncrasy, when it was in fact a response to a prevalent aesthetic and philosophical movement of the time.

Leach posed a new analysis of Dodgson's sexuality. She argues that the allegations of paedophilia rose initially from a misunderstanding of Victorian morals, as well as the mistaken idea, fostered by Dodgson's various biographers, that he had no interest in adult women. She termed the traditional image of Dodgson "the Carroll Myth".

She asserts his diaries show he was also keenly interested in adult women, married and single, and enjoyed several scandalous (by the social standards of his time) relationships with them. In later life many of those he described as "child-friends" were girls in their late teens and even twenties. She argues that suggestions of paedophilia evolved only many years after his death, when his well-meaning family had suppressed all evidence of his relationships with women in an effort to preserve his reputation, thus giving a false impression of a man interested only in little girls.

Similarly, Leach traces the claim that many of Carroll's female friendships ended when the girls reached the age of 14 to a 1932 biography by Langford Reed, who Leach claims intended to suggest from this that Dodgson was a "pure man" untainted by sexual desire.

Sherry L. Ackerman argues that the Carroll Myth also extends to traditional, mainstream views of Carroll's spirituality. Ackerman proposes that Carroll, rather than being a conservative Victorian Anglican, was actually a mystic. She links Carroll to the nineteenth century Neoplatonic Revival in Great Britain, as well as to accompanying trends of theosophy and spiritualism. The concept of the Carroll Myth has been opposed by some leading Carroll scholars, in particular Morton Cohen and Martin Gardner.

Chapter 2

The Annotated Hunting of the Snark

Nonsense may well be the most misunderstood of literary genres. Many have mistaken it for mere loony and meandering piffle—fun, but chaotic stuff. Yet, as the novelist and critic Elizabeth Sewell discovered in her insightful study The Field of Nonsense, a well-made nonsense world is strictly regulated. It resembles a game whose moves are ordained: they can't go in just any direction. Guests at the Mad Tea-Party have to keep moving on to the next seat; indeed, the plot of Through the Looking-Glass follows the sequence of a game of chess. Sewell sees nonsense as a logical construct which, unlike poetry, excludes deep emotion. If she is right, the phrase "nonsense poem" seems an oxymoron.

Fond of arbitrary order, nonsense has no truck with lunacy, with which it has sometimes been confounded. Whenever madness intrudes on a Carroll-designed world, this disturbing element must soon be ejected. Alice quits the Mad Tea-Party in disgust, and when, in The Hunting of the Snark, a character known only as the Banker starts chanting words "whose utter inanity proved his insanity" his fellow travelers react in horror and abandon him. True, the limericks of Edward Lear are peopled with mental cases like the Old Man of Whitehaven who danced a quadrille with a raven, but we glimpse each of them for only five lines, and clearly we are to think them pretty silly.

In nonsense, it seems clear, a fussy, orderly mind goes out to play, fully aware that it is kidding. Moreover, reading the

Alice books and Carroll's verse, one begins to suspect the author of playfully trying on the mantle of the Almighty. His creations are self-contained, little worlds made cunningly. This may be the very insight James Joyce had when, in Finnegans Wake, he likens Lewis Carroll to the Trinity: "Dodgfather, Dodgson, & Coo." Certainly there's a curious streak of impiety in the Reverend Mr. Dodgson. In the Alice books, parodies poke fun at poems of moral uplift and the hymns of Isaac Watts. "'Tis the voice of the sluggard" becomes "'Tis the voice of the lobster" and Watts's "busy bee" turns into a "little crocodile."

In The Hunting of the Snark, Carroll's verse narrative of 1876, abstract ideas are deflated to the level of objects in everyday use:

They sought it with thimbles, they sought it with care;
They pursued it with forks and hope,
They threatened its life with a railway-share;
They charmed it with smiles and soap.

Ever the mathematician, Carroll assumes that numbers are trustworthy things to be clung to like the Old Rugged Cross. Alice, even as she falls down the rabbit-hole, is calculating the radius of the earth. In The Hunting of the Snark, the Bellman, leader of the hunt, asserts, "What I tell you three times is true"—which declaration sets off his companion the Butcher on an involved calculation to demonstrate that 2 + 1 = 3.

Understandably, The Hunting of the Snark, An Agony in Eight Fits has been much less harried by critics than the earlier, vastly more popular Alice books. But as Martin Gardner records in his extensive bibliography, it has inspired two operas, an operetta, a couple of musicals, and some websites; among its many translations are two in Latin and others in Japanese, Hebrew, Russian, and Faroese. The talc is a sort of nonsensical Moby-Dick. In a hundred and forty-one bouncy quatrains, it tells how an expedition sails away to follow a blank chart, on a ship manned by a captain and crew all of whose names alliterate: a Bellman, a Butcher, a Baker, a Banker, a Broker, a Barrister, a Boots, a Bonnetmaker, a Billiard-marker, and a Beaver. They seek the mysterious Snark—we don't know why—on a quest that looks hopeless from the word go. According to the Baker, should the Snark prove to be a Boojum (whatever that is), then "You will softly and suddenly vanish away,/ And never be met with again." I trust it isn't to spoil any surprise to note that that is exactly what happens in the end: "For the Snark was a Boojum, you see."

For the reader who cares to explore this curious work, Gardner's painstakingly annotated edition will be a reliable guide. It reproduces the original illustrations by Henry Holiday, including one that the author objected to because it depicted the Boojum, a creature that Carroll wanted left to the reader's imagination. For the most part, Holiday's work seems realistic, except that all the human characters have swollen heads like Humpty Dumpties.

Helpfully, Gardner packs in some ancillary material of interest mainly to the devout Snarkophile: Holiday's recollections of working with Dodgson (the artist's job expanded as the author added fits); a mock-serious commentary by the philosopher F. C. S. Schiller; an additional fit by that masterful versifier J. A. Lindon; and a tract that the author inserted in each copy of the first edition, "An Easter Greeting to Every Child Who Loves Alice," perhaps to counter his story's final tone of bleak despair.

Well might he have worried about his effect on the little ones. As a child once myself, I found the Alice books terrifying. Empathizing with Alice, I thought her position as the helpless pawn of arbitrary forces, at the mercy of whimsical and imperious adults like the Red Queen and the King and Queen of Hearts, was a picture of childhood too real to take lightly. I recall being surprised that my teacher, whom I had trusted, was pushing these unsettling books on me; I suspected her of conspiring to make children feel powerless. It is true that Carroll's heroine maintains a remarkably English upper lip throughout her disturbing adventures, and yet in the end of each book she suddenly turns into a giant among pygmies, jerked out of a menacing dream world and rocketed back to reality. It is hard not to heave a sigh of relief.

At the conclusion of the Snark, there is no such rescue

operation. An ultimately despairing work, it seems too alarming to deserve a PG rating. I wouldn't want to venture into it again if I didn't have Martin Gardner by my side. At the age of ninety-two, with more than a hundred volumes to his credit, Gardner has long been one of our most useful deflators of flaky New Age fads in pseudoscience, an expert on mathematical and other puzzles, and an erudite annotator of classics, among them Alice. Had Gardner been around at the time, he might have spared Dante Gabriel Rossetti the pain of mistaking the Snark for a veiled attack on himself.

The book is particularly valuable for its patient and extensive notes and for Gardner's preface, in which he sets forth various interpretations of Carroll's fictive hunt. Critics haven't been able to resist reading the story as symbolism or allegory, and Gardner's own guess is that its story of a failed quest brings us to "the end of all searching ... final, absolute extinction—that dreaded return to nothingness with which the human race continues to flirt. Carroll said that when he wrote it he didn't have any deep meanings in mind, but that, if people insisted, they could take the hunt "as an allegory for the pursuit of happiness" Fair enough, although the Snark seems a kind of Rorschach test that lets us read it however we like: an account of any difficult and uncertain quest that comes to naught. Still, that it's such fun along the way ought to insure that this guessing game will go on indefinitely. And surely Martin Gardner's conscientious job of explication shouldn't need reattempting for a good long while.

COSMIC AND PSYCHOLOGICAL REDEMPTION IN GEORGE MACDONALD'S LILITH

George MacDonald, Scottish Victorian author, wrote the first fantasy novels for adults in English. He dedicated himself to literature after failing as a Congregational minister, ultimately producing over fifty books—novels, fairy tales for children, poetry, sermons, literary criticism. His writing never gained him more fortune than was barely adequate to support his large family, but it did yield fame enough for him to move in a circle of eminent contemporaries: Charles Kingsley,

Matthew Arnold, Henry Crabb Robinson, John Ruskin, Lewis Carroll, and the Rossettis were just some of the family's well-known friends and acquaintances (Greville MacDonald, 300-02).

MacDonald's current literary reputation rests largely on his fairy tales and fantasies. C. S. Lewis considered him a mythopoetic genius pressured by financial need into abandoning the fantastic in favour of the novels preferred by the public (George MacDonald xxix). Whatever the reason, MacDonald produced only two book-length fantasies for adults. These works bracketed his long career: Phantastes, in 1858, was his third publication, while Lilith, in 1895, was almost his last.

The concerns MacDonald expresses in his writing are largely religious. He was devout but heterodox, having been ejected from his first and only pulpit for suggesting in a sermon that the heathen might, after death, be given a chance at salvation (Greville MacDonald 180-83). He eventually found a spiritual home in the developing Broad Church wing of Anglicanism and a mentor in F. D. Maurice, whose church in Vere Street, London, the MacDonalds attended and who shared MacDonald's universalist convictions (Greville MacDonald 397-99). MacDonald was convinced that all humankind, not just Christians, would eventually enjoy reconciliation and unity with God, because God loved all people so much that he would send them deeper and deeper into the Hell of their miserable, isolate natures until—before or after physical death— they finally became desperate enough to repent, turn toward him, and undergo a spiritual education and/or purgation that might take millennia.

In Lilith he goes so far as to join Origen (third century) and John Scottus Eriugena (ninth century) in suggesting that even Satan himself will eventually be saved and brought into the Divine being so that, as St. Paul put it, "God might be all in all" (I Cor. 15:28). MacDonald's wife found Lilith disturbing and protested its publication (Raeper 364), while MacDonald's eldest son Greville hailed it as the best statement yet of "the Revelation of St. George the Divine". The bulk of contemporary reviewers sided with Louisa, but Greville too was correct. As Jeanne Walker has pointed out, Lilith contains its author's strongest affirmation of his doctrine of universal redemption. If, as the story has it, even a Lilith can be saved, who then shall be eternally condemned?

Anyone familiar with Jungian psychology who reads MacDonald (particularly his sermons and criticism) must be struck by the classically Jungian character of MacDonald's views of the soul and its development. Although separated by nationality, professional disciplines, and two generations (MacDonald was 51 years old in 1875, when Jung was born), both Jung and MacDonald rejected the rigid Protestant traditions of their upbringing to produce Neo-Platonic, Hegelian models for human spiritual growth.

Both were widely read in, and show the strong influences of, the German Romantics, Christian mystics, and medieval hermetic philosophy (in MacDonald's case the hermetic influence probably came through Jacob Boehem). Jung theorised that the psychic and the material are but two sides of the same Reality, while MacDonald believed that the material world of Nature is God's direct self-expression. Both believed that God dwells in, and speaks from, the unconscious. Both believed that spiritual growth is achieved through a union of opposites in the soul.

Both were marginalised by the religious establishments of their times, but stubbornly adhered to the Christian tradition. MacDonald all his life considered himself a Christian teacher, while Jung, according to Aniela Jaffe, "explicitly declared his allegiance to Christianity" and was "grieved" that his religious ideas were "not properly understood" (Jung, Memories, x-xi).

MacDonald's theology modifies mainstream Christian orthodoxy in the direction of the influences he shares with Jung. For instance, in mainstream orthodoxy, the agent of spiritual maturation is the indwelling Holy Spirit, which brings Christ's life (new birth) to the Christian soul in baptism (or, in some Protestant denominations, at conversion). Thus God indwells Christians only, and only Christians are able to "be transformed ... by the renewing of your minds" (Romans 12:2) to achieve a spiritual maturity "measured by nothing less than the full stature of Christ" (Ephesians 4:14). MacDonald believed, however, that each individual at his/her deepest core was indissolubly united to deity. He held that God "sits in that chamber of our being in which the candle of our consciousness goes out in darkness" (Orts 25). MacDonald distinguishes between the "bastard self" of our consciousness, subject to sin and error, and the true self, or "Christ-self" (Diary 17), the true God-made individuality of which God is root and ground (Sermons 3 80.) The "Christ-self" is the agent of spiritual development in all people, and destines all for union with God.

MacDonald's "Christ-self" thus has obvious similarities to Jung's concept of the "Self." Jung distinguishes the Self from the conscious ego as being the totality of the personality, conscious and unconscious, and the origin of the drive toward psychological development, or individuation. Individuation, though productive of a "larger" and more complete personality, is painful because it requires people to withdraw their projections and acquire self-knowledge they find repellent. People dread becoming more conscious, and every advance toward individuation entails suffering. The suffering caused by unwanted self-knowledge is also an inextricable part of spiritual growth for MacDonald. Before one can repent of sin and thrust it from oneself, one must see the sin in oneself, in all its ugliness. This is a major component of the purgatorial agony, and is graphically pictured in Lilith.

Besides the similarities in their models of the human personality, there is also a theoretical connection between the psychology of Carl Jung and the literary works of George MacDonald. Edmund Cusick's article "George MacDonald and Jung," lays out the case that much of MacDonald's work, particularly his fantasies, falls into Jung's category of "visionary" art. As contrasted with what Jung calls "psychological" art, which is based upon the materials of conscious life, visionary art presents material from the collective unconscious, and therefore teems with archetypal images and characters, and depicts archetypal processes. Jung cites Dante's Divine Comedy, Part II of Goethe's Faust, and Blake's poetry as examples of visionary literature. Cusick contends, I think rightly, that MacDonald's fantasies fit Jung's descriptions of visionary literature in their dreamlike quality, and their employment of the mythological, the monstrous, the grotesque, and the archetypal. His exploration of MacDonald's use of anima figures pays particular attention to Lilith.

Jung says that visionary works "flow more or less complete and perfect from the author's pen.... Here the artist is not identical with the process of creation; he is aware that he is subordinate to his work or stands outside it, as though he were a second person ... (15:72-73). MacDonald felt a divine mandate to write Lilith, and he completed the first draft seamlessly and nearly without correction, a method Greville MacDonald describes as "unlike anything else he ever did". Greville MacDonald also reports that even fans of his father's other work disliked the book. Jung says that visionary literature is usually "repudiated" by a public "astonished, confused, bewildered, put on ... guard or even repelled; we [readers] demand commentaries and explanations" (15:91).

I wish to suggest that the most illuminating commentary and explanation of Lilith is produced by consideration of MacDonald's Neo-Platonist Christianity and the archetypal psychology of Jung himself. ike the Divine Comedy to which MacDonald alludes (213-16), Lilith can be read on an individual, psychological level as well as on a universal one. On one hand it re-tells the story of humanity's fall and foresees its redemption, following a universalist model of Christian history and eschatology. On the other, it sketches a process of individual redemption much resembling the progress toward psychic wholeness described in Jungian psychology.

The Lilith of legend is a figure as shadowy, and with as many antecedents, as King Arthur. In Kabalistic tradition she was Adam's first wife, created like Adam out of earth, who rebelled against the inferior position in intercourse and the subservience it implied, and left him. When a hundred of her demon children were killed as punishment, in revenge she became a slayer of infants and seducer of sleeping men. She seems to be a Jewish adaptation of the Babylonian incubi and succubae, and in the fourth century she was identified with the Greek Lamiae, who were vampires.

MacDonald's Lilith tells the story of a young aristocrat named Vane who, through his encounters with the ghost of an ancient librarian (who sometimes appears in the form of a raven) finds his way into the "world of seven dimensions." The librarian/raven (who also claims to be a sexton) has a wife who presides over a cavernous chamber filled with corpselike sleepers who are waiting to "grow young enough" to rise. When she offers Vane a place among her dead, he flees in terror. In subsequent travels around this new world Vane comes to an orchard valley, in which a band of charming children are mothered by Lona, the oldest girl among them.

They either remain children perpetually or grow up to become stupid, vicious giants. Leaving the valley to seek help for them, Vane is sheltered one night in the cottage of Mara, a beautiful, solitary woman. She warns him of an evil giant-princess who has imprisoned the waters of the country in an egg and become queen of the city of Bulika, where she now murders all infants born. Continuing his travels, Vane discovers a skeletal, unconscious woman and spends months nursing her back to health in the hope that she will be a companion for him. But when she finally wakes she spurns him. He follows her to Bulika, where he is frightened by an "opaque shadow" in the form of a man, discovers she whom he revived as a princess in the palace, and is tricked by her back into his own world.

Mr. Raven, meeting Vane again in his own garden, reveals himself to be "Adam, the old and the new man; and ... his wife, ministering in the house of the dead, was Eve, the mother of us all, the lady of the New Jerusalem". The princess is Lilith, the "angelic splendour" that was Adam's first wife, who, after Adam refused to worship her, committed suicide and espoused the great Shadow, who made her queen of Hell. She had one child by Adam, Lona, who is now the eldest and adoptive mother of the Little Ones and whom, with the rest of the children, she is seeking to kill, for "her daughter appears to her an open channel through which her immortality—which she yet counts self-inherent—is flowing fast away". She has tricked Vane back into his own world so that she could follow, thus using his world as a detour around the stream that Mara has enchanted to block her direct access to the children.

At this point we can make some observations about these characters and the relationships between them. Adam, Eve, and Mara form a trinity of archetypes of the collective unconscious that represent a glorified humanity, outside of time in the Divine mind. One of the leading characteristics of archetypes is wholeness, meaning that they unite opposites, having a light and a dark side. This wholeness or quality of paradox is one of the most prominent features of these three characters.

Adam, for instance, first appears to Vane as the ghost of an ancient librarian who later claims to have read all the books in Vane's enormous library; thus he is a repository of human culture through the ages. He next appears as a raven—a bird that has negative as well as positive associations; it is the devil's bird, cursed for not returning to Noah's ark, the bird of the underworld, but also the bird sacred to Apollo and the God-sent bringer of food to Elijah the Tishbite. Adam's appearance as a raven demonstrates his protean quality, later confirmed by his observation that everyone has "a beast-self—and a bird-self, and a stupid fish-self, ay, and a creeping serpent-self.... he has also a tree-self and a crystal-self, and I don't know how many selves more—all to get into harmony". Adam, in other words, is the true microcosmic man, who has balanced and can manifest the whole human and sub-human creation.

He unites and contains culture and nature, spirit and body. His raven-self is a corrective opposite to his librarian-self; as a raven he exhumes worms and flings them into the air, where they become glorious winged creatures. This, he says, represents his role as sexton, in which he watches "for the hour to ring the resurrection-bell, and wake those that are still asleep".

The true role of a sexton, imaged in the raven, is to raise the dead, and, "except you are a true sexton, books are but dead bodies to you, and a library nothing but a catacomb!". Truth which is but intellectually perceived, MacDonald believed, is dead; a live truth is a lived truth. A librarian who is a true sexton, therefore, must not simply know, but he must realise—resurrect and embody—all truth expressed in human culture.

MacDonald's Adam is indeed Man, with a capital M. Vane calls him "the old and new man"—biblically, that is to say, humanity both fallen and redeemed, corrupted and incorrupt. In Vane's final vision of him, he appears as a kingly man "in the prime of strength, beautiful ... large and grand, clothed in a white robe, with the moon in his hair". Notice that the kingly man, who in traditional symbolism we would expect to be accompanied by the sun (sun = man and king) is instead lighted and crowned by the traditionally feminine moon—another paradox, or indication of completeness. This final appearance of Adam is not Man as the male half of a male/female polarity, but Man as incorporating the feminine, and therefore Man as whole.

We find in Eve the same archetypal quality of paradox. Biblically Eve is "the mother of all living." MacDonald says her "still face might be a primeval perfection; the live eyes were a continuous creation"; they have "life in them for a nation". Yet this vision of life comes to Vane through a door that looks like an upended coffin, in a dark cottage room illuminated by a candle and invaded by a wild-looking black cat, and she ushers him into a deathly cold room filled with the dead. When these sleepers mature—grow young enough, in the text's terms—they will awaken, rise and go. As with Gimbutas's Neolithic goddess, this cavernous tomb is Eve's womb (cf Schaafsma 54). The House of Death belongs specifically to her; Adam calls it "my wife's house". Even her sleepers are described with opposing metaphors. Adam says the dead out on the moor "lie thick as the leaves of a forest after the first blast of your winter" and later makes the reference to Dante even more explicit with a direct quote: "Thick as autumnal leaves that strow the brooks / In Vallombrosa". Yet in the same breath he adds another description: "... thick, let me say rather, as if the great white rose of heaven had shed its petals over it". Eve's dead are likened, therefore, both to the damned and to the redeemed in the Divine Comedy, and she is a Beatrice surrounded by the traditional paraphernalia of witchery (cottage, candle, coffin, cat). We remember that witches, in folktale and rumor, eat children—even, and sometimes especially, their own (Russell 239-40). Eve is thus the great all-Mother: all-birthing, all-nurturing, yet all-devouring.

Mara, daughter of Adam and Eve, is also a paradoxical, ambiguous figure. Her face is beautiful, yet she muffles it as if it were ugly; she is graciously hospitable, yet entertains her guests with dry bread and water, a cold attic and a hard cot. The Little Ones fear her as they fear the giant-princess, yet she seems benign and honest enough with Vane. She tells Vane that "Cat-woman" is "not my name" yet she sends cats, large and small, on her errands. When Adam has explained Lilith's history and nature to Vane, Lilith escapes them in the form of a spotted leopard, bursting through Vane's attic mirror back into the seven-dimensional world. Adam and Vane follow her to protect the children, Vane promising Adam that he will sleep that night in the House of Death before acting. But upon seeing the magnificent horse he is to ride in the morning, Vane, infatuated with the sense of power the horse gives him, breaks his promise and speeds off on the horse toward the children's orchard valley.

Upon crossing Mara's enchanted stream, however, the horse dies under him. Mara then sends a horde of cats which first save Vane from a menacing pack of wolves, then turn on Vane and drive him all night, relentlessly scratching and biting when he would stop, on the smoothest and shortest way to the Little Ones. This incident expresses Mara's essential paradox: she takes Vane where he needs to go by hurting him until he goes there. Mara is a savior, but her name means bitter (Ruth 1:20) and she incarnates MacDonald's notion of life (and, if necessary, an afterlife) as purgatory: human suffering as the necessary instrument of sanctification. In Jungian terms, this parallels the individuation process, in which the attainment of salvation (psychic wholeness) is preceded by the ego's crucifixion, an agonizing suspension between irreconcilable opposites. It is neatly appropriate that Mara is the daughter of Eve, for when Eve plunged herself and Adam into despair, she brought Sorrow into the world. This child is blessed indeed, however, for she is the redemptrix of her parents and all their other progeny, her brothers and sisters. Vane calls her the "shepherd whose wolves hunt the wandering sheep home ere the shadow rise and the night grow dark".

In contrast to this archetypal trinity whose leading characteristic is wholeness, we have a mirroring trinity of incomplete or fragmented humanity: Vane, Lona and Lilith, who end up sharing adjoining couches in the House of Death. Lona is an underdeveloped Eve. Innocent and maternal, she rules over the Little Ones as Eve rules her dead.

The name Little Ones is almost certainly an allusion to the passage in Matthew 18 which, with its cognates, MacDonald utilised heavily in developing his notions about the divine nature. Jesus here tells his disciples "Unless ye be converted and become as little children, ye shall not enter into the kingdom of heaven ... But whoso shall offend one of these little ones which believe in me, it were better for him that ... he were drowned in the depths of the sea" (Mt. 18: 3, 6).

The Little Ones might represent actual children, whom MacDonald saw as fresh from God and therefore generally morally superior to adults, or the adults who, during their lives on earth, have become as little children and so entered the kingdom of heaven—or both. As the Little Ones correspond to Eve's sleepers, the bad giants and the inhabitants of Lilith's city Bulika are an equivalent, on earth and in time, of the dead being purged in the Evil Wood and the Dance of Skulls. There clearly seems to be a relationship between the giants and the Bulikans. While the Little Ones presumably come from Bulika, brought to the orchard valley by the white leopardess Astarte or by their own mothers to save them from Lilith's programme of infanticide, some of them grow into bad giants—possibly Bulikans without the cultural advantages of civilization! Lona, upon entering Bulika, describes its citizens as "just bad giants". The situation of the Little Ones at the beginning of the novel, then, though they seem happy enough, is hardly satisfactory by most standards. They either remain children or grow into bad giants. Without water to cry with, Adam says, they cannot grow into a true maturity.

Lona is thus the immature counterpart to Eve the eternal Mother. Though she cannot stop some of her children from growing into bad giants, she cares for them as well as she can. She is described as a sort of Holy Innocent on the verge of womanhood. The distinguished MacDonald scholar Roderick McGillis finds her insipid compared to her dynamic mother ("Phantastes" 51), and the characterization is hard to dispute. At least to modern taste, Lona is insipid, but there is good reason for this. Lona, too, is a Little One, though the tallest of the lot. She has never cried, never developed any depth or complexity of character. She is the "heart's wife" of Vane, who according to Adam is "but beginning to become an individual". She is simply, blandly, good.

Opposing Lona's one-sided goodness in this trinity of fragments is her mother, Lilith. MacDonald's Lilith is Evil incarnate; the ultimate negative goddess. As the consort of the great Shadow, she represents cosmic evil; as the princess of Bulika who taught avarice and brutality to an innocent agrarian people, she represents evil as institutionalized in society; as a vampire who lives on the blood of others, she represents exploitative evil in human relationships; as the enforcer of sterility, enemy of children (who in MacDonald almost always evoke Christ or the Christ-self) and eventual slayer of her own daughter, she represents the self-destructive evil in the human psyche.

Vane, the third figure in the trinity of incomplete humanity, is described as a young man so isolated among his books that he has hardly developed a personality. His loneliness in the world of seven dimensions makes him realise that he is, in fact, "but a consciousness with an outlook". He has "preferred the company of book or pen to that of man or woman," and "if the author of a tale I was enjoying appeared, would wish him away that I might return to his story. I had chosen the dead rather than the living, the thing thought rather than the thing thinking!" These preferences of Vane's are dramatized when he grasps after the Raven's bird-butterfly only to have it become a dead book in his hand, thus acting the part of those whom Wordsworth described as murdering to dissect. But from this psychologically embryonic state, Vane retraces the developmental steps of the archetypal Adam from bookworm to butterfly. Symbolically, Vane too first espouses Lilith, then Lona (Eve). In the events of the story recounted to this point, Vane, like Adam, has loved Lilith, been rejected by her as an equal partner in a love relationship, and finally suspected her evil nature. As Lilith attempted to use Adam to establish her own dominance, so she used Vane.

When Vane (cat-driven or cat-guided) returns to the Little One's valley, he is not needed there to protect the children, for Mara's white leopardess Astarte fights off Lilith. What in fact he does do, in this stay in the other world, is reenact the second phase of Adam's prehistory.

He falls in love with Lona, Lilith's daughter and the children's acting mother, and is received as king by the children, who in his absence have made friends with the animals of the forest and taken to sleeping in trees. This is a sweet, sexless Eden, complete with serpent—a woman from Bulika, who fled from Lilith with her baby, and now wishes to return. She has started the children on the project of invading and liberating Bulika and taught them to use stones as weapons.

To determine MacDonald's attitude toward this military project, we may consult his sermon on the wilderness temptations of Christ. Christ did well to reject Satan's offer of the world's kingdoms, MacDonald argues, because true good must be rooted in people's hearts, and therefore lasting good cannot be achieved by conquest and rule, even if it were the conquest and rule of Jesus (Sermons 1 154-60). The mission to Bulika is, then, doomed to futility, but Lona in her innocence supports the plan, and Vane lacks both wisdom and will to do anything but agree—thus, in leading the venture, eating the apple himself. (In the midst of their preparations for this invasion, Vane makes Lona a mantle. This reminds the reader of his making clothes for Lilith, and suggests that Lona might fill the place that Lilith spurned. Appropriately enough, where Lilith scorned the clothes he made, Lona returns the gesture by making Vane a similar garment.)

This interesting re-rendering of Eve's temptation and fall in terms of the wilderness temptations of Christ is reinforced in Bulika, where Lona quickly discovers her mistake ("Let us leave the horrible place ... This people is not worth delivering") and her mother. She flings herself into Lilith's arms, Lilith dashes Lona to the floor and kills her, and Lilith is immediately withered back into the skeletal form in which she first appeared to Vane. Lona's death, like Christ's, has disabled Evil.

The equivalent in religious imagery is found in the early Christus Victor theological tradition, which sees Christ crucified as the bait God dangles before the ever-greedy Devil who, by swallowing Christ into death and taking him to hell, imported his own ruin as surely as did the Trojans. Lilith, the slayer and consumer, wishes to absorb Lona's life back into her own, but in thus swallowing her daughter and opposite she finds herself immobilized rather than rejuvenated.

Lilith seeks, in Lona's destruction, to stop up the open channel through which she conceives her own life might leak away. But in thus consuming her daughter she cannot, in fact, gain new life—energy and strength—for her evil purposes. Just as, in life, Lona's adoption of the Little Ones foiled Lilith's efforts to kill the children of Bulika, in death, too, Lona's goodness counteracts rather than potentiates her mother's wickedness.

There are a couple noteworthy points about this retelling of the Eden myth. First, though Lona gives heed to the temptress, whatever fault is involved is shifted to Vane, who, if he'd slept in the House of Death as he promised, presumably would have known better than to endorse the Bulikan scheme. Second, this Eden, though charming, is not conceived of even by its inhabitants as perfect. It is, in fact, a state of arrested development. The children need to grow, and they badly want mothers; in fact, hope of finding their mothers largely motivates their interest in invading Bulika. Static, sexless innocence may be preferable to evil, but is not MacDonald's idea of a terminal Paradise. Third, it presents a highly condensed version of the Christian history of creation, fall, and crucifixion/redemption.

Vane's situation now is like Adam's after the fall; between them, his Eves have plunged him into despair. Like Adam, his natural innocence (symbolized by Lona) has been slain by his capacity for evil (Lilith) and now he must eat his bread in sorrow (Gen. 3:17). Appropriately enough, his next stop is at the House of Bitterness, where Mara brings Lilith to repentance.

The conversion of Lilith says much about MacDonald's definition of evil and its cure. Lilith's essential sin is her insistence upon sovereignty over her own being: "I am content to be to myself what I would be. What I choose to seem to myself makes me what I am.... My own thought of myself is me. Another shall not make me!". In Jungian terms, she insists upon her ego's right to define and control her self, the right of her consciousness to dictate to her unconscious. The "Law of Liberty" to which Mara refers (384, cf James 1:24-25) is a simple reality of MacDonald's universe: "freedom" is the liberty to obey the God Within, or in other words, to live out our true selves. To disobey the inner God is not liberty; it is slavery to the false ego-self. Or, as Mara puts it, it is to "do as the Shadow, overshadowing your Self inclines you".

The human capacity for evil, therefore, in MacDonald's terms, is simply the human capacity for perverting our true natures, for refusing to be the selves God made. Evil is essentially an individual phenomenon (though its outworkings are corporate and pervasive) and the cure must be administered to people as individuals: that cure being a long hard look (enforced, if necessary) at reality. When Vane brings Lilith to Mara's house, Mara sends an inchworm-like creature into the fire until it glows with heat, and allows it to crawl into the dark spot on Lilith's side, whereupon Lilith begins to writhe and sweat in horror. Yet this torturing worm (or serpent) is nothing but self-knowledge—knowledge of herself as she is, not as she prefers to think herself. Vane says the worm "was piercing through the joints and marrow to the thoughts and intents of the heart". This phraseology echoes Hebrews 4:12: "For the word of God is ... sharper than any two-edged sword, piercing even to the dividing asunder of soul and spirit, and of the joints and marrow, and is a discerner of the thoughts and intents of the heart."

The torture pictured here is clearly a physical representation of the psychological suffering entailed by, first, a clear vision of the distorted self of one's own making; second, an experience of one's powerlessness over the nature of one's own being; and third, an experience of what a person becomes who insists on killing her true Self to feed the self of her fancy: "one who [knows] existence but not love ... nor life, nor joy, nor good ... a live death". Both the word of God (which, in John's gospel, is Christ himself) and the serpent are associated with wisdom. The agony Lilith finds so excruciating is nothing more than the truth. Similarly, the psychic suffering involved in Jung's individuation process is caused by the painful and relentless alteration of one's own self-image: withdrawal of projections, integration of one's contra-sexual characteristics (anima or animus) and acknowledgement of one's shadow, characteristics repressed because they are socially or morally unacceptable.

Her resistance blasted by these unremitting doses of reality, Lilith abandons her defiance. But the process of purification requires more than passive yielding. The only way for Lilith to complete the process is for her to open her closed hand; that is, to restore that which she has taken. The hand is clenched so that the fingers have grown into the palm; Lilith cannot open it, so Mara, Vane and the children take her to Adam and Eve for help. As Adam and Eve escort Lilith to the chamber of death, the Shadow shakes the house. Lilith, terrified, asks if the children are inside, and "at the word the heart of Eve began to love her." When Lilith cannot rise to her feet, "[t]he Mother lifted, and carried her inward". Thus Lilith's arrival upon her couch of death and regeneration has proceeded through transforming encounters with each of the three positive feminine principles. In absorbing her daughter and opposite she paralyzed her own evil nature; in the House of Bitterness she was led to turn from that evil and share Mara's tears; in the House of the Mother she speaks as a mother herself. Yet even having attained that couch, Lilith is told she will not be able to sleep until she opens her hand.

In Jungian terms, Lilith's development is blocked. She cannot make the required gesture by force of conscious will. She needs the intervention of the unconscious, or God Within, and that is what happens: at her request, Adam cuts off the hand with the sword of the angel who used to guard the gate to Paradise. Biblically, as noted above, the sword symbolizes the word of God, or Christ, who in Revelation is described as having a two edged-sword coming out of his mouth. Jung, quoting Simon Magus, associates the flaming sword of the angel at the gate with the divine pneuma (spirit) and says Simon's description of the pneuma corresponds to alchemical descriptions of the uroboros—the serpent! The sword, therefore, has the same associations as the "worm" that tortured Lilith with self-knowledge: It is God's spirit, holy wisdom, that transforms the natural being into the divine.

The symbolism of the clenched hand is rich, but its basic significance is clear enough that we need not explore its many possible correspondences. Though this is never explicitly stated in the text, Schaafsma, reasonably enough, infers that in that clenched hand Lilith holds the egg containing the land's waters, for Vane must bury the hand in the desert to restore the river that once ran in the orchard valley and the lake that will drown the monsters in the Bad Burrow—or, as MacDonald explicates the image in his text, the inhabitants of the unwholesome mind. But the process resembles surgery far more than mutilation. The wound does not even need dressing, for it is "healing and not hurt"; in place of the dead deformity, "the true, lovely hand is already growing". The image is certainly violent, but the violence is not of MacDonald's making; rather, he has provided some mitigation (the new hand) for Jesus's uncompromising direction: "If thy right hand offend thee, cut it off, and cast it from thee: for it is profitable for thee that one of thy members should perish, and not that thy whole body should be cast into hell".

Lilith, her offending member purged from her, sleeps. The agent of cosmic, social, interpersonal, and psychic destruction has given herself up right heartily to the Divine transformation. Reading the text on its universal level, Lilith's reclamation sets the stage for the folding up of the two trinities: the incorporation of the immature, fragmented humanity represented by the Vane/Lona/Lilith trinity into the glorified humanity symbolized by the "little family" of Adam/Eve/ Mara. The body of the white leopard Astarte, who died in crossing the Bad Burrow, is brought in and laid at the feet of Lilith, who was the spotted leopard. As McGillis has observed, Astarte is Lilith's "inmost soul" ("George MacDonald" 8), which will wake when she does. Astarte is Mara's agent, and to say she is Lilith's inmost soul is to say that, at the end of time, Lilith the Slayer will be raised as Mara the Savior. In other words, humanity's capacity for evil and the suffering it has caused will be truly perceived to have been midwife to human sanctification and bliss. In his book The Great Divorce, MacDonald's best-known disciple, C. S. Lewis, puts these words into the mouth of a dead and glorified George MacDonald:

> The good man's past begins to change so that his forgiven sins and remembered sorrows take on the quality of Heaven.... [A]t the end of things, ... the Blessed will say, "We have never lived anywhere except in Heaven.... What seemed, when they entered it, to be the vale of misery turns out, when they look back, to have been a well; and where present experience saw only salt deserts memory truthfully records that the pools were full of water.

Not only will Lilith become Mara, but Vane and Lona will become (or, in the language of St. Paul, become incorporate in) Adam and Eve. After burying Lilith's hand and restoring the country to fertility, his own act of atonement for "both [his] cowardice and [his] self-confidence" (391, cf Mendelson 211), Vane lies down beside Lona in the House of Death and begins to dream. His last and most climactic vision is that of the eschaton, when the golden cock crows and he, Lona, the Little Ones, and their animals, representing the world family (Mendelson 313) and animal creation, cross the new earth, are welcomed into the new heaven, and begin to ascend the throne of God. On the new earth, Vane says,

The microcosm and macrocosm were at length atoned, at length in harmony! I lived in everything; everything entered and lived in me.

To be aware of a thing, was to know its life at once and mine, to know whence we came, and where we were at home-was to know that we are all what we are, because Another is what he is!

Humanity again communes freely with nature and finds that they "mean the same". This is the flower and fulfillment, the fertile maturity, of that perfection of which the Eden of the Orchard Valley was but the seed. Vane's two espousals, the Bulikan invasion, and Lona's death retell the stories of the creation, fall, and redemption; Lilith's repentance ushers in the last judgment. Vane is the Adam, and Lona the Eve, of the new Creation.

In the symbolic tradition of Christian orthodoxy, this trinitarian imagery works perfectly. To be orthodox Jungians, though, we must ask ourselves, Where is the fourth? Wholeness is symbolized by quaternios: we have here instead, at the end of space and time, an Adam/Eve pair (which incorporates Vane/Lona), plus Mara their daughter (who incorporates Lilith). Who or what might be Mara's missing male complement?

For answer, we must look to figures on the fringe of the text, but hardly on the fringe of the Christian tradition out of which MacDonald operates. Mara incorporates Lilith, and Lilith's male complement is the great Shadow. The Shadow's significance is demonstrated when he attacks the army of Little Ones invading Bulika. He possesses the children upon whom he falls: "He did me quite different. I felt like bad. I was not Odu any more—not the Odu I knew. I wanted to tear Sozo to pieces ...". Mendelson identifies the Shadow as "Satan and

Death" and certainly the Shadow performs the functions of those traditional concepts in estranging people from their true selves and so spiritually murdering them. He is the agent of spiritual devolution. Mara casts him in the role of the false or ego-self, for to do evil is to do "as the Shadow, overshadowing your Self inclines you." Interestingly, when Vane sees the Shadow in Bulika, he (the Shadow) is closely followed by Astarte. The black void of death, therefore, possesses a "white shadow" named for a goddess of fertility—suggesting that the principle of Evil is itself shadowed by a divine agent ready to redeem the harm it does. Where the Shadow falls, Mara will be near to save.

Who, then, is Mara's male complement-the male figure who throws the Shadow into space/time as Mara, the Lady of Sorrows, throws Lilith? The Man of Sorrows, of course—the agent of spiritual evolution that MacDonald terms the Christ-self and the true self. He, like Mara, is the child of Adam and Eve as well as their redeemer.

He appears in the text only as the "beautifullest man" who comes to claim the Little Ones as they approach the heavenly city. Jung saw the Satan of Western culture as the split-off shadow of its Christ, and here we see that image working more than psychologically. Jung made no metaphysical truth-claims for his reading of Western mythology as psychological projection, but such a metaphysical truth-claim is necessary for MacDonald. If it is true that "only good where evil was, is evil dead", then all evil must be transformed, not conquered, subdued, or even annihilated.

In terms of the text, the Shadow, too, will come to the House of Death to "lie down and sleep also". In leaving, essentially, a textual hole where the figure of Christ belongs and working out the incorporation motif through the goddess-figures of Lilith and Mara, MacDonald proposes as metaphysical truth a linkage that, more clearly stated, might have disturbed his Victorian Christian audience far more than the book actually did. The male counterpart of Mara, who does/will incorporate Lilith, is a Christ who does/will incorporate the great Shadow, or Satan.

So much for the tale as an eschatological prediction. Obviously there is another level that strikes us closer to home. We can also read it as imaging an individual's struggle after psychic wholeness. On this level, the characters become personifications of psychic entities and potentials within Vane himself. The Adam/Eve pair become a representation of psychic wholeness in the tradition of the prince/princess marriage in fairy tales or the hermaphrodite in alchemy, with Adam representing the consciousness of a male personality, Eve the unconscious. Note the night imagery MacDonald uses to describe Eve in her first appearance in the novel: "A whole night-heaven lay condensed in each pupil; all the stars were in its blackness, and flashed; while round it for a horizon lay coiled an iris of the eternal twilight". The night, of course, is a classic symbol of the unconscious in Jungian thought. And, as mentioned above, in Vane's last encounter with the Eternal Trinity he does not see Adam and Eve, but a kingly man with the moon in his hair.

The inner fragmentation that reflects Vane's immaturity is represented by the division of his anima into Lona/Lilith, who between them constitute his Eve. Their mutually disabling encounter represents, in Jungian terms, that suspension between irreconcilable opposites that immobilizes the psyche. At the novel's end, when he brings Lona and Lilith to Eve's house and lies down beside them, he is, in the world of seven dimensions, on his way to the healing transformation, which will unite them. Mara, Bitterness, is here the agent of the transformation; as Sorrow led Adam and Eve to repentance, so she is the one who takes Vane and his Eves to the House of Death.

Therefore Vane's eschatological vision at the novel's end, in which he is united not only with Lona, but also with the Little Ones and the beasts in approaching the heavenly city, represents his own future as a whole human being—a microcosmic Adam—as well as the redemption of the universe. And indeed this is a true vision of Vane's telios, but he has not realized it yet. Although in the world of seven dimensions Vane has, through the crucible of guilt, self-knowledge, repentance, and atonement, attained sufficient spiritual maturity to yield right heartily to the Divine sleep of remaking, in his own world he is still a Little One who must weep before he can grow. And to that world he must return. As he is ascending God's throne, Vane is drawn to a little door with a golden lock and pushed through to discover himself, once more, alone in his library.

This conclusion of the book is certainly an anticlimactic shock for the reader, and has been interpreted by many critics as a negation or reversal of the hope promised by the eschatological vision. However, as Mendelson observes, a return to the real world is a convention of the quest romance, and does not belie the visionary experience. In this case, I think the significance of the return is made clear by the final chapter. Another has given Vane this dream that he did not seek and did not willingly leave; therefore, as he says, "that Other is able to fulfill it". Such an end was foretold when Vane first met Mara, and she predicted, "The time will come when you must house with me many days and many nights ... not willingly!"

This prophecy is never fulfilled in the world of seven dimensions, but the first thing Vane says to the reader about his post-visionary condition is, "I have not yet found Lona, but Mara is much with me. She has taught me many things, and is teaching me more". Vane, with his dead Lona and his bound Lilith, is once more in the House of Bitterness, suffering until hard-won self-knowledge will through repentance send his capacity for evil into a transforming sleep, until he by faithful obedience restores that which it has taken, and until his primal innocence, which has died as the virginal Kore, is resurrected as Eve, the goddess who, through her bearing of ancient sorrow, has become the true and fertile mother of our Father's children.

In the final chapter, Vane is uncertain whether he is still sleeping in the House of Death and dreaming his return to his "own" world, or whether the whole other world experience itself was a dream. The deliberate blurring of the distinction between dream and waking makes what was for MacDonald an essential point about the nature of human life, which he asserts both here and in Phantastes in the quotation from Novalis: "'Our life is no dream, but it should and will perhaps become one.'" When, in this life or the next, Vane "wakes" as his true self, the reality he perceives with his cleared vision (or, in Blakean terms, through his cleansed doors of perception) will make everything he experienced while his self was overshadowed into a cloudy dream that has passed. Then, as he says, "I shall know that I wake, and shall doubt no more". And then, in and as the eternal Adam, he will indeed walk on the new earth, under the new heaven, and ascend the throne of God.

In this essay I have emphasized the commonality of MacDonald's thought with Jung's, but I do not wish to overstate the similarity. Both men criticized Western Christianity's tendency toward dualism in setting up an opposing principle as the implicit or practical (if not the technical, theological) equal of God, and anticipating an eternity divided into two camps: the Good God and his adherents forever separated from and triumphant over the Bad God (Satan) and his. Jung resolved the difficulty by approaching the problem from the psychological angle, dealing with the "God-image" in the human psyche rather than God as a metaphysical concept. Evil, he insisted, has real psychological existence; that is, the Self, the whole of the psyche, contains evil as well as good.

The end of the individuation process is not goodness, but wholeness, which means recognizing, in ourselves, both good and its opposite. Christ, the Perfect Man, is only an adequate symbol of the Self if we include an opposite—Satan or Antichrist—to complement Christ's goodness. Following the logic of prioritizing the psychological, Jung in one of his most famous works, Answer to Job analyzed the Biblical God as a rather undifferentiated consciousness in which benevolence and tyranny were uncritically mixed, who was seeking to complete his own individualization process through union with humanity. Thus, Jung avoids dualism by seeing evil as part of God.

MacDonald takes a more traditional approach, affirming God as Summum Bonum and denying, as do the Church fathers, that evil has actual existence, being rather a lack or perversion of goodness. MacDonald's Christ-self, unlike Jung's Self, does not include evil. MacDonald is only more self-consistent than mainstream Christian tradition in his insistence that because evil is no thing, it will be eradicated from God's creation as soon as God's creatures—slowly and painfully—cease to prefer phantoms of their own manufacture to the selves that God made, and that much of what people call "evil" (sorrow, pain and death, for instance) is actually the Shadow of the Good—or, if one prefers, the refining fire of purgatory. Thus our text's last word on Lilith, the primal carrier of evil, is given in answer to Lona's question, "Who were her parents?" My father,'" answered Adam, "'is her father also'".

Chapter 3

The Search for Non-Being

Humpty Dumpty informs Alice that 'there are three hundred and sixty four days when you might get un-birthday presents'. It is obvious to him that un-birthdays are real Beings and not mere utterances. His statement is another augmentation to one of the oldest and rudimentary philosophical controversies: whether Non-Being, like Being, exists. Footprints of this controversy, which was initially conceived by Greek philosophy, can be tracked all over the two books of Alice. Carroll conveys, through Alice's discourses with the various figures she meets on her way, his belief that Non-Being does indeed exist. This stand can be inferred not just from Humpty Dumpty's statement but from other passages in Alice as well.

The beginning of the 6th Century B.C. was a defining moment in the history of mankind intellectual thought. From this time on, for a period that lasted around 150 years, some Greeks, in later years called the 'pre-Socratics', began to ask new questions and propound new answers about the nature of the universe. (Most of the pre-Socratics flourished not in Athens, nor even on mainland Greece, but in Asia Minor, Lower Italy and Sicily. 'Greek', in this context, is a cultural expression rather than a geographical one.) The pre-Socratics were the first to formulate tenets that were based on reasonable arguments rather than on theological doctrines, and they set the foundation on which the future intellectual revolution in philosophy would be created by Socrates, Plato and Aristotle.

But before we follow Alice into Wonderland, we should recall the roots of the controversy, in Elea in Lower Italy, in the early 5th Century BC. There, Parmenides, asserted in a poem that he had composed, that only the 'Is' is, whilst to speak of the 'Is not' is to take a '. . . wholly incredible course, since you cannot recognise Not Being (for this is impossible), nor could you speak of it, for thought and Being are the same thing.' The grammar used by Parmenides in his poetic assertion gave rise to different interpretations. Did he mean 'is' as a predicate, as for instance in a sentence like: 'Parmenides is Greek', or is it the 'is' of Existence? It seems most likely that the 'IS' means Existence since, later on in the poem, he characterise the 'IS' as a well-rounded ball, namely having material properties. Accordingly, to Parmenides, Non-Being was analogous to Non-existence.

Parmenides' concept, embraced by his disciples (the Eleatics) is considered to be a refutation of the teachings of his predecessor, Pythagoras, who claimed that a kind of Non-Being does indeed exist. Other pre-Socratics, such as Democritus of Abdera, the most prominent of the atomist scholars, and one who wrote and taught some decades after Parmenides, also insisted, like Pythagoras, that Non-Being must in fact exist, in spite of Parmenides' rigorous logic. Certainly, the pre-Socratic philosophers conceived Being as (being) made of matter. Democritus for instance, and other Atomists, viewed Being as comprised of an infinite number of small particles- the word 'atoms' literally meaning 'indivisible'. Atoms combine to form all the objects in the universe. They are solid, microscopic, move in space and join one another to form more complex objects. Movement of atoms is possible since imbetween each one of them there is a void.

The void is not nothing at all - it is Non-Being. A Non-being that, however, exists. But Greek philosophy had to pass through another thinking revolution in order to postulate the existence of non material Beings; The leading figure in this revolution was Plato who conceived the tenet of the Forms (Ideai). The Forms are the ultimate real Beings, having no spatial nor material properties.

In the *Sophist* dialogue, Plato argues that what 'is not' in some sense also 'is', refuting Parmenides' concept of the impossibility of the Non-Being to exist. Non-Being is just a being characterised only by its difference from 'another' being. He asserted that the antinomy between Being and Non-Being is false. The only real antinomy is that of a single object of consciousness and all other things from which it is distinguished. Carroll was no stranger to Greek philosophy, which was one of the subjects he studied as part of the Classics curriculum at Christ Church. It seems that he embraced Platonic Ideational thought by asseverating the existence of un-birthdays - un-birthdays are non-material beings. Nor are they the only ones to be found in Carroll's realm of non-material beings. There also is the dog's temper. The Red Queen urges Alice:

'Try another Subtraction sum.

Take a bone from a dog: what remains?

Alice considered. 'The bone wouldn't remain, of course, if I took it -and the dog wouldn't remain; it would come to bite me — and I'm sure I shouldn't remain!'

'Then you think nothing would remain?' said the Red Queen.

'I think that's the answer.'

'Wrong, as usual,' said the Red Queen: 'the dog's temper would remain.'

'But I don't see how -'

'Why, look here!' the Red Queen cried. 'The dog would lose its temper, wouldn't it?'

'Perhaps it would,' Alice replied cautiously.

'Then if the dog went away, its temper would remain!' the Queen exclaimed triumphantly.'

Carroll is over and over again seen to be fascinated by the idea that Nothingness is more than what meets the eye:

Take some more tea,' the March Hare said to Alice, very earnestly.

'I've had nothing yet,' Alice replied in an offended tone, 'so I can't take more.'

'You mean you can't take LESS,' said the Hatter: 'it's very easy to take MORE than nothing.'

The Cheshire cat's grin too is a non-material being. The

cat appears from the void and slowly vanishes back into it leaving behind him just a grin. Can a cat's grin exist without its master? Carroll does not hesitate, he is certain that it does. For it is clear that to Carroll a grin is just a Platonic Form - a nonmaterial being which has real existence. He is not at a loss to see the phenomena of the cat's head without its body, the possibility of which brings about a heated disputation between the king and the executioner.

The executioner's argues that: 'You couldn't cut off a head unless there was a body to cut off from', but the king is not at all convinced. To him, like to Carroll: ''anything that had a head could be beheaded.' and the executioner's philosophical observations are just 'talking nonsense'. However, there is a philosophical hurdle for un-birthdays. Birthdays and Un-birthdays are of course also expressions of time. Plato did not consider time as a form. He held that: 'The moving images of eternity we call time, days and nights, are the parts of time' (Timaeus). One must therefore question whether Birthdays or Un-birthdays are indeed Platonic Forms.

Humpty Dumpty is not in the least troubled by this philosophical hurdle. He remembers well that the Hatter told Alice that he 'knew Time' and that one cannot 'talk about wasting it' because Time is 'him'. Time, says the Hatter, is someone that if you only 'knew how to keep on good terms with him, he'd do almost anything you liked with the clock', for instance 'you could keep it to half-past one as long as you liked'.

To Humpty Dumpty, as well as to the Hatter, Time is a real entity. Once we become aware of this reality, Plato's concept presents no hindrance to the existence of either birthdays or un-birthdays. As with Time, Numbers too are portrayed by Carroll as real entities. Upon entering the garden Alice comes up to three card gardeners presented by Carroll as Two, Five and Seven. To Carroll, the Christ Church mathematician, Numbers, like Time, are more than just abstract figures - they are real Beings. Carroll venerates here Pythagoras' concept about Numbers. Aristotle records that the Pythagoreans held that Numbers were: the first things in the whole of nature' and that 'the elements of numbers are the elements of all things'

Numbers also play an important role in Plato's philosophy. It is commonly construed that he inclined to interpret his theory of the Forms in terms of mathematics as in the *Timaeus* dialogue; Mathematical entities have real existence; they are nonmaterial entities that exist in the realm of the Forms.

Aristotle however held (in the *Metaphysics*) that Plato thought of the Number as an intermediate substance between the Forms and the world of appearances. The Neo-Platonics, who flourished after Aristotle, believed, contrariwise, that numbers were identified by Plato with Forms. Whatever is the right meaning that Plato intended for the numbers, it is widely agreed that the Pythagorean number theory is the direct ancestor of the Platonic theory of Forms.

Numbers afford Carroll creative freedom. The gardeners' numbers are equivalent to their identities, so it is only natural for the Queen, coming upon the gardeners, to ask: 'And who are these?' Since the gardeners 'were lying on their faces', 'she could not tell whether they were gardeners or soldiers, or courtiers, or three of her own children'.

Plato, as part of the cave allegory, asserts that the identity of a human being is not derived from their body but from the character of the their soul. Carroll, in pure Platonic reasoning, professed that a Number like the soul, is a nonmaterial entity that harbours the true identity of its subject. The gardeners' bodies are visible but, alas, their numbers are out of sight, hence their identity vanished and their very existence is in doubt. Another issue that Carroll coped with was the question raised by Greek philosophy about the true nature of the Being. Ever since the pre-Socratics, Greek philosophers have disagreed with each other about the very nature of Being. Is it one or is it many? Can it move or is it immovable? This controversy is interwoven in the two Alice books. In order to follow Carroll's adaptations in this respect, one must go back to the pre-Socratics' tenets and 'Begin at the beginning'.

At the beginning, Parmenides taught that the IS, namely

Being, or sole existence, is characterised as being one and not many, as neither generated nor capable of being extinguished, and as complete, not divisible into parts and immovable. Being is immovable- due to its being one and as such filling the whole universe with nowhere further to extend. Alice, it seems, is aware of this concept. After drinking from the 'DRINK ME' bottle and growing in size to such an extent that her whole Being fills the room completely leaving no space for anything else, she observes : 'Oh, you foolish Alice!' she answered herself. 'How can you learn lessons in here? Why, there's hardly room for YOU, and no room at all for any lesson-books!'

Parmenides' disciple, Zeno of Elea, formulated a few paradoxes to demonstrate his masters' teachings that Being is one and motionless. The most famous of his paradoxes is Achilles and the tortoise. If, in the race, the tortoise has a start on Achilles, then Achilles can never reach the tortoise for, while Achilles traverses the distance from his starting point to that of the tortoise, the tortoise will have gone a certain distance and, while Achilles traverses this distance, the tortoise goes still further, ad infinitum. Consequently, Achilles may run indefinitely without overtaking the tortoise.

The Achilles paradox purported to force upon the listener the truism that motion is impossible and what we see as motion is an illusion. Pursuant to Zeno's paradox Carroll wrote a lovely short piece which he called What the tortoise said to Achilles. Achilles, trying to follow the tortoise's reasoning, is left by the end mentally near despair failing to understand Carroll's adaptation of Zeno's paradox which leads to infinity.

Parmenides further portrayed the IS as: 'perfect from every direction, like the mass of a well-rounded ball, in equipoise every way from the middle'. This portrayal raised a question - if that is so then the IS extends only as far as the periphery of the ball. What exists beyond? Parmenides' pupil, Melissus, was aware of this seeming inconsistency and added his own refinement. He negated every form of void: to him, Being is infinite in space as well as in time. Any other possibility will be inherently contradictory since it will imply a presence of some Non-Being beyond the edge. Another pre-Socratic who conceived a tenet about the nature of Being was Heraclitus of Ephesus, in Asia Minor, a predecessor of Parmenides, who lived about 500 B.C. Unlike Parmenides' 'oneness' concept, Heraclitus taught that existence is dualistic - both 'oneness' and plurality. He further asserted that the nature of all things is governed by one universal principle-that of the logos, the ultimate reality, which is manifested by the interdependence of the opposites and by the process of flux (Panta Rhei) and change. His teaching is defined as the unity of the opposites.

The opposites may appear different but at the same time they are held together in unity as, for instance, health and disease, or hot and cold. They in fact define each other. As Heraclitus put it: 'Justice, which is a good, would be unknown were it not for injustice, which is an evil'. The existence of the opposites depends only on the difference of the motion on 'the way upwards' from that on 'the way downwards'; all things, therefore, are at once identical and not identical.

Humpty Dumpty, a true Heraclitean, asserts that there must exist an opposite to a birthday which is an un-birthday. Alice enters the world where Humpty Dumpty lives through the looking glass, and, as is common in mirror worlds, every image has its opposite. The mirror images are different, right appears as left and vice versa, but at same time they are identical, since after all they are images of the same object. Lewis Carroll rejects Parmenides' concept of oneness and the impossibility of movement; Equally Heraclitean he embraces the view that everything is in an everlasting process of flux, change and transformation, while its essence remains the same. This is evidenced by Alice's encounter with the Caterpillar: Who are you', asks the Caterpillar and Alice answers:

'I - I hardly know, Sir, just at present I know - at least I know who I was when I got up in this morning, but I think I must have been changed several times since then'. Alice is uncertain: 'I can't understand my self, to begin with; and being so many different sizes in a day is very confusing.'

The caterpillar, unlike Alice, is 'not at bit' confused and

does not 'feel queer' at his transformation 'into a chrysalis, some day, and then after that into a butterfly'. And why should he? As an Heraclitean thinker he knows that the process of his transformation does not change his essence and identity.

Carroll submits more evidence that sameness is not lost due to change. In one instance Alice refers to her previous height changes when she briefly suffers an identity crisis:

'I wonder if I've changed in the night? Let me think; was I the same when I got up this morning?'

And the unavoidable question: 'But if I am not the same, who in the world am I?' She ponders whether she 'could have been changed for any one' of the children she knew - Ada or Mabel. For a moment she believes that 'I must be Mabel and shall have to go and live in that poky little house and ever so many lessons to learn!' To avoid such a grim prospect, Alice, still deeply doubtful about her identity, expresses her preference to stay down in words that immediately call to mind Heraclitus' 'up and down' language:

'I'll stay down here! It'll be no use their putting their heads down and saying 'come up again, dear!' I shall only look up and say 'who am I, then? Tell me that first, and then, if I like being that person, I'll come up; if not, I'll stay down here till I'm somebody else.'

After another short cycle of height transformations Alice gains self- confidence and, with indisputable Heraclitean conviction she is 'very glad to find herself still in existence'. Alice still experienced another alarming transformation. After tasting the mushroom she found that 'all she could see, when she looked down, was an immense length of neck'. Luckily she was delighted to find that her 'neck would bend about easily in any direction, like a serpent'.And indeed a Pigeon, protecting his hatched eggs, insists that Alice is a serpent, not just by her snakelike shape but also in accordance with Aristotelian Categorical syllogism, which the pigeon applies in an upside down manner:

All Serpents eat eggs
Alice eats eggs
Alice is 'a kind of serpent'

Carroll, the author of several books on logic, is paying here tribute to Aristotle, the founder of logic as a branch of philosophy, and to Aristotelian syllogistic propositions of two premises and a conclusion like :

All Greeks are mortal
Socrates is Greek
Socrates is mortal.

The right Aristotelian syllogism, the Pigeon should have used, is of course:

Serpents eat eggs
A is a serpent
A eats eggs

One must excuse a Pigeon in distress for such a fallacy when many people, in more relaxed circumstances, reach similar false conclusions. Carroll suggests that in spite of all the changes that have transpired, Alice's existence has not been affected. After the great Greeks, nearly all eminent philosophers, through the ages, have taken part in the disputation about the existence and nature of the Non-Being.

Chapter 4

The Delimitation of Text Worlds in Lewis Carroll's Alice Books

My interest in the work of Lewis Carroll goes back to my childhood, but, more recently, as a linguist, I rediscovered the enormous potential of the Alice books as illustrations of how our language system actually works; this was thanks to Robin Lakoff's (1993) excellent article on the subversive potential of the *Alice* books, which she analyses in general terms from a pragmatic perspective. The reading of this chapter stimulated my own personal reflections and thoughts on the books, in particular regarding the notion of reference and its connection with acts of naming, classifying, categorising and establishing an orientation within a text world. This explores how reference is dealt with in the books *Alice in Wonderland and Through the Looking Glass* by focusing on two aspects:

- The peculiar way in which acts of assigning sense and reference take place in the two fictional worlds,
- How the deictic parameters regarding space, time and person coordinates determine the idiosyncratic nature of *Wonderland* and, especially, of *Looking Glass World*.

The general theoretical assumption underlying the present discussion is that the analysis of language in given texts can provide insights into the workings of our language as a system of communication. This observation is taken by Lakoff (1993) as a point of departure in her article, and it is also a general principle adopted in stylistic analysis in general and in Systemic Functional Linguistics in particular. In this view, which is clearly functionally-oriented and grounded on pragmatics, language is part of socio-cultural behaviour, and, as such, it is both governed by social rules, and at the same time it reflects the way a given community or society works. In this sense, language as a system of classification and categorisation reveals the kinds of mental representations that are coded linguistically in different societies. Language is thus both an instrument of communication and a mirror image of the society which makes use of it.

THE ALICE BOOKS

If we consider the worlds described in the *Alice* books we have two radically different societies: as Lakoff (1993: 370-71) observes, the dream world of *Wonderland,* a kingdom ruled by the Queen and King of a card pack, is a world of total freedom, where no rules seem to apply and arbitrariness characterises social and linguistic behaviour: however, the world of *Looking Glass,* which is modelled upon a game of chess, is a world governed by a rigid system of rules. The cards and the chess pieces as crucial entities already determine the characteristics of the worlds they inhabit, which, as the reader soon finds out, are more like games than a "real world" as we understand it.

As a result, the exchanges between Alice and the creatures she encounters turn out to be puzzling and apparently nonsensical and absurd. However, a more careful reading of the books reveals the fact that they constitute complex reflections on the philosophical questions of the Victorian Age in Britain. From this perspective, there is very little nonsense in these books. It can be said that the adventures of *Alice in Wonderland and Through the Looking Glass* are not only the stories of a little girl in two different dream worlds, they are also the stories of how human reason confronts traditional problems which have troubled mathematicians, logicians, philosophers and linguists.

Reference is usually defined as a major linguistic function, the function which enables us to establish connections between words or linguistic signs and things in the world, and between different words within a text. Reference is thus a crucial aspect of text structure; it enables us to introduce information in discourse and mantain it without repeating time after time the same words, or to change it without incurring in incoherence. In this article, reference is dealt with as a pragmatic function, that is, as a context-dependent function, but it undoubtedly has a strong semantic and structural basis. However, the pragmatic factor is crucial; this can be seen in the well-known examples provided by textbooks, such as those in (1) and (2):

- I will be back tomorrow.
- I told her to leave it there.

Unless these utterances are said in a context, it is impossible to a have full understanding of their complete meaning. More precisely, it is not possible for us to identify exactly the time reference of *tomorrow* in example (1), nor the entities referred to by the pronouns *I*, *her*, and *it*, nor the place reference for the adverb *there* in example (2). The failure to establish a specific connection between these words and corresponding periods of time, entities or places in a context is a failure in assigning reference.

A further crucial aspect of reference is that it is speaker-based, which means that referential and especially deictic expressions determine the orientation or point of view of a discourse from the perspective of a specific speaker. Indeed, authors such as Semino (1997) and Werth (1995, 1999) argue that deictic terms are at the basis of the "world-building process", that is, the process whereby a reader or listener constructs a mental representation of a text. Thus, deictis establish the coordinates for the entities and the setting that characterise a given situation.

In the first part of the article, I define reference as part of the assignment of linguistic meaning and discuss certain problems which have troubled philosophers and semanticists, but which have been solved by means of discourse-based approaches. In the second part of the article I concentrate on deixis, a specific type of reference, and I discuss how deixis helps define a text world. The illustrations from the *Alice* books provide excellent examples of how some philosophical and linguistic questions which have to do with reference and deixis are humorously manifested in the strange behaviour of the creatures which Alice encounters.

They also constitute good examples of how alternative (or different) worlds are defined and constructed according to parameters which differ from those of our own world. The objective is to illustrate the way in which reference actually determines the creation of patterns of text and discourse and the way it conditions the degree of internal coherence of a text and how this is perceived by a reader. Consequently, throughout the discussion we will see that reference has a lot to do, not only with how a specific text or discourse may differ from other texts or discourses, but also, crucially, that reference is a subjective function, that is, it helps define a context from the specific point of view of a given speaker.

THE PRAGMATIC NATURE OF ACTS OF REFERRING

In this section I address some basic aspects regarding the definition of reference focusing on its pragmatic nature and on the relationship between the notion of reference and existential assumptions. The way reference is standardly understood to work when we use language in context (i.e. in a present-day, developed, western society) is contrasted with the peculiarities which can be appreciated in the use of reference in the *Alice* books.

We can say, as many authors have done before that the interpretation or processing of language in context hinges upon the successful assignment of the sense, reference and force of words. By sense, we usually mean the dictionary meaning or meanings of a word. For example, the word *bank* in English may have two senses or dictionary meanings,

- *a place where you keep your money*
- *a river bank or shore*

The precise meaning of a word in a given utterance is determined contextually, thus if I hear (3), I will assume the speaker will be talking about the place where you keep money:

- I went to the bank this morning but it was closed.

In brief, sense is traditionally considered to be inherent

to specific words and, consequently, context-independent; however, this is only relative, since successful communication depends on an adequate identification and processing of the sense that is intended in a given context. Reference, however, is by nature context-dependent and is speaker motivated. For example, the word *dog* alone does not refer, but we need *referring expressions,* such as the possessive genitive *John's dog* or the demonstrative *that dog* in order for an NP to refer in a specific context. Indeed, reference is typically grammaticalised in the form of articles (*the* man, *a* book) and pronouns (*he, she, it, this, that, mine...*), or lexicalised in the form of adverbs (*here, there, now*).

The main types of *referring expressions* are:

- Definite and indefinite NPs - proper names - deictic elements

I wish now to consider some of the characteristics of *referring expressions* and comment on the peculiarities of the worlds described in the *Alice* books according to these observations. We have seen in examples (1) and (2) that in order to assign reference successfully an utterance needs to be interpreted within a specific context. This means that in many situations a discourse-pragmatic interpretation of an utterance will be favoured even if it contradicts the literal semantic component of the proposition. In traditional semantics, it is assumed that on saying an utterance, a speaker is committed to the truth of the proposition uttered and to the fact he or she believes that the entities referred to exist. However, very often in everyday communication we may say utterances which are not strictly speaking true, but which can be understood on the basis of contextual clues. Thus, somebody may utter:

- I like your blouse!

The utterance exemplified in (4) will successfully be understood as referring to the blouse I am wearing at the moment of utterance, even if the speaker may not know that it is not actually *my* blouse, but my sister's, from whom I have borrowed it. An interpretation of this kind favours a context-based inferencing process, rather than the assumption that the literal meaning expressed by the existential presupposition *the blouse belongs to me* must be true. Simple as this may seem, it is a process that does not seem to form part of the linguistic conventions of *Wonderland* and *Looking Glass* creatures. In both books we find different examples which reveal unsuccessful reference assignment due to a literal interpretation of the utterance and an inability (or refusal) to interpret the utterance contextually. Thus, the last episode in *Wonderland* is the trial against the knave of hearts, who has stolen the Queen's tarts; the King asks the Mad Hatter to take off his hat:

- "Take off your hat", the King said to the hatter.

"It isn't mine," said the Hatter.

"Stolen!" the King exclaimed, turning to the jury, who instantly made a memorandum of the fact.

"I keep them to sell", the Hatter added as an explanation: "I've none of my own. I'm a Hatter." (W/147)

Extract (5) illustrates clearly the pragmatic nature of reference and to what extent its successful interpretation depends on the appropriate inferencing on the part of the listener or addressee. As we saw in example (4) above, in ordinary communication we are able to assign reference even if the referring expression may not be, strictly speaking, true. A successful inferencing process would hinge upon the understanding of the reference of the deictic *your* as conveying what is most relevant in the context, that is, interpretation (6) below:

- Take off your hat +> Take off the hat you are wearing.

Instead, the Hatter understands the utterance to express the literal meaning in (7):

- Take off your hat >> Take off the hat which belongs to you.

A similar example may be found when Alice meets the Red Queen in *Looking Glass World* and tells her she has lost her way, as illustrated in extract (8):

- "I don't know what you mean by *your* way," said the Queen: "all the ways about here belong to *me* - "(LG/206)

As we saw in extract (5), in extract (8) again we find an

example of unsuccessful reference assignment linked to a literal interpretation of the meaning of a possessive pronoun. As in (5), it is not the semantic presupposition that must be inferred by the addressee, that is, it is not (9) a. that Alice means, but the relevance-based implicature illustrated in (9b):

- – I have lost my way - The way belongs to me.
  – I have lost my way +> I don't know what direction to go.

Reference is also interpreted literally in the case of time deixis, not only of Noun Phrases describing entities. As I explain, *Looking Glass* World is defined deictically by a different set of parameters and conventions from what we understand to be the case in our world. Thus, when Alice meets the White Queen she asks her to be her maid and offers her a salary and "jam every other day", which Alice rejects:

- *"It's very good jam," said the Queen.*

"Well, I don't want any today, at any rate."

"You couldn't have it if you *did* want it," the Queen said. "The rule is, jam tomorrow and jam yesterday - but never jam *today*."

"It *must* come sometimes to 'jam today'", Alice objected.

"No, it can't," said the Queen. "It's jam every *other* day: today isn't any *other* day, you know." (LG/247)

This passage illustrates the indexical nature of deictic terms. Thus, deictics are traditionally described as indexical symbols, that is, as terms which have a basic meaning component and a variable one which singles out a referent in a specific context. Thus, the deitic *today*, for example, has a lexical meaning component which stands for "the current day", while the indexical component will single out different instances of days depending on the context of utterance. *Today* is a proximal deictic, since it indicates closeness with the time-reference of the speaker and contrasts with other time expressions such as *tomorrow*, and *yesterday* - distal deictics, in that they indicate distant time references from the point of view of the speaker.

The indexical component of the deicitic *today* corresponds to its function as "pointer", or its ability to single out the specific date which corresponds to the expression *today* in a given context. Deictics are thus always relative to their context of utterance. It is this function of the words *today, yesterday* and *tomorrow* that the Queen seems to be ignoring in her exchange with Alice. This point is also made by many owners of shops, bars and restaurants, who have notes put up in their establishments saying that credit is always granted yesterday and tomorrow, but never today. The context-dependent nature of reference makes it possible to use different referring expressions to refer to a single entity; thus, I may refer to the person sitting opposite me as *my brother, that young man* or *Enrique*. There is a playful reference to this feature in the episode where Alice meets Tweedledum and Tweedledee, whose house is signalled by a sign that says:

- *To Tweedledum's house/ To the house of Tweedledee*

In the sign, both indications refer to the same house.

THE PROBLEM OF NON-REFERENTIAL NPS

A standard question when dealing with reference is that referring expressions such as the ones we have seen so far may also be used non-referentially, that is, without pointing in any specific way at an entity in particular or a place or time in particular. Let's consider a typical example:

- *Jim wants to meet a contemporary artist.*

It we interpret this utterance referentially, the speaker will have a specific person in mind, while in a non-referential interpretation we will mean "any" artist, without specifying one in particular. While many noun phrases and deictics may be ambiguous, as indeed (10) is, negative words are standardly understood as being non-referential. Thus, if we face an utterance like (11) we assume that the negative word *nobody* cannot refer to any particular entity, consequently, it is a non-referential NP:

- I saw nobody.

This is not so in Looking Glass world where even negative NPs or pronouns may be interpreted referentially. This may be observed in an episode where Alice meets the White King in Looking Glass world:

- *"I see nobody on the road," said Alice.*

"I only wish *I* had such eyes," the King remarked in a fretful tone."To be able to see Nobody! And at that distance too! Why, it's as much as *I* can do to see real people, by this light!" (LG/279)

In (14) the King interpets *Nobody* to be a specific individual that can be identified by Alice and referred to linguistically. This seems to be a recurrent motif in literary works, rendered famous in the episode in the Odyssey where Ulysses adopts the name *Nobody* to cheat Polyphemus and to escape.

A related example of misinterpretation of a non-referential pronoun is found in an early episode in *Wonderland*, where the Mouse is telling a story:

- '...and even Stigand, the patriotric Archbishop of Canterbury, found it advisable—-'

'Found what?' said the Duck.

'Found *it*,' the Mouse replied rather crossly, 'of course you know what "it" means.'

'I know what "it" means well enough, when *I* find a thing,' said the Duck: 'It's generally a frog or a worm. The question is, what did the archbishop find?'

The Mouse did not notice this question, but hurriedly went on... (W/47)

The pronoun *it* in the example above obviously does not refer, but is a dummy *it* which perfoms a grammatical function, that of occupying the Object position of an extraposed clausal complement. As in other examples, the passage illustrates the tendency of *Wonderland* creatures to believe that all words must invariably have both reference and sense.

In fact, reference has traditionally been linked to questions about the existence of objects and their ontological status. Traditionally, it is assumed that on uttering an NP, like for example, *the unicorn*, the speaker is committed to the belief that such an entity exists, otherwise, reference will not be possible. This is explained by the fact that NPs trigger existential presuppositions. However, common sense tells us that it is actually possible to refer to imaginary or fictional entities as long as we are aware that they only exist in imaginary or fictional worlds (see Lyons 1977: 181-197). Thus, Lyons (1995: 299) makes the following observation:

one cannot successfully refer to something that does not exist. One can, of course, successfully refer to imaginary, fictional and hypothetical entities; but in so doing, one presupposes that they exist in an imaginary, fictional or hypothetical world. Similarly, one can (and frequently does) refer to dead persons.

The possibility of assigning reference to non-existent entities can be formalised in a theory of discourse grounded on possible world theory, which can be defined briefly as a theory where each speech event or discourse situation constitutes a possible world or possible state of affairs. In this view, as Ryan (1991) claims, each world is the centre for its inhabitants. That is, the actual or real world is the centre for you and me, but for a character in a book, like Alice, the centre is her own world.

The *Alice* books are interesting examples from this perspective because there is a shift from the actual world of Alice or Alice's world to a dream world, *Wonderland* first and then to *Looking Glass*. This shift from one world to another has a consequent shift in the centre of reference or deictic orientation, a point I come back to in section 2.4., and it may be illustrated by two episodes in *Looking Glass World,* where Alice meets the unicorn and where she meets the Red King:

- *'What - is - this?' he [the unicorn] said at last.*

'This is a child!' Haigha replied eagerly, coming in front of Alice, and spreading out both his hands towards her in Anglo-Saxon attitude. 'We only found it today. It's as large as life, and twice as natural!'

'I always thought they were fabulous monsters!' said the unicorn. 'Is it alive?'

'It can talk', said Haigha solemnly.

The Unicorn looked dreamily at Alice and said: 'Talk, child'.

Alice could not help her lips curling up into a smile as she began: 'Do you know, I always thoguht Unicorns were fabulous monsters, too? I never saw one alive before!'

'Well, now that we *have* seen each other', said the Unicorn, 'if you'll believe in me, I'll believe in you. Is that a bargain?'

'Yes, if you like,' said Alice. (LG/287)

This episode playfully reflects on reference and existence. In Looking Glass World, not only do unicorns exist and it is consequently possible to refer to them - and to talk to them! - but, what is more, the world they inhabit is oriented from *their* perspective, so that it is not the existence of unicorns that is questioned, but the existence of children, such as Alice, and the possibility of referring to them and interacting with them.

This relativisation of cultural understanding is taken to an extreme in the episode where Alice meets the Red King, illustrated in (17) below; in this episode, Alice comes across the Red King, who is lying asleep against a tree in the wood:

- "He's dreaming now", said Tweedledee: "and what do you think he's dreaming about?"

Alice said: "Nobody can guess that."

"Why, about *you*!" Tweedledee exclaimed, clapping his hands triumphantly. "And if he left off dreaming about you, where do you suppose you'd be?"

"Where I am now, of course," said Alice.

"Not you!" Tweedledee retorted contemptuously. "You'd be nowhere. Why, you're only a sort of thing in his dream!" (LG/238)

In passage (17), the deictic centre placed from the point of view of Alice is questioned, in such a way that Alice is described as *a sort of thing* in the Red King's dream. But at the same time we have been told that Alice enters Looking Glass world in a dream, which means that the Red King is *a sort of thing* in her own dream. The result is a recursive structure where Alice dreams of the King who dreams of Alice who dreams of the King...a paradoxical structure which lacks a deictic or referential centre and which is typical of the mirror image effects of Looking Glass World.

SENSE, REFERENCE, NAMING AND CATEGORISATION

Naming is the very essence of language, and, as such, it

encloses what we understand by the meaning of a word (both reference and sense) and how that meaning conventionally stands for something in the world. The human habit of naming things, as Alice says, is useful for people who name them though it may seem pointless or arbitrary to the creatures themselves. This is reflected in the conversation between Alice and a gnat in Wonderland, where Alice tells the gnat that she is not fond of insects but that she can tell him the names of some of those that inhabit her world. To this the gnat answers:

- 'Of course they answer to their names?' the gnat remarked carelessly.

'I never knew them to do it.'

'What's the use of their having names', the gnat said,' if they won't answer to them?'

'No use to *them*', said Alice; 'but it's useful to the people that name them, I suppose. If not, why do people have names?' (LG/222)

The gnat seems to believe that a name has mainly a pragmatic or interactive function - so that people can 'call' things - but not a classificatory function. The gnat goes on to say he does not know the answer to the question 'Why do people have names?', but that further on there is a wood where the creatures have no names. Alice meets a friendly fawn in the wood, and they walk together for a while, until they leave the wood and they both remember their names:

- 'I'm a fawn it cried out in a voice of delight. 'And, dear me! you're a human child!' A sudden look of alarm came into its beautiful brown eyes, and in another moment it had darted away at full speed. (LG/227)

Here there is a distinction between the 'pure' state of creatures, without interpretation or classification, and the understanding, through the knowledge of who is stronger and more aggressive, of the relations between the creatures. This is expressed as a kind of pragmatic relation which takes place by means of the act of naming something. Thus, because a creature is called "fawn", it knows immediately that it is weaker than many other creatures and that the others can attack him. What is striking in this passage is that the awareness of what an entity is, either a fawn, or a little girl, comes through language, not through the direct experience of the world. This is an extremely important point, which has been the point of departure for many philosophical writings on how language not only describes reality but how it also controls and, to some extent determines that reality. This view leads quite naturally into issues of language and power and language and ideology, a theme also touched upon in the Alice books, as can be observed from the episode where Alice meets Humpty Dumpty, which I turn to now.

A consistent failure to assign reference and sense to words in context leads necessarily to arbitrariness. What *is* the meaning of a word or sequence of words? How can one ever be sure? The arbitrary nature of language as a convention and the consequent arbitrariness of acts of naming and referring is mentioned explicitly by Humpty Dumpty in his famous conversation with Alice. His peculiar views of language are expressed as soon as Alice introduces herself, as we can observe in extract (12) where Alice answers to Humpty's question about her name:

- *"My name is Alice, but -"*

"It's a stupid name enough!" Humpty Dumpty interrupted impatiently. "What does it mean?"

"*Must* a name mean something?" Alice asked doubtfully.

"Of course it must," Humpty Dumtpy said with a short laugh: "*my* name means the shape I am -and a good handsome shape it is, too. With a name like yours, you might be any shape, almost." (LG/263)

While in our western society noun phrases and other referring expressions have both sense and reference, proper names are standardly understood as having only reference but not necessarily sense. Humpty Dumpty assumes the contrary to be the case, so that a proper name like *Alice must have* a meaning and may be used to refer to *almost any kind of entity*. Similarly, Humpty Dumpty is fully aware of the arbitrary relation that governs acts of denoting and referring, as he tells Alice in a famous passage reproduced under (13); here

Humpty Dumpty replies to Alice who protests about his arbitrary use of the word 'glory':

- "When *I* use a word," Humpty Dumpty said, in rather a scornful tone, "it means just what I choose it to mean - neither more nor less."

"The question is," said Alice, "whether you *can* make words mean so many different things."

"The question is," said Humpty Dumpty, "which is to be master - that's all." (LG/269)

This passage illustrates not only the arbitrary nature of acts of denoting and referring, but also, as Robin Lakoff points out (1993: 372), to what extent these acts are speaker-dependent and governed by ideological questions. Those who have power have the power to decide on the meaning of words, including what we may refer to. This leads to a reading of the Alice books as potentially subversive, since they reveal the fact that linguistic power is real power.

DEICTIC REFERENCE AND THE DEFINITION OF A TEXT WORLD

In the discussion of examples (16) and (17) above I have mentioned the notions of deictic centre and orientation. I wish now to focus on these aspects and discuss the notion of deixis, a special type of reference. Deictic terms are what I described above as grammaticalisations and lexicalisations of referential information which is processed contextually. Thus, deixis is a special type of reference which is manifested in specific word classes, such as personal, demonstrative and possessive pronouns, adverbs specifying time and space coordinates and the tense system.

It can be said that deictic terms introduce the spatio-temporal coordinates of a discourse situation with regard to a deictic centre or point of reference, which is egocentric, or oriented from the point of view of the speaker. This point is usually described as the *zero point*, or the I-here-and-now, and it also receives the name of *index*. Each index, or orientation centre, distinguishes a possible world or discourse situation from an alternative.

Deixis is considered to be egocentric or an expression of subjectivity because an opposition is usually established between the *I-here-now,* which contextually indicates what is close to the speaker, and distant terms such as those in the table below:

Deictic centre or zero point Distal terms

I here/this now you him/her/it there/that then

In the time-tense system, a contrast is established between the now and what precedes and follows it. Also, it is assumed that time develops linearly from past to present over to future, and that this sequence cannot be altered:

yesterday now tomorrow

Radical alterations in the spatio-temporal system give rise to what traditionally are defined as impossible worlds. Ryan (1991) rejects the notion of impossible world in favour of a view of different worlds as alternative and governed by different rules from the rules that govern the actual or real world. Her proposal is briefly outlined at the end of this section in order to account for deviations in the time system in *Looking Glass World*.

The spatio-temporal coordinates, which are expressed by means of deictic terms, define the boundaries of a given world, be it a real or a fictional situation. This view of deixis is particularly interesting if we consider its applications to the understanding of text and discourse structures. Following Werth (1995, 1999), a text world may be defined as a conceptual domain which is organised in hierarchical structures, each level delimited by its own set of deictic and modal parameters. According to Werth (1995: 49) "deixis is in fact part of the modality function of language, i.e. the situating of the information with respect to the current context." As such, deixis as a function may be subdivided into three main types (ibid.):

Viewpoint

Probability

Interaction

Of these three it is viewpoint that corresponds to what we standardly understand by deixis, which in Werth deals mainly with spatio-temporal specifications. I now consider some examples from the *Alice* books and analyse how examples from situations in the fictional worlds are defined deicitcally and how they are oriented from the perspective of a particular speaker. Extract (18) below describes how Alice feels when she has grown to huge proportions and cannot get out of the White Rabbit's house:

- "It was much pleasanter at home", thought poor Alice, "when one wasn't growing larger and smaller, and being ordered about by mice and rabbits. I almost wish I hadn't gone down that rabbit hole - and yet - and yet - it's rather curious, you know, this sort of life!" (W/58)

In this extract we see a contrast between the situation in which Alice finds herself at present, *this sort of life,* and what used to be her life at home.

The deictic centre is situated in Alice's perception of the situation and a shift is described from a distant spatio-temporal situation *was...at home* and the present situation (*this sort of life*). This shift indicates clearly that there has been a change in possible world or discourse world in linguistic terms. The deictic centre itself is made more complex by the fact that Alice talks to herself, creating the impression that the centre is a multiple consciousness, rather than a single one:

- "Oh, you foolish Alice!" she answered herself. "How can you learn lessons in here? Why, there's hardly any room for *you,* and no room at all for any lesson books!" (W/59)

The split in the consciousness creates the illusion of an internal distance between different parts of *Alice,* even if physically this is not possible, as both are situated within the same body.

The difficulty of identifying the *I* as one single unitary entity is a recurrent motif in the *Alice* books, where Alice's identity is often not recognised by other creatures, who are not able to assign a conceptual category to the child they are facing, and, consequently, are not able to refer to her. Alice herself is well aware of the problems of identity she is going through; this problem is first manifested as a problem in defining the *I*, the centre of consciousness:

- Dear, dear! How queer everything is today! and yesterday things went on just as usual. I wonder if I've been changed in the night? Let me think: *was* I the same when I got up this morning? I almost think I remember feeling a little different. But, if I'm not the same, the next question is 'Who in the world am I?' Ah, that's the great puzzle!" And she began thinking of all the children she knew that were of the same age as herself, to see if she could have been changed for any of them." (W/37)

While the shift from Alice's real world to Wonderland only implies a change in space and time coordinates in that *Wonderland* is a projection of a dream world, in *Looking Glass World* the shift becomes more complex, as the space-time relations are inverted with respect to the real or actual world. This is so because *Looking Glass World* is supposed to be a mirror image of the real or actual world. Alice finds it very difficult to understand the way space and time are understood in *Looking Glass World*. In extract (20), Alice is running together with the Red Queen, but they do not move at all, no matter how fast they run:

- Alice looked round her in great surprise. "Why, I do believe we've been under this tree the whole time! Everything's just as it was!"

"Of course it is," said the Queen. "What would you have it?"

"Well, in *our* country," said Alice panting a Little, "you'd generally get to somewhere else - if you ran very fast for a long time as we've been doing."

"A slow sort of country!" said the Queen. "Now, *here*, you see, it takes all the running you can do to keep in the same place. If you want to get somewhere else, you must run at least twice as fast as that." (LG/210)

As in the examples discussed above, the deitic terms establish a comparison between an alternate situation or state of affairs (*In our country you'd generally get to somewhere else - if you ran very fast as we've been doing*) and the present situation (*here*). Distance or remoteness (see Werth, 1999: 239-40) is marked by means of hypotheticality (*if you ran*) and the exclusive use of the third person pronoun *our*.

Similarly, in *Looking Glass World*, the chronological order of events is inverted with respect to the order that is followed in our world. This can be seen in the episode where Alice meets the White Queen:

- "What sort of things do you remember best?" Alice ventured to ask.

"Oh, things that happened the week after next," the Queen replied in a careless tone. "For instance, now...there's the King's Messenger. He's in prison now, being punished: and the trial doesn't even begin till next Wednesday: and of course the crime comes last of all." (LG/248)

In fact, the general rule regarding the way time develops in *Looking Glass World* seems to be that events occur in inverted relationships with regard to the progression they follow in the real world.

In *Looking Glass World* effects happen first and are then followed by causes. For this reason the messenger is imprisoned before he commits the crime in passage (26) above. This inversion of chronological sequences is illustrated further in other episodes such as the ones reproduced below. In (27) the White Queen is still talking to Alice and suddenlt starts shouting:

- 'Oh, oh, oh!' shouted the Queen, shaking her hand about as if she wanted to shake it off. "My finger's bleeding! Oh, oh, oh!' (...)

'What *is* the matter?' [Alice] said, as soon as there was a chance of making herself heard. 'Have you pricked your finger?'

'I haven't pricked it *yet*,' the Queen said, but I soon shall - oh, oh, oh!'

'When do you expect to do it?' Alice asked, feeling very much inclined to laugh.

'When I fasten my shawl again', the poor Queen groaned out. (...) As she said the words the brooch flew open, and the

Queen clutched wildly at it and tried to clasp it again. (LG/349)

As is expected, the Queen does not hold the brooch properly and pricks her finger. The cause-effect relation between the pricking and the bleeding is inverted, so that chronologically the bleeding is previous to the pricking.

A similar scene takes place in the episode where Alice meets the Unicorn in *Looking Glass World*. In this passage, the Lion and the Unicorn have asked Alice - to whom they refer as 'The Monster' - to cut up a cake in slices for all to eat. However, Alice is not aware that this action needs to follow *Looking Glass World* laws and not the natural laws she is used to:

- Alice seated herself on the bank of a little brook, with the great dish on her knees, and was sawing away diligently with the knife. 'It's very provoking!' she said, in reply to the Lion (...). 'I've cut several slices already, but they always join on again!'

'You don't know how to manage Looking Glass cakes' the Unicorn remarked. 'Hand it round first, and cut it afterwards!'

This sounded nonsense, but Alice very obediently got up, and carried the dish round, and the cake divided itself into three pieces as she did so. '*Now* cut it up,' said the Lion, as she returned to her place with the empty dish. (LG/290)

As in example (27) above, in extract (28) the relation of cause-effect between cutting and handing out slices is inverted.

The peculiarities of the spatio-temporal system of *Looking Glass World* may be analysed more in depth by considering exactly in what way the alternate world depicted in the fictional world differs from the actual world or real world. Ryan (1991) proposes a complex taxonomy which allows us to identify the different types of accessibility relations between alternate worlds and the actual world, where we, as readers, are situated. For the purposes of the present discussion we may include the following variables (Ryan 1991: 32-33):

- *Physical compatibility*. A world is accessible from AW if they share the same natural laws.
- *Taxonomic compatibility*. A world is accessible

from AW if both worlds contain the same species and they have the same properties.

If we consider the characteristics of *Wonderland* and *Looking Glass World* according to these variables we may observe that both differ from the real world along these parameters since animals and inanimate objects can talk, and in both worlds we find animate entities such as chess pieces or cards and extinct species, like dodos. Moreover, *Looking Glass World* differs further along the parameter of physical compatibility in that the natural laws that govern time progression are not respected.

Reference is crucial in order to account for the process of communication and it depends on pragmatic clues for its adequate interpretation. This has been illustrated by means of different passages from the *Alice* books, which are two idiosyncratic worlds where pragmatic principles in general and reference in particular are not understood to work in the way we (or Alice) would expect. An analysis of the defeat of expected uses provides interesting insights regarding the implied reflections on the validity of our language systems as systems of communication. This leads to the conclusion that the *Alice* books, rather than 'nonsense' or 'children' literature constitute playful reflections on issues which have been the concern of linguists and philosophers for many years.

To end, an analysis of deictic terms as a special type of reference in the fictional worlds of the *Alice* books may provide insights regarding the importance of such terms in their function of delimiting the text world boundaries and in illustrating the laws that rule spatio-temporal relations. By providing distorted versions or mirror images of our own world, the fictional worlds of *Wonderland* and *Looking Glass* invite the reader to meditate about the characteristics of the world we inhabit and how such characteristics are systematised by means of language.

Chapter 5

In the Shadow of the Dreamchild: A New Understanding

Some books, like David Friedrich Strauss' *The Life of Jesus,* forever change the direction of scholarly inquiry. Just as Strauss attempted to reveal the historical Jesus behind the gospel formulations and the deposits of centuries of faith and tradition, so Karoline Leach attempts to find the historical Charles L. Dodgson behind, as she would have it, the Lewis Carroll myth. It is impossible to say whether the Rev. Charles Dodgson would have been more upset by the comparison of his newest biographer's work with that of Strauss (Dodgson having been a very devout and conservative Christian and ordained a deacon in the Anglican Church) or with the surprising conclusions Leach reaches, or rather suggests, about his love life.

Leach's heretical thesis, which scandalizes and enrages orthodox Carrollians, is that C.L. Dodgson was primarily interested not in little girls but in sexually mature women. And if that were not blasphemous enough, she further argues, albeit considerably less convincingly, that the main object of the Rev. Dodgson's affections was none other than Lorina Liddell, nee Reeve, wife of the Dean of Christ Church and mother of the real Alice, the inspiration for Carroll's classic *Alice's Adventures in Wonderland* and the "dreamchild" of Leach's title.

Although Leach's book is no biography in the conventional sense, she does begin with the basic facts: "Charles Lutwidge Dodgson was born on 27 January 1832. He died on 14 January 1898. "Lewis Carroll" was born on 1 March 1856 and is still very much alive." Ever since the first occurrence in print of Dodgson's famous pseudonym, the historical record has become confused. The primary sources to which one would normally turn are a problem: Dodgson's family burned many of his personal papers in Oxford after his death and the manuscript of his diaries was made available to no one outside the immediate family for more than half a century.

The main source for his life, until the rather recent efforts to publish the unexpurgated diaries and the appearance of such thorough biographical studies as Morton Cohen's recent book, informed by decades spent assembling and editing Carroll's correspondence, was the official family biography written in the Victorian hagiographic tradition by Carroll's nephew Stuart Dodgson Collingwood. This latter work, Leach argues, fixed and popularized the notion of Lewis Carroll as an eternal child, the Oxford don comfortable only in the company of female children, a mathematician untouched by life's more normal male-female relations. True, Collingwood did have access to the original diaries and perhaps much other material, but the last two chapters of his biography were solely his own invention, Leach believes.

Leach argues that Dodgson was more interested in sex than calculus from the time of his undergraduate mathematical reading vacation at Whitby in 1854. To make a possible case here she relies on a highly biographical reading, a technique she employs several times in this work, of both the poem and short story Dodgson wrote at that time and contributed to the *Whitby Gazette*. In the former, the hero falls in love with a cook named Matilda, in the latter the barmaid Sukie. *Pace* Leach, there is little to suggest that art imitated life here anymore than it did in the rabbit hole of Wonderland. Dodgson, like most of his generation, was for too class-conscious for any such dalliance.

A major contribution of this book, however, is to focus attention on the fact that many of Dodgson's "child friends" were hardly children by any standard. She examines these "friendships," from that with the actress Isa Bowman, who was above the age of consent when she first met Dodgson, to

Gertrude Chataway who was still seeing Dodgson when, at the age of 27, she was invited to spend a week with him at Eastbourne. Some of the facts about the ages of his "young" friends are not new, but Leach's emphasis on what is at least an emotional if not necessarily sexual involvement with young women does constitute a difficult-to-counter revisionist reinterpretation of Lewis Carroll. To support her thesis of an affair between Charles Dodgson and Lorina Liddell, Leach presents an almost stereotypical view of the great Greek scholar who, in her view, had little interest in his attractive wife. Based on some of the Liddell correspondence to which she had access, she posits a homosexual relationship between Liddell and his friend Arthur Stanley of University College. And if the *Greek-English Lexicon,* on the compilation of which he spent most of his adult life, was his second love, then Lorina must come third in this curious view. Leach strangely overlooks Liddell's own romantic lyrics, such as his 1844 elegy, in which he exclaims:

Seven years are flown since first I seemed
To know thee as thou art;
Since first the flame arose that soon
Burnt hot within my heart.

Here one would have expected the kind of biographical excursus Leach makes when treating Carroll's own lyrics. But no. Does she really think that Liddell's long and intimate acquaintance with Greek lyric poets led to some kind of amatory inhibition? Four children would seem to argue otherwise.

Alice as "dreamchild" is another tenet of the Carrollian faith which Leach tries to contest. The direct evidence for Carroll's infatuation with young Alice Liddell being so strong that it led to a proposal of marriage is thin. In his 17 October 1866 journal Dodgson writes: "On Sunday Uncle S. dined with me, we had a good deal of conversation about Wilfrid [one of Dodgson's brothers] and about A.L.—it is a very anxious subject." Opinion has been that the initials A.L. must refer to Alice Liddell. The second source is a rumor quoted by Lord Salisbury in a letter of 1878 to the effect that Dodgson had asked for the real Alice's hand and, being refused, had "gone out of his mind." Salisbury's comment is dismissed as a mere rumor made a decade and a half after the "fact," and yet Leach is quite willing to give credence to other rumors of about the same time regarding Dodgson's escapades with young women. Furthermore, she simply disbelieves Stuart Collingwood's comment in a letter to Violet Dodgson (another of Carroll's nieces):

Whereas, in regard to the Liddells, it was Alice who was undoubtedly his pet, and it was his intense love for her (though she was only a child) which pulled the trigger and released his genius. Indeed it is quite likely that Alice's marriage to Hargreaves may have seemed the greatest tragedy of his life.

Certainly a break in relations leading to an estrangement between Charles Dodgson and the Liddell family occurred in 1863. The most authoritative documentation for what caused the riff would have been the pages of Dodgson's journal for 27—29 June of that year, pages mysteriously missing from the notebook. While working in the Dodgson family archives, however, Leach did discover a hitherto neglected note in the hand of Violet which she claims summarizes the now missing pages:

L.C. learns from Mrs. Liddell that he is supposed to be using the children as a means of paying court to the governess—He is also supposed [unreadable text] to be courting Ina. This is quite important to the construction of Leach's thesis. She strikes out on a path first, I believe, suggested by Raphael Shaberman in his privately printed 1982 pamphlet on the suggestion of a relationship between Dodgson and Mrs. Liddell. She interprets the name "Ina" to refer not to Alice's sister Lorina but rather to Alice's mother, the wife of Dean Liddell, Lorina Liddell. Carroll's photographing of the Liddell children, especially Alice, his entertaining of them, his many visits to the Deanery, all become a sort of cover for an affair with Lorina. In order to substantiate this interpretation it becomes necessary for Leach to enlist numerous "child friends," biographers, and family members in a conspiracy to hide Carroll's affair with Mrs. Liddell and then later with other not so young girls. Conspiracy theories often begin with an anomaly or uncertainty or two which are pushed beyond credulity in the service of unmasking some fiendish deception. They simply go too far and Leach, alas, is here no exception.

There are a few other troubling aspects of the book for which Leach's editors bear some responsibility. Speculation offered in one chapter becomes solid evidence later on (e.g., the Lorina thesis, having been raised as a possibility, is treated as fact). Material drawn from Dodgson's journals and elsewhere is not always footnoted (e. g. , the discussion of what Dean Liddell and Dodgson said to one another regarding the important matter of his remaining at Christ Church in his studentship without proceeding to take Holy Orders). Finally, footnotes fail to adequately document important charges (e.g., that Carroll had a large collection of "nudities") or offer confusing attribution (e.g., in citing "one biographer" in her text, the footnote lists three).

Like the protagonist of her play ("The Mysterious Mr. Love"), Leach knows what she is after and what she wants. For her, that is a total revision of the long-standing popular myth of Lewis Carroll. This is an extremely well-written book of powerful, though not always persuasive argumentation. Nabokov once commented on the possibilities of literary biography as "a kind of double paper-chase: first the biographer pursues his quarry through letters and diaries, and across bogs of conjecture and then a rival authority pursues the muddy biographer." If Ms. Leach comes through the bogs of conjecture bespattered with the mud, that is inevitable when one tries to dig deeply.

Chapter 6

Tenniel as Carroll's Reader

When John Tenniel was providing 42 illustrations for Alice's Adventures in Wonderland in 1864 he was in his mid-forties, an established illustrator and a Punch cartoonist. At that time C. L. Dodgson and Lewis Carroll were equally unknown as authors, for adults or children. Tenniel, on the other hand, already had a professional understanding of the visual codes and illustrative techniques of his day, and already had an audience—an adult rather than a child audience—who would expect from him a certain level of technical proficiency, humour, and social nous.

Tenniel's illustrations should therefore interest us today not just for their remarkable and continuing success as a felicitous adjunct to Carroll's text, but also as the first—arguably, the best—Victorian reading or interpretation of Carroll's text. After all, as a reader Tenniel enjoyed considerable advantages, including his personal position and experience, his access to the author's own illustrations to the manuscript version of the story, and access to the author himself.

In his study of illustration in children's literature, Words about Pictures, Perry Nodelman has argued that "the pictures in a sequence act as schemata for each other"—that is, all the expectations, understanding, and information we bring to reading an illustrated book, and all the information we accumulate as our reading proceeds, "becomes a schema for each new page of words and each new picture as we continue throughout a book." If this is so, all Tenniel's choices relating to subject matter, size, position, and style of illustration must come to operate, as we proceed through Alice in Wonderland, as a kind of guide to reading Carroll's text. An examination of Tenniel's opening sequence of illustrations as they appeared on the page in the 1866 edition of Alice in Wonderland will therefore begin to reveal Tenniel's preoccupations, the kind of interpretation of Carroll's text he is interested in making.

As William Empson pointed out in 1935, two aspects of Alice are traditional in children's stories: the idea of characters of unusual size (miniatures and giants) and the idea of the talking beast. Tenniel's opening drawing, the White Rabbit at the head of chapter 1, draws on both these traditions.

The rabbit occupies a point between animal and human, simultaneously both these things and neither of them, an implication hardly made so firmly by Carroll's text. The rabbitness of the rabbit is emphasized by the meadow setting, the absence of trousers, and the careful attention paid to anatomy and proportion. But the rabbit is slightly distorted towards the human by his upright posture, his clothing and accessories, his pose, and his human eye and hand.

Less obviously, Tenniel also extends Carroll's text by offering information about the size of the rabbit. From the grass and dandelion clock (a visual joke) in the background the reader grasps the rabbit as rather larger than normal bunny size: about the size of a toddler or small child, perhaps.

As this illustration was invented by Tenniel (Carroll's headpiece illustration shows Alice, her sister, and the book), the contrast is clear between Carroll, whose picture draws attention to the frame of the story, to the affectionate relationship of sisters, and thereby to Alice's membership of the human family, and Tenniel, who selects a traditional story idea that shifts the focus another way, toward a mediation between different kinds familiar from those many forms of art in which animal behaviour is used to represent human behaviour.

In further illustrations, Tenniel offers more images suggestive of unusual relative size. Alice too large to go through the little door. She holds the bottle labeled "DRINK ME" which will shrink her; on page 15 she is growing taller, with the text elongated to match. Then comes page 18, where the frame and larger size suggest that here is an important picture. In it the human/animal rabbit and the idea of Alice's unusual size occur together. Alice looks gigantic in relation to the hallway, and the White Rabbit, normal size for the hallway (it appears) but perhaps (in that case) outsize for a rabbit, is much reduced from the importance he assumed in the first illustration and is shown fleeing from her terrifying figure.

The pool of tears illustration on page 26 also relates to these themes. Here a fully dad human, Alice, is depicted much the same size as the unclothed mouse with which she swims. Note, too, that in the text, Alice frightens the mouse away as she had previously frightened the rabbit, although this time it is by talking about her pet, her cat Dinah.

The reader who ponders this opening sequence of illustrations might reflect that Alice would also be frightened of Dinah if she met her while still mouse-sized. The schemata, then, direct the reader towards a cluster of ideas in which animal fears and anxieties about survival are connected with images of lesser or greater relative size.

Tenniel appears to have arrived at this interpretation independently: while he does frequently follow Carroll's designs closely in the subject and overall approach to an illustration (Michael Hancher provides some useful opportunities to make comparisons), of the pictures just discussed only the one of Alice growing taller at the head of chapter 2 very much resembles a parallel drawing in Carroll's manuscript. Moreover, when Tenniel does follow Carroll in choice of subject he usually makes significant changes in treatment: Tenniel's Alice, for instance, having slipped into the pool of tears, is very much more alarmed than Carroll's Alice.

Edward Hodnett, who reviewed Tenniel's work for the Alice books picture by picture, makes rather slighting remarks about several of the designs in this opening sequence: those on pages 8 and 10 are "too matter-of-fact to be necessary," the "elongated Alice stands merely looking round-eyed," and the second vignette of Alice swimming with the mouse "makes the first superfluous." Hodnett seems to me to have missed the point. These designs are in my view extremely consistent in seeking and developing a particular nexus of ideas.

Despite the evident connection between many Tenniel illustrations and Carroll's own illustrations, then, this is clearly Tenniel's own interpretation. But if this is so, what is to be made of it? My thesis in this paper is that through his animal drawings, Tenniel offers a visual angle on the text of Alice in Wonderland that evokes the life sciences, natural history, and Darwinian ideas about evolution, ideas closely related by Tenniel to Alice's size changes, and to how these affect the animals she meets. As I will show, this is partly a matter of Tenniel's "drawing out" an underlying field of reference in Carroll's text.

I will also argue, however, that when Tenniel's approach to his animal subjects is compared to that in earlier and contemporary illustrated natural history books, the viewer is conscious of resemblances which indicate that Tenniel's pictures are best situated and read in that context.

The effect of the initial sequence described above, for instance, is that as chapter 3 unfolds Alice's encounters with various different creatures, the illustrations begin to re-create Alice itself as a kind of zany natural history for children. Our post-Freudian view of Alice in Wonderland tends to be of a private, heavily encoded, inward exploration or adventure. But Tenniel's reading, I would argue, offers us an outward-looking text, a public adventure, a jocular reflection on the natural history craze, on reading about natural history, and on Darwin's controversial new theory of natural selection.

I will return to Tenniel as reader later, but in order to establish that this interpretation is no mere add-on but a genuine response to the text, I must first deal with science, natural history, and evolutionary ideas as themes that Carroll himself originates.

Interest in contemporary ideas about the animal kingdom is signaled early on in Alice in Wonderland, in chapter 2, when Alice finds that the well-known children's recitation piece "How doth the little busy bee" has been mysteriously ousted from her mind by new verses that celebrate a predator, the crocodile. Carroll's parody of Isaac Watts's pious poem for children thereby establishes his book's reference to a newer, more scientific view of nature—approaching a controversially Darwinist view. It does this by mocking and displacing the worldview often called natural theology. According to natural theology, a set of convictions much touted in children's reading, God's existence can be deduced from the wondrous design of his creation.

The universe is benign and meaningful, a book of signs (like the industrious bee) of God's benevolent and educative intentions just waiting to be read by humans. Carroll's crocodile, all tooth and claw, signifies other things: amorality, the struggle for existence, predation of the weaker by the stronger.

Readers of Alice in Wonderland are also likely to notice that the animal characters do not behave or talk much like animals in traditional fairy tales or fables. They are neither helpers nor donors nor monsters nor prophetic truthtellers, the main narrative functions of animals in traditional fairy tales, but nor are they the exemplary figures illustrative of human fallibilities and moralities familiar from fables.

They do not teach lessons about kindness to animals, as animals in children's stories often did, and they do not much resemble the creatures in nursery rhymes or jingles or Edward Lear's nonsensical poems either. Instead, they talk, chopping logic, competing with Alice and each other, and often mentioning things "natural" animals might be imagined to talk about, like fear, death, and being eaten.

I think Denis Crutch is also roughly right when he points out that there is in Alice a hierarchy of animals equivalent to the Victorian class system but also suggesting a competitive model of nature: the white rabbit, caterpillar, and March Hare seem to be gentlemen, frog and fish are footmen, Bill the lizard is bullied by everybody, hedgehogs and flamingos are made use of, and the dormouse and the guinea pigs are victimized by larger animals and by humans. William Empson's 1935 essay notes how Carroll's ideas and manuscript illustrations associate evolutionary theories with Alice in Wonderland.

This is a crucial point and, I believe, the best explanation for the presence of so many animals in Wonderland. It was after all Carroll who put a dodo, best known for being extinct, into the text, and Carroll who first included an ape, that key symbol of evolutionary debate, in his drawing of the motley crowd of beasts in the pool of tears. But Carroll's evolutionary reference is much more extensive than Empson found it, for a Darwinist view of life as competitive struggle is also promoted by Alice, who—apparently unconsciously, as if she really cannot help it—repeatedly reminds us that in life one must either eat or be eaten. Alice will keep talking about Dinah to the little creatures she meets who are the natural victims of cats (26-27), she has to admit to the pigeon that she herself has eaten eggs, and in the Mock Turtle scene she has to check herself rather than reveal that she has eaten lobster and whiting (148, 152).

The Mock Turtle, of course, is a very creature of the table, while Dinah the predator, the aboveground cat, has a place maintained for her in Wonderland by the Cheshire Cat, a friendly but slightly sinister appearing and disappearing cat whose most significant body part is his grinning, tooth-filled mouth (he grins like the crocodile, as Nina Auerbach has noted). The "little bright-eyed terrier" of which the aboveground Alice is so fond also has other-selves in Wonderland, Fury in the Mouse's Tale, the puppy in chapter 4. Moreover, the Mouse's Tale—the next poem in the book after the crocodile poem—talks about predation as if it were a legal process.

The reader should therefore take the hint and connect the animal "eat or be eaten" motif elsewhere in the story with the trial scene in the last stage of the book. Carroll has the White Rabbit make this association of ideas when he mutters "The Duchess! The Duchess! Oh my dear paws! Oh my fur and whiskers! She'll get me executed, as sure as ferrets are ferrets!". This is one of those moments when Alice reveals its ferocious undercurrent.

The White Rabbit here anticipates legal execution as simultaneous with the process of being prepared for table: that is, these "civilized" human behaviors are proffered by Carroll as analogous to predation by a "natural" enemy, ferrets.

Alice herself, by kicking Bill the Lizard up the chimney (an incident memorably illustrated by Tenniel in a very funny picture) and by looking on approvingly while the guinea pigs are so unkindly treated in court, inverts the theme of kindness to animals established in more orthodox children's literature like Maria Edgeworth's tale of "Simple Susan," where a girl's pet lamb is saved from the slaughterer's knife.

In Alice in Wonderland there is humorous delight in the misappropriation of the creatures in the croquet scene, and there are many other versions of a cruel carnival in the book: for instance, Alice imagines herself being set to watch a mousehole by her own cat. She also resents "being ordered about by mice and rabbits"—a phrase that suggests the "world upside down" of carnival but which might also be taken as summing up the new evolutionary predicament of humanity. Fallen down the rabbit hole from her lordly position at the top of the Great Chain of Being, Alice instead finds herself, through a series of size changes, continually being repositioned in the food chain.

The importance of the theme of predation, "the motif of eating and being eaten," is such that it has attracted a number of commentaries. It is fully described by Margaret Boe Birns in "Solving the Mad Hatter's Riddle" and by Nina Auerbach in "Alice and Wonderland: A Curious Child." Birns remarks in opening her essay that "Most of the creatures in Wonderland are relentless carnivores, and they eat creatures who, save for some outer physical differences, are very like themselves, united, in fact, by a common 'humanity.'" Birns therefore even cites a crocodile-eating fish as a case of "cannibalism," quoting in support of this idea Alice's "Nurse!

Do let's pretend that I'm a hungry hyaena and you're a bone!" (Looking-Glass, 8). She also remarks that Wonderland contains creatures whose only degree of self-definition is expressing a desire to be eaten or drunk, and offers other comments on scenes in Through the Looking-Glass where, as she puts it, "food can become human, human beings can become food." I do not always find "cannibal" readings supported by the parts of the text in question. Auerbach also makes claims about cannibalism, but a little differently, referring the idea of "eat or be eaten" back to Alice, her "subtly cannibalistic hunger," the "unconscious cannibalism involved in the very fact of eating and the desire to eat." Auerbach associates this interpretation with Dodgson's own attitude to food. But textual support for the quality Auerbach calls Alice's cannibalism seems lacking. Alice does not really eye the other animals in her pool of tears with "a strange hunger" as Auerbach suggests, nor do the Hatter and the Duchess "sing savage songs about eating" as Auerbach claims.

To describe a panther eating an owl as cannibalism, Auerbach must assume (like Birns) that the creatures in Alice are definitely to be read as humans in fur and feathers. My argument is that they need not be so read: the point might be their and Alice's animal nature. Nor does the food at Queen Alice's dinner party at the end of Through the Looking-Glass "begin to eat the guests" as Auerbach claims, although food does misbehave in Looking-Glass and the Pudding might have this in mind (Looking-Glass, 206). Overall, however, in my view the preoccupation of Alice in Wonderland with creatures eating other creatures is much better accounted for by the "more sinister and Darwinian aspects of nature" which Auerbach and Birns also recognize as a part of the Alice books.

I now return to my main argument, that Tenniel's illustrations pick up on but also extend this Darwinist and natural history field of reference in Carroll's text. As already noted, Tenniel's drawings of animals do not stylistically suggest a "children's fairy tale" but rather produce Alice as a kind of natural history by resembling those in the plentiful and lavishly illustrated popular natural histories of the day. My argument therefore differs from Michael Hancher's, which emphasizes social and satirical contexts by comparing pictures of various Wonderland and Looking-Glass creatures to those in Tenniel's and others' Punch cartoons.

While Hancher establishes the relationship with Punch as an important one, however, the most convincing animal resemblances he reproduces from Alice in Wonderland (I am not here concerned with Through the Looking-Glass) amount to only two pictures, the Cheshire Cat in a tree resembling the "Up a Tree" cartoon of a raccoon, and the ape on page 35 of Alice resembling the ape in "Bomba's Big Brother." Tenniel's frog footman and fish footman are Grandvillian figures with animal heads but human bodies, and also evidently suggest social commentary. But they stand apart from the argument I am presenting here because no effort is made by Tenniel to present them as animals.

The satiric side of Tenniel's animal illustrations in Alice, hinted at by echoes of Punch, is never very dominant, then, and should not be seen as precluding another field of reference in natural history reading.

The scope, persistence, eccentricity, and variety of the natural history craze—or rather, series of crazes—that swept Britain between 1820 and 1870 are described for the general reader by Lynn Barber in The Heyday of Natural History and by others in more specialized publications, and need not be redescribed here.

The importance of illustration in contemporary natural history publishing, however, is central to my argument and must be touched on briefly. Even in the midcentury climate of Victorian self-improvement and self-education, the volume of this well-established branch of publishing is impressive: the standard of illustration in popular periodicals and books was high, and sales were also impressively high in Victorian terms.

Rev. John George Wood, according to his son and biographer Theodore Wood, a pioneer in writing natural history in nontechnical language, had reasonable sales for his one-volume The Illustrated Natural History in 1851 and very good sales for Common Objects of the Sea Shore in 1857. But when Routledge brought out his lavishly illustrated Common Objects of the Country in 1858 it sold 100,000 copies within a week of publication, and the first edition was followed by many others, a figure worth comparing with Darwin's more modest first-edition sell-out of 1,250 copies—or, indeed, with Dickens's sales of Bleak House (1852), which were 35,000 in the first two years. The result of Wood's success was a much grander publishing venture by Routledge, Wain and Routledge, a three-volume The Illustrated Natural History with new drawings including some by Joseph Wolf: volume 1 (1859) was on mammals, volume 2 (1862) on birds—the frontispiece is reproduced in figure 2—and volume 3 (1863) on reptiles, fish, and mollusks.

Wood's astonishingly prolific career as a popularizer, however, of which I have described only a tiny fraction (he was dashing off such productions as Anecdotes of Animal Life, Every Boy's Book, and Feathered Friends in this decade as well), is in line with much other more or less theologically inclined and intellectually respectable natural history publishing in the 1850s and 1860s, often by clergymen.

Children were important consumers of such books and periodicals and sometimes are obviously their main market, and a number of fictional works, such as Charles Kingsley's The Water-Babies (1863) and Margaret Gatty's Parables from Nature, of which the first four series appeared between 1855 and 1864 (that is, in the decade prior to Carroll's publication of Alice in Wonderland), capitalize on the contemporary conviction that natural history was a subject especially appropriate for children. Tenniel connects his Alice and natural history illustration by a number of stylistic allusions.

He borrows the conventional techniques of realism, such as the cross-hatching and fine lines used to suggest light, shade, and solidity of form in the Mock Turtle's shell and flippers, or the crabs' and lobster's claws. Accuracy in proportion and a high level of anatomical detail are equally important. the grouping of subjects may also be suggestive—a point first noted by Narda Schwartz, who also drew attention to the resemblance between the etching of the dodo in Wood's three-volume natural history and Tenniel's dodo. Also significant is the way Tenniel's design showing the creatures recently emerged from the pool of tears includes a rather furry-haired Alice among, and on a level with, the beasts and birds. Carroll's own pictures for the pool of tears sequence have the quite different effect of separating Alice from the animal world, a point I will return to. Another Tenniel habit that suggests natural history illustration is his provision of sketchy but realistic and appropriate backgrounds. Here Tenniel's viewpoint sometimes miniaturizes the reader, setting the viewpoint low and thus letting us in on the ground level of a woodland world magnified for our information (compare figs. 3 and 4).

When Alice stands on tiptoe to peep over the edge of a mushroom, when she carries the pig baby in the woods or talks to the Cheshire Cat, Tenniel uses a typical natural history technique, placing a familiar woodland flower—a foxglove—in the background in such a way as to remind the reader of Alice's size at that time. Similarly, Tenniel makes use of the difference between vignettes for simple or single subjects, and framed illustrations, including full-page illustrations, for larger-scale and more important and complex subjects, in a way that very closely resembles a similar distinction in natural history illustration—popular natural histories like Wood's tend to use large, framed illustrations to make generalized statements, showing, for instance, a group of different kinds of rodent, while vignettes present an individual of one species. And above all, although Tenniel certainly endows his creatures with personality and facial expressions, his animals, unlike his humans, are never grotesques.

In fact, nineteenth-century natural history illustration also delights in endowing the most solidly "realistic" creatures with near-human personality or expressiveness, a quality that Tenniel builds on to good effect, for instance, in his depiction of the lawyer-parrots, which remind one of Edward Lear's magnificent macaws.

Thus while Tenniel's animal portraits reflect the Victorians' pleasure in their expanding knowledge of the variety of creatures in the world, they also faithfully reproduce the contemporary assimilation of this variety to familiar human social types, a sleight of hand of which Audubon, for example, is a master: his Great Blue Heron manages also to subtly suggest a sly old gentleman, probably shortsighted, and with side-whiskers.

In the visual world inhabited by Tenniel, then, the differing works of Audubon and Grandville (the latter could depict a heron as a priest merely by giving the bird spectacles) slide together. Where few of Tenniel's successors have been able to resist the temptation to turn the animals in Alice in Wonderland into cartoon or humorous creations, though, it is Tenniel's triumph that he drew his creatures straight, or almost straight: the Times review of Alice in Wonderland particularly noted for praise Tenniel's "truthfulness ... in the delineation of animal forms." It was, indeed, his skill in drawing animals that first established his reputation as an illustrator, when he provided illustrations for Rev. Thomas James's Aesop's Fables in 1848.

Can sources for Tenniel's remarkable animal drawings be more precisely identified? An early biographer of Tenniel records his acknowledgment that he liked to spend time observing the animals at the zoos However, comparisons between pictures reveal that in addition Tenniel almost certainly consulted scientific illustrations or recalled them for his Alice in Wonderland drawings. For example, in the mid-eighteenth century George Edwards produced a hand-colored engraving of a dodo which, he wrote, he had copied from a painting of a live dodo brought from Mauritius to Holland.

The original painting was acquired by Sir Hans Sloane, passed on to Edwards, and given by him to the British Museum. In 1847 C. A. Marlborough painted a picture of a dodo, which is now in the Ashmolean Museum. And in 1862 the second volume of J. G. Wood's The Illustrated Natural History includes a picture of a dodo. Compare all these with Tenniel's dodo: they surely either have a common ancestor or are copies one from the other.

The dodo is a special case in that Tenniel could hardly have studied one at the London zoo. But I wish to put forward a claim that Wood's 1851 one-volume and, later, expanded three-volume Illustrated Natural History were very probably familiar to Carroll and the small Liddells and also to Tenniel, not only because Wood's dodo illustration is a possible source for Tenniel's but because these volumes also display smiling crocodiles, baby eagles in their nest, and the lory, as well as illustrations of numerous more familiar animals that appear in the words and/or pictures of Alice, including the edible crab, the lobster, the frog, the dormouse, guinea pigs, flamingos, varieties of fancy pigeon, and so forth. Given the compendious nature of Wood's works, this is hardly surprising, of course. But Wood must be favored as the source of animal drawings most probably known to Tenniel for the further reason that Wood illustrations often quite strongly resemble Tenniel illustrations, as readers may judge by comparing figures 12, 13, 14, 15, and 16, to the toucan, eagle, and crab from Alice and the lobster and dormouse.

No matter how good Tenniel's famous visual memory, he is unlikely to have drawn such a menagerie without some research. Hancher noted the strong resemblance between a Bewick hedgehog (from the General History of Quadrupeds, 1790, often reprinted) and the evasive croquet-ball hedgehog at Alice's feet on page 121. Bewick's hedgehog, however, had already been recycled by William Harvey for Wood's one-volume Illustrated Natural History where Tenniel is equally likely to have seen and remembered it: all three hedgehogs have the same dragging rear foot.

This is another case, like that of the dodo, where scientific natural history illustrations have been copied, recopied, or reworked for reprinting. A similar argument could be presented about the large number of depictions of sinuous flamingos that Tenniel might have consulted. The volume of contemporary natural history publishing for children and adults, the evident contemporary interest in illustrations of animals, and the resemblance between Tenniel's and contemporary natural history drawings have important implications: the resemblance indicates that Tenniel is here creating the context within which he wants his pictures to be read. He shows us that he saw (and wanted the viewer to be able to see) Carroll's animals as "real" animals, like those that were the objects of current scientific study and theories, at least as much as he saw them as Grandville or Punch-type instruments of social satire, or fairy-tale or fable talking beasts.

In line with his scientific interpretation, then, Tenniel in illustrating Alice in Wonderland intensifies Carroll's reference to Darwin's theory of evolution by carrying out his own visual editing of the Carroll illustrations in the manuscript. Tenniel makes the ape appear in two consecutive illustrations: in the second, it stares thoughtfully into the eyes of the reader—appearing to claim kinship. Tenniel includes among the creatures in these illustrations on pages 29 and 35 a fancy pigeon, perhaps a fantail or a pouter, which should in my view be taken as a direct reference to Darwin's argument from the selective breeding of fancy pigeon varieties in chapter 1 of The Orion of Species.

A visual detail that Tenniel introduced into the book, the glass dome in the background to the royal garden scene on page 117, looks like the dome at the old Surrey Zoological Gardens and therefore constitutes another reference to the study of animals. And as already noted, Tenniel does not reproduce Carroll's rather lonely image of Alice abandoned by the animals, which would have had the effect of separating her human figure from the animal ones and thus emphasizing Alice's difference from them. Instead, Tenniel provides two images of Alice among, and almost of, the animal world, developing a radical implication of Carroll's text of which Carroll himself was possibly unaware.

On the other hand, Carroll's interest in predation, in the motif of "eat or be eaten," is not one on which Tenniel expands. No doubt it would have been thought too frightening for children: one must recall the care taken by Carroll over the positioning of the Jabberwocky illustration in Through the Looking-Glass. But while Carroll's text here develops emphatically—albeit peripherally—some ideas that Tenniel could only leave aside, Tenniel's recognition of the importance of such themes is strongly demonstrated by the puppy picture.

This illustration is a particularly large one, dominating the page on which it appears. It is framed, and therefore gives an impression of completion and independent significance, very different from that given by the more common vignette with its intimate and fluid relationship to the text. These things make it probable that the puppy scene and its illustration were especially important in Tenniel's reading of Alice in Wonderland. Yet commentaries on Alice in Wonderland tend to ignore the puppy scene, perhaps because critics are often most interested by Carroll's verbal nonsense, and the puppy is speechless. Indeed, Denis Crutch disapproves of the puppy as "an intruder from the 'real' world" and Goldthwaite takes up this point, commenting that the puppy was Carroll's "most glaring aesthetic mistake in ... Alice"—neither seems to have noticed that the hedgehogs and flamingos are also not talking beasts.

Another reader of Tenniel's illustrations, Isabelle Nitres, takes a similar line, remarking that "the full-page illustration is perhaps placing too much emphasis on Alice's encounter with the puppy." But what Tenniel's puppy illustration encapsulates, in my view, is the theme of the importance of relative size. Here is Alice's fearful moment of uncertainty about whether she is meeting a predator or a pet. As reader and Alice will discover, the puppy only wants to play. But Alice is "terribly frightened all the time at the thought it might be hungry, in which case it would be very likely to eat her up in spite of all her coaxing", and Tenniel's illustration with the thistle in the foreground towering over the tiny Alice, like many of his memorable illustrations, primarily signifies her anxiety.

Later, too, Tenniel's choice of the lobster as the subject of a drawing is a visual reminder of the transformation of animals into meat: it brings the viewer uncomfortably close to recognition of kinship with the devoured, so human is the lobster and so warily is his eye fixed on the viewer's.

The lobster is another illustration that Hodnett found an inexplicable presence in the text: the song in the text "provides insufficient excuse for an illustration," he remarks. My analysis of Tenniel's composite verbal/visual Alice in Wonderland is very different. Possibly going well beyond Carroll's conscious intentions, Tenniel offers a Wonderland that concurs with the evolutionist view of creation by showing animals and humans as a continuum within which the stronger or larger prey upon the smaller or weaker. The implication—one many readers of Darwin were most reluctant to accept is that if animals are semihuman, humans may conversely be nothing but evolved animals.

Alice's extraordinary size changes—in which Tenniel is so interested-therefore play a significant role in this new world, for as I already pointed out, it is through her series of size changes that Alice finds herself continually being repositioned in the food chain. Wonderland is truly the place of reversals: its theme of a world upside down is traditional, as Ronald Reichertz has reminded us in an illuminating study that positions Alice in Wonderland in relation to earlier children's reading.

Size changes can represent the topsy-turvy, of course. But while Alice has some recognizably Jack-in-Giant-land experiences—like struggling to climb up the leg of a table—and some Tom Thumb experiences—like hiding behind a thistle—what is so weird or Wonderlandish about her story is not her sudden growth spurts but that she transforms rapidly from the small to the large and vice versa.

Alice's body changes at times suggest being outsize and aggressive—for example, when she is trapped in the White Rabbit's house and terrifies the little creatures outside, or when she is accused of being an egg-stealing serpent or predator by the pigeon. But she is undersized and therefore vulnerable when she slips into the pool of tears or when she meets the puppy.

The size changes connect back to "eat or be eaten" where the dangers of large and small size, a theme especially horrifying to children, is a traditional one, found in tales of giants and ogres, Hop-o' my Thumb or Mally Whuppie. But as we have seen, the Tenniel/Carroll Alice in Wonderland links forward to ideas of predator and prey, eat or be eaten, and the "animal" nature of humanity, all recently given new urgency by Darwin.

A contemporary illustration worth pondering that deals with these important ideas (it appeared at almost exactly the time of the publication of Alice in Wonderland) is the cover of

Hardwicke's Science-Gossip: A Monthly Medium of Interchange & Gossip for Students and Lovers of Nature (January 1866). This cover represents the scientific technology that interested Carroll, as well as, more sentimentally, the small creatures and plants of woodland and seashore that are a part of the "natural history" background.

These subjects, however, make a mere frame to the central illustration, both grisly and amusing, which is a depiction of the chain of predation, eat or be eaten, in action. One could hardly ask for a more succinct visual summary of this important element in the contemporary contexts of Alice. Recognition of this theme will, as well as accounting for lobster and puppy illustrations, also account for the otherwise somewhat puzzling centrality of Dinah and the Cheshire Cat in Carroll's text. Nina Auerbach quotes Florence Becker Lennon's insight that the Cheshire Cat is "Dinah's dream-self," and certainly one or the other is more or less everwhere in Wonderland. I think the reason for this must be that this familiar household pet best emphasizes the paradoxical difference between being large, in which state the cat is a delightful little furry companion, and being small, in which state the cat might kill you and eat you. In the Darwinian world, size can be the key to survival.

And yet, Carroll selected a smiling crocodile to stand for the new view of creation. The cruelty of the Darwinian world is, in his view, somehow inseparable from delight. To suggest a context for this unexpected but quintessentially nineteenth-century state of mind, a comparison may be made here between Carroll's poetic vision of his particular predator and Henry de la Beche's 1830 cartoon of life in A More Ancient Dorset; or, Durior Antiquior. De la Beche was English despite his name, and was the first director of the British Geological Survey. According to Stephen Jay Gould, who includes it in his preface to The Book of Life, de la Beche's spirited cartoon, simultaneously grim and humorous, was "reproduced endlessly (in both legitimate and pirated editions)" and is an important model, becoming "the canonical figure of ancient life at the inception of this genre." In short, this is the first dinosaur picture. Victorian paintings of nature (showing a similar pleasure to Carroll's in his crocodile) do tend to centre on hunting and predation—see The Stag at Bay—and de la Beche's infLuential image, Gould explains, became a thoroughly conventional depiction of prehistory, first, in showing a pond unnaturally crowded with wildlife (rather like Carroll's pool of tears), and second, in depicting virtually every creature in it as "either a feaster or a meal" —something one may also feel about Carroll's characters.

Particularly striking is the gusto, the pleasurably half-horrified enjoyment of bloody prehistory, in de la Beche's cartoon, which in my view is very comparable to the enjoyment of the image of the devouring crocodile in Lewis's brilliant little parody. A slightly unpleasant gusto also animates Alice in Wonderland, a book that fairly crackles with energy although the energy has always been rather hard to account for. While on the official levels of his consciousness Carroll "stood apart from the theological storms of the time," is it possible that the news of evolution through natural selection was, on another level of his mind, good news to him as to many other Victorians, coming as a kind of mental liberation?

Humanity might well have found crushing, at times, the requirements of moral responsibility and constant self-improvement imposed by mid-Victorian ideals of Christian duty. Alice, for one, young as she is, has already thoroughly internalized many rules of conduct, and Alice's creator, equipped as he was with what Donald Rackin has called a "rage for standards and order," revels in the over-setting of order (as well as disowning this oversetting thoroughly when Alice awakens from her dream). The exhilaration of an amoral anti-society in Alice in Wonderland may he, therefore, in part the exhilaration of a Darwinist dream, of selfishness without restraint.

As we all know, Alice's route out of Wonderland is to grow out of it. In closing this essay a final suggestion may be made about Carroll and his self-depiction in Wonderland. If the book is full of expressions of anxiety about relative size—and the dangers of largeness and smallness—this may not merely be because a new theory of evolution by natural selection had enlivened this ancient theme. Possibly Carroll had adapted this theory as a private way of symbolizing for himself the anxieties and dangers of his relationship with Alice and the other Liddell children. In Morton N. Cohen's biography Lewis Carroll, a table numbers the occurrences of guilty self-reproach and resolves to amend in Carroll's diaries and shows how these peaked at the time of his deepest involvement with the Liddell family.

Is it possible that Carroll, far from suffering a repressed interest in little girls, consciously acknowledged and wrestled in private prayer with his own impossible desires? It seems to become ever more difficult, rather than easier, to read this aspect of Carroll's life.

In a recent Times Literary Supplement (February 8, 2002), Karoline Leach argues that Carroll's friendships with children were emphasized in his nephew Stuart Collingwood's biography to distract attention from the potentially more scandalous fact of the older Carroll's friendships with mature women. A letter in response by Jenny Woolf, on February 15, points out that Carroll's sisters continued to recognize Carroll's women friends, so obviously perceived these friendships as chaste, but reminds us of the possibility that Dodgson may have cultivated girl children as friends because of their innocence, because they were sexually "safe" to him, rather than because they were dangerously enticing.

A response to this position, of course, would be that the assiduity with which Carroll cultivated friendships with small girls seems out of proportion to such a purpose. Whatever the truth of these matters, it appears to me that Carroll, distressed by the emotional battles documented in his diary, might well have developd a set of imaginative scenarios in which a little girl's growing up or down is reversible according to her own desire: this offers one kind of explanation of some of the more mysterious events of Wonderland.

The dangerous but exhilarating aspects of Carroll's relationship with his little friends seems to fit neatly into a "tooth and claw" model of society, too, for each party to such a friendship, although acting in innocence and affection, has a kind of reserve capacity to destroy, to switch from pet to predator. Carroll might even have dramatized himself as a beast in a Darwinian world in relation to these little girls who are never the right size for him.

At times he is only the pet—a romping, anxious-to-please, but oversized puppy. But there are other times when he might fear becoming the predator, a crocodile whose welcoming smile masks the potential to devour. And conversely, of course, Carroll's beloved little friends had the monstrous capacity to destroy him, morally and socially, if he should ever overstep the boundaries of decency and trust. Tenniel, presumably unaware of any secret underside to Carroll's life, was anyway debarred by Victorian regard for children as viewers from depicting the savage underside of Alice. But by referring the reader outward to current controversies and current interests in the natural sciences, he has succeeded wonderfully in rendering in art both Carroll's, and his own, grasp of the importance of a new worldview, and of the explosive anxiety and exhilaration to which it gave birth.

Chapter 7

Wordsworth, Carroll and the 'Aged, Aged Man'

The question that lies behind this essay could not be simpler: what happens when a self meets or encounters an other? Its a simple, almost banal, question, but one that has important and far-reaching implications. It is the crucial question posed in Emmanuel Levinas's ethics; a theory of ethics which has, in turn, influenced thinkers such as Jean-Luc Nancy, Jacques Derrida and Jean-Francois Lyotard.

I don't want to engage in an abstract argument here - that's not the point of this essay - but I will point to one key premise underlying my question. For Levinas, the self-other relationship is based on a fundamental and violent disequilibrium: the self experiences, thinks, comprehend and represent the other - it is active; the other is experienced, thought, comprehended, represented - passive.

This is unavoidable: if the other were to remain wholly other to the self - unknown, unrepresented - no encounter could take place and knowledge would be impossible. The ethical implications concern the way in which this inevitable process of representation is performed and seeks to recognise and to think the violence that it entails.

So, what happens when a self meets an other? I want to contrast two versions of the same, quite simple, event: a meeting that happens and is subsequently reported, represented, by a narrator. I'll start with the second, revisionary, version of the encounter, the "report" of which begins:

I'll tell thee everything I can:
There's little to relate.
I saw an aged aged man
A-sitting on a gate.
"Who are you, aged man?" I said.
"And how is it you live?"
And his answer trickled through my head,
Like water through a sieve.

The encounter depicted in this passage is, of course, already familiar from Wordsworth's "Resolution and Independence"; and yet, everything seems to have changed. The "White Knight's Song" from Lewis Carroll's *Through the Looking-Glass* parodies the meeting between the narrator and the Leech-Gatherer that occurs in the second half of Wordsworth's poem, a meeting that strives to resolve the conflict which sets that poem in motion. A very brief precis of the conflict to refresh memories... As I'm sure you recall, "Resolution and Independence" opens with the narrator out for a stroll, feeling "as happy as a boy" because "The pleasant season did my heart employ: / My old remembrances went from me wholly; / And all the ways of men, so vain and melancholy".

When suddenly, and apparently inexplicably, he undergoes a violent mood-swing: "As high as we have mounted in delight / In our dejection do we sink so low; / To me that morning did it happen so;". It is at this stage that the meeting occurs: the narrator is greeted by the sight of an old man beside a pond whom he engages in conversation; and it is the recognition of this old man's cheerful demeanour that finally inspires the narrator to prayer: "'God,' said I, 'be my help and stay secure; / I'll think of the Leech-Gatherer on the lonely moor!'".

While critical accounts of "Resolution and Independence" often differ quite widely in their opinions about the poem's precise meaning, a consensus seems to have emerged about its general tenor. This consensus places Wordsworth's poem at the centre of, what we might call, the liberal humanist tradition: through perceiving, and identifying with, the old man's perseverance, the narrator learns the value of resolution and independence in the face of suffering and adversity. The self is healed through an empathy with the suffering of the other - an old and familiar story. Recently, Richard Bourke, in a comprehensive review of approaches to this poem, has cited Albert Gerard's and Jane Worthington's accounts as paradigmatic readings of the text, whose conclusions recur with little substantial alteration in a great deal of recent criticism. Gerard's argument is that through "identification with the leech-gatherer' ... the poet is released from 'puzzled recognition' and led to a 'mature acceptance of the position and value of suffering'"; and Worthington's earlier idea is that the poem presents a "stoic precept" that "warns against the anxious anticipation of misfortunes".

So, from this, we have "Resolution and Independence" as a quintessentially humanist text charting the individual's progress towards enlightenment through a recognition of the value of stoicism in the face of suffering. In terms of the self-other problem however, it seems that this reading of the poem can secure its closure only at the cost of reducing the other, suppressing its otherness by converting it into a mere instrument in the self's process of maturation. Lewis Carroll's poem will have nothing to do with this process; in fact, it is the violent reduction of the other by humanism that appears to be the main target of his satire.

His parodic re-writing of Wordsworth refuses any notion of an "ennobling recognition of misfortune" by excluding any explanatory framing narrative and thereby presenting the meeting as a naked fact. Thus, what occurs in the encounter between the narrator and the old man expands to occupy the entire poem: there is no thematic introduction that sets the scene for the meeting and smoothes the relation between self and other by setting up a context in which the focus of all attention can become the self and its reactions. Of course, other changes have also taken place: the Leech-Gatherer who teaches the fortitude of resolution and independence to the narrator of Wordsworth's poem is replaced with a half-crazed "Aged Aged Man" whose explanations of the bizarre schemes by which he earns his living are utterly ignored by a narrator who has his own, equally outrageous, plans to consider. I suspect Carroll's version of the encounter is familiar, but I'll cite a short section of it to refresh memories:

"Who are you, aged man?" I said.
"And how is it you live?"
And his answer trickled through my head,
Like water through a sieve.
He said "I look for butterflies
That sleep among the wheat:
I make them into mutton pies,
And sell them in the street.
I sell them unto men," he said,
"Who sail on stormy seas;
And that's the way I get my bread -
A trifle, if you please."
But I was thinking of a plan
To dye one's whiskers green,
And always use so large a fan
That they could not be seen.
So, having no reply to give
To what the old man said,
I cried "Come, tell me how you live!"
And thumped him on the head.

And so it continues... In Carroll's poem, the violence of the encounter comes straight to the fore. The Aged Man is forced to repeat his story under the duress of ever increasing physical abuse - in the *Looking-Glass* version he is "thumped on the head", shaken "well from side to side / Until his face was blue" and, in an earlier version of the poem intended for the less delicate taste of Carroll's fellow Oxford dons, he is "kicked", "pinched", his ears are boxed, his "grey and reverend locks" are "tweaked" and he is generally "put into pain". And, after all of this, all that the Aged Man manages to communicate to the narrator is that he is willing to "drink" his "noble health". The conclusions the narrator draws from his encounter, conclusions that clearly echo Wordsworth's, illustrate - through their wholly arbitrary relation to what has gone before - the problematic status of the closure of resolution discovered by the humanist reading of "Resolution and Independence" and the work of suppression undertaken by such an approach to the poem.

As I have already said, things are quite different in the later poem: the ludicrous schemes and the physical violence of Carroll's poem have an exuberance that is utterly foreign to Wordsworth's original. And yet, as a parodic rendering of the encounter that takes place in Wordsworth it also seems to be extremely apt. One is left with the impression that Carroll has discovered, has uncovered, a violent subtext that cannot - and perhaps should not - be wholly excised from a reading of the poem. Carroll's reading presents an injunction, a demand to the reader of "Resolution and Independence": "you must recognise the violence to which the other, the old man, is subjected".

What Carroll has picked up on and exposed quite mercilessly is the inattention of the narrator of Wordsworth's poem to the Leech-Gatherer's tale. The narrator's relationship with the Leech-Gatherer is characterised by what Steven Knapp identifies as "the speaker's well-known but still mysterious inability to *concentrate* on what he himself wants to interpret as a providential answer to his needs". This loss of attention within Wordsworth's poem - as contact with the old man gives way to internal musings about the self - seems to indicate what materialist critics have over the past few years identified as Romantic poetry's way of dealing with its objects.

Perhaps the most influential, and certainly the most well known, reading of this type is that offered by Jerome McGann in his book, *The Romantic Ideology*. McGann's general thesis is this: Romantic aesthetics indulges in political quietism by escaping from material reality to questions of self-reflection and self-consciousness - it is engaged in what McGann refers to as a "self-regarding spiritual economy" - and the modern critic must beware of identifying with the writers to the extent that his or her own account falls prey to this "Romantic ideology". Now, as I have just said, this also seems to be the thrust of Carroll's parody. In fact, that this is so is even clearer in the earlier version of the poem which begins: "I met an aged, aged man / Upon the lonely moor: / I knew I was a gentleman, / And he was but a boor. / So I stopped and roughly questioned him... " Here, the explicit cultural reference to gentility is what allows Carroll's narrator to bully the aged man and thereby frames the nonsense verse with distinct social bounds. In Carroll's version of the meeting, there is no possibility of the development of a "spiritual economy", but simply the representation of the material reality of a violent class relation.

Yet, once one begins to take notice of the differences between Wordsworth's and Carroll's poems, questions emerge about the sort of reading that a materialist might propose. The thrust of McGann's critique is that Romanticism submits to an ideology of "spiritual economy" that negates the materiality of the other; but it seems that it is just this economy that is put on stage in "Resolution and Independence". Although a "spiritual economy" might legitimately be said to characterise the first half of the poem while the narrator walks "Far from the world, and from all care"; it is this economy that leads to the anxiety which the old man interrupts. Furthermore, the narrator appears aware of his "displacement" of the Leech-Gatherer, and his inability to listen to the story is explicitly discussed. In other words, the poem appears to contain its own self-conscious reflection on the supposedly unconscious ideological structure of Romantic art: within the narrative of the poem, the narrator carefully sets up and inhabits the very categories - performs the very actions - that are supposed to shape the poem's production.

However, simply noting that "Resolution and Independence" anticipates the critique levelled at it by materialism is not saying that the poem thereby becomes exempt from it. The "White Knight's song" is not critically redundant, but rather bears witness to a conflict at the heart of Wordsworth's text which that text cannot resolve or sublate: an awkwardness in the shape of the old man. How does this awkwardness manifest itself? Stated in a brief and somewhat peremptory manner, it takes the form of an other that cannot be wholly sublated - comprehended and represented - by the narratorial self (this is the recognition pointed to by what I referred to earlier as Carroll's injunction). The poem presents the demand in the shape of the other that the narrative recognise the presence of this other in its material otherness. What I have just called "the demand for the recognition of the other in its otherness" sounds suspiciously like sloganeering. I hope that it is more than this, and I want to try to explain what I am talking about by very briefly outlining a reading of the meeting that retains an idea of Carroll's injunction in the background.

It has become a bit of a commonplace to say that "Resolution and Independence", indicates a paradigmatic shift in the style and content of Wordsworth's poetry: at the same time it marks a move away from the style of the *Lyrical Ballads* and also suggests the trajectory that will be undertaken by Wordsworth's changing poetic practice. As such, it is a liminal text, a poem caught up in a transition towards the more orthodox Christian world-view of Wordsworth's later work, that is unable either to fully encompass this view or to retain the earlier modes of understanding that characterise the *Lyrical Ballads* .

One can see the transition at work in the changes that occur in the poem between its first version of 1802 and the revision of 1807. The earlier version of the poem is very clearly in the *Lyrical Ballads* tradition and bears a striking resemblance to poems such as "The Sailor's Mother", "Alice Fell" and "Beggars" that were written during the same period. They are all, what one might call "encounter poems", as they relate the conversation of people that the narrator meets during his travels.

When Wordsworth revises the poem however, everything changes: the speech of the Leech-Gatherer that comprised the second half of the poem is excised, and the status of the old man undergoes a transformation.

The change in the old man is first marked by the deletion of the opening description which stated simply that "the old man was" there (a description, the power of which Wordsworth had insisted upon at length in a letter to Sarah

Hutchinson). In the second version, this is replaced by the famous simile of the rock and the sea beast:

As a huge stone is sometimes seen to lie
Couched on the bald top of an eminence;
Wonder to all who do the same espy,
By what means it could thither come and whence;
So that it seemed a thing endued with sense:
Like a sea-beast crawled forth, that on a shelf
Of rock or sand reposeth, there to sun itself;
Such seemed this Man, not all alive or dead,
Nor all asleep...

The terms of description have changed: the ontological "was" has been transformed into an aesthetic "seemed" that changes the man into "a thing endued with sense", a signifier, who requires decoding. And yet, as Wordsworth's own comments in the "Preface" to his *Poems* of 1815 make clear, decoding is almost impossible as the description refuses to stand still: rather, it veers between a "stone ... endowed with something of the power of life", "a sea-beast stripped of some of its vital qualities" and the old man "divested" of the "indications of life and motion" to produce a point where the "objects unite and coalesce in just comparison".

The suggestions of resolution in the terms "unite" and "coalesce", however, mask a profound indeterminacy: the "just comparison" that the image suggests - and the ethical implication of this phrase calls for a whole essay of its own - indicates a point of contact between the narrator and the old man in which the latter is represented as neither material nor ideal, and is certainly not a synthesis of the two.

It is this slippage that underpins the description of the Leech-Gatherer: from his first appearance that "befalls" the narrator, breaking forcefully into his "spiritual economy", attempts at comprehension are thwarted by the multiplication of identities. The first question the narrator asks is about the providential nature of the meeting - does it occur "by peculiar grace, / A leading from above, a something given" (and one should not consider these possibilities as merely equivalent) - is a question that remains unanswered. Equally, the old man's "flash of mild surprise" that occurs before he replies to the narrator's question has all of the destabilising power that Paul de Man detects in a similar phrase during his reading of "The Winander Boy".

As their conversation proceeds, the narrator's inability to listen to the Leech-Gatherer's story is not simply inattention but the result of a failure to comprehend the other. As the old man continues speaking, epithets slide off him: he is neither alive, nor dead, nor a dream, nor a gift of providence; or else he is all of these things. The poem thus specifically and explicitly depicts the refusal of a resolution in the knowledge that arises from the comprehension and fixation of the other.

The indeterminacy of the old man reaches its climax in the penultimate stanza, directly following his most material appearance in the poem with the direct quotation of his speech:

While he was talking thus, the lonely place,
The old Man's shape, and speech - all troubled me:
In my minds eye I seemed to see him pace
About the very moors continually,
Wandering about alone and silently.
While I these thoughts within myself pursued,
He, having made a pause the same discourse renewed.

By this stage, he seems both wholly external to the narrator: a material other, identified with and assimilated into the landscape; an other who is impossible to comprehend or even to hear. And yet he is also invested with a powerful metaphorical presence: internalised as a "troubling" image in the "mind's eye" that provides assistance as the narratorial self desperately attempts to seek the solace of firm knowledge and adequate representation. The poem thus internalises McGann's "spiritual economy", doing violence not to the represented other but rather to the process of representation itself through a writing that invokes the absence of totalisation and of closure.

And so, the reference to the man's "firm mind" and the invocation of "God's help" in the final stanza marks, neither the humanist certainty of resolution and independence nor the displacement from the world for which it is condemned by the materialist, but rather the desperate but impossible desire for knowledge and self-certainty in the face of the finally irreducible heterogeneity of the other.

BUT THERE ARE NO SUCH THINGS AS WORDS

Remember the Jabberwocky's song in Carroll's *Through the Looking-Glass*? Pretty meaningless, huh? Still, it sounds "English" rather than, say, French or German or Italian. That is why it is so amusing: it sounds like perfect English yet we cannot understand it. Actually, we understand quite a bit about the poem even though we don't understand it as a whole. For example, what do we know about *toves*?

Well, we know that there are more than one of them and that those mentioned here are *slithy*, whatever that is. We know that *slithy* describes the *toves* as either like a slithe or having slithes. We know that these slithy toves *gyred* and *gimbled*, and even though we don't know what these actions are we know they are actions and something about when they took place. How do we know all this, not knowing what any of the boldface parts of the words mean?

The reason we know so much about the meaningless words in Carroll's poem is that some of the words and parts of words are, in fact, English. The English words are small, less prominent words, barely more prominent in their pronunciation than the parts of words, the prefixes and suffixes. These small words and parts of words (in plain type above) are expressions that tell us nothing about the world, but only about the grammatical categories of the English language; let's call them morphemes, just to have a term for them.

The nonsense parts of the words in the Jabberwocky song above are all noun, verb, and adjective stems, the main parts of words without prefixes or suffixes. Stems are also the linguistic things that refer to the world we live in. Let's call whole words and stems lexemes; they are anything we use in speech that names or refers to things in the real world. Morphemes will then be the words or parts of words that mark the categories of grammar which are the crucial stuff of language. That is why they control whether we sense a spoken or written utterance is English or French or German.

No one has ever been able to define the word *word* despite gargantuan efforts to do so. *The Linguistic Concept of Word: An Analytic Bibliography* by Alphonse Juilland and Alexandra Roceric lists 118 PAGES of books and articles (unsuccessfully) attempting to define the word *word* over the past 3 millennia. Why can no one define *word*? Maybe because words simply do not exist; rather, the sentences we speak are composed of lexemes and morphemes and these two linguistic objects differ too much to be subsumed under one concept.

The differences between these two linguistic elements are dramatic. Here are the major ones.

Comparison of Lexemes and Morphemes

Lexemes *Morphemes*

Refer to real world *Refer to grammatical categories*

May be derived *Cannot be derived*

Always associated with sound Often not associated with sound Sounds always predetermined Sounds often depend on stem Are infinite in number Belong to a small, closed class Let's examine these differences. Lexemes, remember, are basically noun, verb, and adjective stems or whole words: *violin, play, small* are lexemes. They refer to things, actions, states, and qualities in the real world. Suffixes like *-ing, -s, -ed,* prefixes like *re-, ex-, un-,* particles like *the, not, so* and prepositions like *of, for, to* are morphemes. They refer to grammatical categories like Progressive Aspect (*-ing*: *am going*), Plural Number (*-s*: *cars*), Past Tense (*-ed*: *walked*), Negation (*un-, not*: *unwanted*), Definite (*the*: *the cat*), Possession (*of*: *of my friend*).

Lexemes like *violin, play,* and *small* are subject to derivation, a process which generates new words from others: *violin* > *violin-ist, play* > *play-er, small* > *small-ness*. Morphemes do not undergo derivation even if they are not affixes which mark derivations themselves. We do not find words derived from *the, that, of, for, it*.

Lexemes always comprise a sound plus a meaning but morphemes may have either one but not the other. For example, if *-er* means "someone who does something", as in *runner, player, driver,* what sound has that meaning in *(a) cook, (a) guide, (a) cut-up*? With these verbs, all we have to do is use them in a noun position, e.g. *the cook guided us through the kitchen,* and we know that the speaker is using the noun, not the verb. (Leads one to wonder why we have affixes at all, doesn't it?)

On the other hand, morphemes some time show up with sound but not meaning. Take the adjectives that end on *-ic,* e.g. *histor-ic,* meaning "having the property of history" from *history*. There are lots of these derivations: *climat-ic, theatr-ic, semant-ic*. But look at this series: *dram-at-ic, spasm-at-ic, enigm-at-ic*. The meaning of these adjectives is the same as that of the "syntactic" class: "having the properties of X", where "X" is the meaning of the underlying word. However, they contain an extra morpheme, *-at*. Why is that? Well, for some reason known only to the ancient Greeks, who enjoyed the same derivation, before adding *-ic* you had to insert a suffix *-at* if the stem ended on an [m]. So, when English borrowed these words from Greece, the rule came with it. The suffix *-at* probably had no meaning in Greek but it certainly has none in English, where it is simply required of all words borrowed from Greek ending on [m] when the suffix *-ic* is applied. So not only do we find morpheme meanings without morphemes, we find morphemes without morphemic meaning.

The sounds of lexemes are always predetermined and remain (more or less) the same wherever they occur in a phrase. The sound of a morpheme on the other hand, especially prefixes and suffixes may vary wildly. The future tense in Tagalog (or Philippino) is formed by adding a prefix. For example, *bili* is the verb stem meaning "buy" and *bi-bili* means "will buy". So, if *kuha* means "get", "will get" should be *bi-kuha,* right? Wrong. The future of *kuha* is *ku-kuha*. Hey, what's going on here? The verb meaning "laugh" is *tawa;* "will laugh" is *ta-tawa*. Catch on? What do you think the future of *sulat* "write" is? You are right if you guessed *su-sulat*. Tagalog reduplicates the first syllable of the verb stem to make a prefix. In other words, the sound of the prefix is not predetermined, but is determined by the sound of the stem. The morpheme here is not a sound but a rule for creating sound. Only morphemes may be rules for retrieving sound, never lexemes.

Tagalog Future Tense

Stem	Future
bili "buy"	*bi-bili "will buy"*
kuha "get"	*ku-kuha "will get"*
punta "go"	*pu-punta "will go"*
sulat "write"	*su-sulat "will write"*
tawa "laugh"	*ta-tawa "will laugh"*

An important difference between lexemes and morphemes is that the former, but not the latter, belong to an open, unlimited class. That means that there is no limit on the number of noun, verb, and adjective stems in any language. New lexemes may be derived by compounding, affixation, and other rules; they may be borrowed from other languages or simply made up.

The number of morphemes, however, is limited to around 200. Proto-Indo-European languages have fewer than 100.

We are currently being inundated by new lexemes describing the categories, states and qualities of new technology.

We never meet a new preposition (*of, for, by, with*), pronoun (*he, she, it*), or article like *a* or *the*. The fact that the number of morphemes and the categories they refer to is fixed suggests that they determine the grammar of a language. That is why the Jabberwocky Song 'sounds' like English even though it is incomprehensible. It is English with nonsense lexemes but real morphemes.

So, speaking is a bit more subtle than stringing 'words' together in phrases. Assuming that *on* is a word does not distinguish between the lexeme *on* in *the oven is on,* and the morpheme *on* in *on the table.*

Why is this important? It helps us understand the important difference between grammar and vocabulary. The meaning of on the morpheme, but not that of the lexeme may expressed by a suffix in some languages, such as Finnish and Hungarian.

It helps us understand why children begin learning lexemes around the age of one, about a year before they begin learning grammar, represented by morphemes. They only begin picking up morphemes around the age of two, when they begin using phrases. Finally, it helps explain why chimpanzees can learn what seem to be lexemes but not morphemes (morphemes represent grammar, the essential core of language). Morphemes convey the categories of grammar itself, so if we want to understand language itself, we must understand first and foremost morphemes. Lexemes are not going to tell us much about language.

Remember, the magic word is LINGUISTICS, a very new science, indeed. Morphology is the study of words and their parts: morphemes and lexemes. It examines the grammatical and semantic categories they convey as well as the sounds and sound changes caused by combining them. It also explores the relations of words in sentences.

Chapter 8

The Lost Girlhood of the Victorian Gentleman

"A boy phenomenon, perhaps?" suggested Nicholas. "There is only one phenomenon, sir," replied Mr. Crummles impressively, "and that's a girl." *(Charles Dickens, "Nicholas Nickleby")*

This Book explores the intimate relationship between middle-class men and little girls in nineteenth-century British culture. *Men in Wonderland* traces the ways in which a number of male authors in this period construct girlhood and analyzes the exact nature of their investment in the figure of the girl.

The idealization and idolization of little girls, long acknowledged features of the Victorian era, cannot be thought of without reference to a pervasive fantasy of male development in which men become masculine only after an initial feminine stage. In this light, little girls represent not just the true essence of childhood, but an adult male's best opportunity of reconnecting with his own lost self.

The works of the individuals discussed at length in the study ahead—Wordsworth, De Quincey, Dickens, Ruskin, and Carroll—exhibit in various ways this male myth of feminized origin. Juxtaposing these literary texts and art forms with a range of other cultural productions such as philanthropic tracts, conduct books, government reports, fine art, and popular journalism, *Men in Wonderland* demonstrates both the evolution of the idea of the ideal girl in the nineteenth century, and the manifestation of the concept of original girlhood in genres that would seem less driven by personal motivations.

Although this fantasy of development by no means holds universal sway, it nevertheless makes its way into general currency because of its appeal to an important and influential strain in nineteenth-century discourse, a strain that is noticeably middle class, religious, paternalist, sentimental, nostalgic, and conservative.

Recognizing the existence of such a historical phenomenon brings numerous benefits to Victorian studies. In particular, this perception fuels the reassessment of the oeuvres of a variety of literary artists, especially inasmuch as it complicates the narratives of pedophilic desire that have habitually been employed to explain the work of the nineteenth century's most infamous girl-lovers (Ruskin and Carroll figuring here as the two most familiar examples of the type). More broadly, the identification of such a paradigm advances our understanding of such important characteristics of the age as its fraught constructions of masculinity, its obsession with loss, its rampant sentimentality, and its intense valorization of the little girl at the expense of mature femininity.

In many ways, to point out that the Victorians thought of early childhood as a feminine era is to state the obvious. After all, here at the beginning of the twenty-first century, the world of infancy and young childhood is still largely perceived as a female domain: not only does the care of little children continue to be primarily woman's responsibility, but the terms with which the early period of childhood is characterized—a time of "softness" and "vulnerability," requiring "gentleness" and "protection"—remain resolutely feminized. For these reasons, Freud's account of the process by which human beings come to understand sexual differentiation remains problematic: because of the feminine aura of those early days, it is hard to swallow his theory that all children initially believe themselves to be "little men," and that only upon noticing their "lack" do little girls regretfully give up this fantasy.

If childhood is a feminized world now, it was even more so in the nineteenth century: whereas male babies today are soon dressed in clearly coded "masculine" apparel and colors, large numbers of Victorian photographs of scowling boys in short frocks exist to remind us that brothers and sisters used to be "clothed alike," as Coleridge wistfully recalls in "Frost at Midnight." Although the breeching ceremony of the early modern period—the great day when a six- or seven-year-old boy would shed his girlish dress and don trousers—had more or less fallen into obscurity for the Victorians, it was not until the twentieth century that boys, in any of the social classes, would wear obviously gendered clothing before this relatively advanced age.

Perhaps more significantly, for many boys of the middle and upper classes the age of six or seven signaled the removal from maternal or feminine care in the home into the masculine world of the school: up until this point, their lessons would have taken place alongside their sisters in a female-staffed nursery.

Trousers and school thus marked the end of the first phase of existence for boys; girls of these classes, still wearing petticoats and pursuing their education, for the most part, at home, experienced no such division between early and later childhood. Given that the garments and worlds left behind continued to be female, then, the first six years of male life in the nineteenth century carried a clear stamp of femininity, especially when viewed in retrospect. While it may be a critical commonplace that the Victorians adhered to a rigid system of gender separation, in this particular instance it seems that young boyhood crossed the line, and actually looked more like girlhood.

It is, however, one thing to notice that the early lives of boys found them wearing versions of female clothing and lodged in the female-controlled zones of the house, and quite another to register the depth of passionate investment in nineteenth-century writings that both insist that perfect childhood is always exemplified by a little girl, and that, despite the logical and biological impossibilities of the stance, lament a man's lost girlhood. To understand the climate that fostered the growth of a fantasy of primary and ideal femininity, it is necessary to examine the beliefs that informed the Victorians' fascination with the idea of the child. The account here begins with a brief summary of the general historiography of childhood in eighteenth- and nineteenth-century studies, and then moves to a consideration of the complicated and contradictory origins of the concept.

Since the publication of Philippe Ariès's *Centuries of Childhood* in 1962, it has generally been accepted that the idea of childhood is a fairly recent invention. According to current explanations, childhood's birth is coincident with the rise of the middle class in late-seventeenth- and eighteenth-century Europe, and its infancy appears to draw strength from the twin sustenances of the Evangelical movement and Romantic thought.

Historians document the growth of philanthropic concern for children, which manifests itself in institutions like the Foundling Hospital, the burgeoning Sunday school movement, and early campaigns for the abolition of exploitative labour, while those on the literary trail register the central importance of the child in the writings of Jean-Jacques Rousseau, William Blake, and William Wordsworth.

Contemporary scholarship claims that this interest in the child grows ever more particularized as the nineteenth century progresses: by virtue of the rapid pace of industrialization and population expansion, runs the argument, the plight of the laboring and the indigent child becomes hugely obvious and eventually energizes massive legislative reform and the erection of comprehensive educational and social welfare systems for the working-class child. Investigating Victorian domestic ideology's construction of the inviolable middle-class home, feminist critics and historians contend that the life experience of the child of comfortable means came to be shaped with comparable rigor in this period.

This is also an era, it is maintained, in which the child and its properties become the subject of specialized legal and medical discourse. Furthermore, the figure of the child evolves into a dominant icon both for elite and popular consumption: six hundred thousand copies of *Cherry Ripe,* an engraving by the Royal Academician John Everett Millais, are not enough to satisfy public demand in 1880, while Charles Dickens's thirty-year career furnishes a veritable kindergarten of child heroes and heroines for the collective mind.

This overview gives a sense of the highly visible centrality of the child in any number of arenas and at all class levels in Victorian life. More difficult to describe is the meaning carried by the idea of the child in this period for the influential middle-class community that constitutes the primary focus of this study. Because the era of childhood was of paramount significance to two powerful, and apparently opposed, systems of thought, one would expect to find deep and irresolvable contradictions embedded at the heart of the nineteenth century's perception of children.

On the one hand, to thinkers as various as Locke, Rousseau, and Wordsworth the child represents a pure point of origin, deeply connected to the natural and primitive world, and as yet unmired by the sullying forces of language, sexuality, and society. On the other, the eighteenth-century revival of hard-line Puritan attitudes in some strains of the Evangelical movement brought to the fore the doctrine of the primary corruption of human nature: the child comes into this world as a bearer of original sin, a creature of fundamental depravity. And yet in spite of this radical disagreement, these two different visions of the child turn out to be remarkably amenable to each other in the daily practice of nineteenth-century life and discourse.

Up until fairly recently, the secular bent of literary and historical studies has resulted in a disproportionate emphasis upon the prominence of the Romantic idea of the child in the Victorian period: consequently the Evangelical perspective, and its perceived extremism, has been given relatively short shrift. In the past fifteen years or so, however, the importance of acknowledging the deeply religious, if complicated and often conflicted, character of at least the first two-thirds of the nineteenth century has become more widely appreciated. In consequence a more balanced view of the child's combined heritage is now beginning to emerge.

Between the 1730s and 1830s the Evangelical movement galvanized British Christianity, affecting practically all denominations from the established to the Nonconformist sects. While Evangelicals came to be active in every sphere of social reform in the nineteenth century, the primary tenor of this new religious enthusiasm was essentially personal and domestic: adherents were encouraged to scrutinize with unprecedented intensity the states of their own souls and those of others, especially family members, and to conduct with great reverence such home-centered activities as private and family prayers, meditation, and Bible study. Within such a regimen of spiritual examination, attention to the child was particularly marked. This watchfulness, however, took various different and sometimes competing forms. For those Evangelicals, both inside and outside the Church of England, who subscribed to Calvinistic doctrines of original sin, it was imperative to guide and educate children to give them the best opportunity of redeeming themselves, so they might obtain God's grace.

To modern, and even to many contemporary standards of judgment, the strict codes of supervision and punishment levied by zealots endeavoring to save children from their corrupt natures often ran dangerously close to cruelty. Even though this residue of earlier theological thinking insisted on the fundamental wickedness of children, it nevertheless concurred with the otherwise opposed Romantic code in placing tremendous emphasis on the care of the child, and in seeing the world as a continual source of moral danger.

Many other Evangelically minded Christians, however, found themselves turning away from theories of original sin toward ideas more overtly compatible with Romanticism's idealization of children: in this frame of mind, Scripture could, for example, be reinterpreted in line with Wordsworth's ideas about the child, and thus "texts urging us to become as little children were now about innocence, rather than, as in Puritan dogma, about obedience." Children, then, were to be closely observed because they offered adults glimpses of an original heavenly purity. Perhaps not surprisingly, those whose secular or religious beliefs promoted such a glorified view of childhood could on occasion be just as exacting as the most doctrinaire Calvinist on the subject of acceptable child behaviour. These different strains of Victorian Christianity, then, found themselves variously in contention and agreement with Romanticism's view of the child as pure and innocent, but ultimately colluded with its insistence upon the central importance of childhood. While such theoretical positions had obvious implications for the ways in which children were perceived, just as significant were the derived effects of Evangelical Christianity's relocation of the sacred from the supernatural and ecclesiastical, to the personal and familial, realm. In this essentially domestic religion, the ideal Christian home and its occupants became "objects of sentimentalization, bordering on worship."

The mid-nineteenth-century crisis of belief that famously struck down many middle-class Evangelicals, causing them to turn away from institutional religion and search elsewhere for salvation, strengthened this sense that the family, and most particularly, the child at its heart, offered an alternative access to grace and purity. On a still deeper level, the story of Adam's ejection from Paradise in Genesis, previously important to the perception of childhood because of its explanation of the source of original sin, increasingly offered itself as a myth of personal development to middle-class Victorian individuals, both religious and otherwise.

Evangelical Christianity's drive toward self-examination had led the way to making religious narratives much more personally applicable: now, as John Gillis puts it, whether or not orthodox belief was present, the Garden of Eden "ceased to be a place, and became a stage of life," the time of childhood. In a move that has huge significance for this particular project, such retrospective imagining of the early years of life as a paradise of innocence and purity not only placed an absolute line of division between childhood and adulthood, but also declared that same adulthood to be a time of postlapsarian guilt and gloom.

Understanding both why this model was so compelling to middle-class men and why those childhood years were most satisfyingly embodied in the figure of a little girl will be a major task in the chapters ahead. For now, we can notice in broad outline a couple of factors touched upon earlier. Men from comfortable backgrounds in this period were far more likely to have experienced a definitive break between those early years in the feminized nursery and their subsequent careers in the wider world than women of their class, whose lives were generally expected to be bounded by the home.

Furthermore, this same gendering of the home, and its concurrent transformation into the locus of the sacred, not only had the effect of creating that domestic, and now much vilified, paragon, the Angel in the House, but also her ideal daughter. On those occasions when paradise was imagined as the primary, lost stage in the journey of life, rather than the sanctified home, then the perfect little girl formed its most apt symbol.

While this project plainly situates itself within the historiography of childhood, it simultaneously has relevance and allegiance to a number of other important scholarly arenas. My analysis owes a huge debt to the pioneering labors of academic feminism over the past twenty years, particularly to its careful explication of nineteenth-century constructions of the feminine, and the concomitant emergence and consolidation of domestic ideology.

Furthermore, this study finds a home in the burgeoning world of masculinity studies, a field that has recently grown out of the work of these feminist precursors. Like many of the works in this area, the present investigation is part of the movement to complicate our understanding of the complexities and contradictions that both challenged and supported nineteenth-century gender ideology: while earlier historical and critical studies often reproduced the Victorians' division of the "separate spheres," now "the 'private' is being reformulated to take account of men, in the same way that the scope of the 'public' has been progressively enlarged to take account of women."

Although my work has benefited from contemporary examinations of the subtle stratifications and shifting patterns within the English class system, and of the anxious constructions of different styles of masculinity, in the nineteenth century, *Men in Wonderland* takes a relatively broad swathe of middle-class male life as its area of investigation. The term *gentleman* is thus included in the book's full title simply to indicate that the principal subjects of this study are of the well-to-do classes.

If this project participates in both childhood and masculinity studies, then it also aims to contribute to the current investigation into the construction of transgressive sexualities in the Victorian period. For the first two-thirds of the twentieth century, nineteenth-century figures who appear to display desires other than those expected within normative conjugality were generally analyzed in the light of a single, and now largely outmoded, theory that invoked the familiar narrative of a repressive Victorian culture.

In this hydraulic account, the sexual urge was forced underground by prudish proprieties, only to burst out triumphantly and obscenely in aberrant and unnatural forms. Carroll's and Ruskin's evident fascination with little girls, to be named "paidophilia" in 1906 and catalogued under "Abnormality" by Havelock Ellis in his *Study of the Psychology of Sex*, constitutes one of the various eruptions in this story. Literary critics working in the shadow of this model had few options open to them in their study of Carroll and Ruskin, for they could only support, deny, or ignore (and this last course was the road most taken) the portrait of the artist as pervert.

Michel Foucault's challenge to the repression hypothesis, however, excited a wealth of investigation into the constructed nature of sexuality and the historical emergence of different categories of "deviants." Consequently it became possible to examine the case of the Victorian girl-lover from different perspectives, and to consider how his obsessions might be related to those of his society.

Foremost amongst today's investigators is James R. Kincaid, whose *Child-Loving* assimilates Arie 's to Foucault. Kincaid concurs with *Centuries of Childhood*'s basic argument about the recent emergence of the concept of the child, but adds his own twist. Given that the apparent absence or presence of sexuality became a key actor in the separation of adult and child, it was inevitable that both the dividing line, and the child itself, should have become heavily eroticized. The very act of creating a pure, asexual, blank child produces sexual desire: the emptiness cries out to be filled. The child, then, was created as the infinitely desirable Other. According to Kincaid, the pedophile becomes an indispensable figure in the drama: he is the imaginary monster that we have created to reassure ourselves that our own desires for the lovely child are proportionate.

Kincaid's argument is compelling, but it is important here not to collapse together two historically distinct moments or to ignore the question of gender (boys and girls appear to be equally fascinating in his account). The beginning of widespread cultural interest in the child and the recognition of the figure of the pedophile are not simultaneous events, but are separated by over a hundred years.

The point is not to deny that sexual desire may be present in the gentleman's obsession with the child, but to ask questions about the cultural origins of that desire, to consider what *else* that adult interest might be signifying in the period before the pronouncements of medicalized discourse effectively closed down all explanations other than the diagnosis of individual pathology. Concentrating upon certain male writers' conceptualization of their childhood selves suggests that temporally displaced self-love is a major theme not only in the cultural productions of the Victorian era, but also in its famous programs of social reform. Likewise, insisting on a marked tendency in this period to reimagine the young self as feminine brings gender issues to the fore and highlights the crucial links between attitudes toward children and domestic ideology.

On this latter point, I make a more concerted argument for the primary importance of girls to the Victorian imagination than Carolyn Steedman, who in *Strange Dislocations: Childhood and the Idea of Human Interiority* agrees with Kincaid that in the nineteenth century, children were "distributed across the sex-gender system" in ways that are now impossible to recover. Yet she cannot help noticing that "when the child was watched, written about and wanted, it was usually a feminised set of qualities (if not a female child) whose image was left behind for our analysis." Steedman's admission is hardly surprising: while her project is a wonderfully broad scrutiny of "the social and psychic consequences of embodying what is lost and gone in the shape and form of a child" (viii), she conducts this inquiry through a very particular search for avatars of Goethe's Mignon, who "after all the cultivated androgyny of her presentation, turns out to be a girl in the end".

Men in Wonderland, most notably in its final chapter, turns up its own share of Mignons, but it is rather Steedman's attention to the wide-ranging effects of the adult's retrospective construction of the state of childhood that makes her book so important: this work, I hope, draws strength from her clear-sighted and often moving exploration of the investments adults place in the child through their beliefs, desires, and fantasies, and their use of "living bodies as expressions of the deepest springs of the self". Ultimately, however, *Strange Dislocations* is interested in recovering the child, and registering the distortions forced upon it by the adult's perspective: *Men in Wonderland* gives precedence to the adult fantasizer and thus tells a significantly different story.

This elucidation of the distinction between Steedman's work and my own preoccupations suggests a number of other important lines of demarcation. Of primary concern here is the male figure who constructs, in one way or another, a fantasy of his feminine childhood. Although ventures into related areas will help substantiate the argument, this emphasis necessarily excludes a range of undoubtedly interesting fields of inquiry.

This book by no means attempts a comprehensive overview of the origins and appearances of the idealized girl in nineteenth-century literature and culture. It says very little about how women writers in this period manipulated the figure of the child in their works, autobiographical, fictional, or otherwise. Similarly, although Lewis Carroll's writings are examined, it generally avoids the genre of children's literature.

Furthermore, juvenile masculinity, which is obviously the main interest of Claudia Nelson's *Boys Will Be Girls*, gets scant attention in this study. All in all, then, I concentrate on the essential peculiarity of my central finding and trace only the twists and turns of a singular narrative through the nineteenth century.

The narrative told is of the rise and fall of the ideal girl, revealing the concomitant progress of the myth of the gentleman's lost girlhood. While the principle of organization is broadly chronological, and while all sections set examinations of the works of single figures against considerations of wider historical contexts, the exact approach to different types of cultural materials varies from chapter to chapter. Certainly there are strong threads that run throughout the entire project: first, the preceding discussion of the influence of religious belief and practice on the social and individual perception of childhood resumes at junctures in all chapters, most noticeably in the first three. Other connections are formed, second, by the continual invocations of two key literary texts and, third, by the repetitions of an iconic vision of the adult male and the little girl.

The nineteenth century learns how to think about the sacred content of childhood and the blasphemy of child labour *through* Wordsworth's *Ode: Intimations of Immortality* and Barrett's "Cry of the Children": lines from these poems recur as touchstones in the public and private discourses of the child examined in chapters 1, 2, and 5. In one way or another, all five chapters present pictures of man and girl together.

On some occasions the couple appears in the mainstream of everyday Victorian life—Little Nell and her grandfather walk hand in hand away from the wildly popular *Old Curiosity Shop*; Carroll's Alice stops to listen to the White Knight's song; most ominously, sensational literature of the 1880s depicts the girl and the man in danger in *Dr. Jekyll and Mr. Hyde,* and the girl in danger *from* the man in the scandal sheets of muckraking journalism. More often, however, the image of man and girl is buried in little-read texts or private correspondence—summoned up in De Quincey's tear-stained reconstruction of the night of tenderness he shared with young Kate Wordsworth; excitedly recreated in Ruskin's celebration of his breathless dancing with an Irish schoolgirl; or figured in Carroll's enigmatic photographs of girls even when the adult male is ostensibly absent. All three of these recurrent features, then, unify a project that deliberately adopts a range of methodological techniques.

Chapter 1 places accounts of childhood development in the poetry and prose of William Wordsworth and Thomas De Quincey in relation to one of the numerous trajectories within the history of childhood. A study of the emerging concept of the juvenile delinquent and the provision of specialized care for young offenders provides a representative demonstration of the ways in which ideas about the child evolved between the last quarter of the eighteenth century and the midpoint of the nineteenth. General theories of childhood come to rely on absolute divisions between adult and child, corruption and innocence, masculineand feminine: by 1850 it is a truism that there is nothing so unlike a criminal as a little girl.

Wordsworth presents two important images of the child: the vital boyish self of *The Prelude,* and the otherworldly girl, variously depicted as Lucy or his sister Dorothy, whose experience is ruptured in death, or allowed no maturation. De Quincey appropriates solely the latter half of the representation and applies it to his own autobiography, identifying the young self as consistently feminine, and definitively cut off from the adult by the fact of death. This is the paradigm that will provide the Victorians with an increasingly attractive image of the innocent self of childhood, isolated from a progressively threatening world.

Chapter 2 considers the ramifications of this mode of perception by scrutinizing a constellation of texts from the early 1840s. Readings of Dickens's *Old Curiosity Shop* and Sarah Stickney Ellis's *Daughters of England* show how the model works as both personal and national fantasy, for the young girls in novel and conduct book alike are imagined as memorializing not only the past selves of their older male relatives, but also the rural idyll of a bygone England.

Juxtaposing these works with the report by a royal commission in 1842 on children's employment in the mines and Elizabeth Barrett's short poem "The Cry of the Children," I examine the contradictions inherent within Victorian society's views of girlhood. While Little Nell and Ellis's exemplary daughters embody the deathly perfection of the era's idealizing depiction of young femininity, the government report, and Barrett's response to it, constructs a radically different picture of the distinctly nonideal existence of a large proportion of the nation's little girls.

The horrifying visions of exploited girl-labour brought to the public eye make it abundantly clear that innocent girlhood is not an universal phenomenon, but an economically contingent construction; more particularly, focus upon the active body of the working-class girl reveals it to be disturbingly sexual. Contained within these unresolved conflicts of the 1840s are the elements that will ultimately destroy the conception of the little girl as both repository of purity and moral worth, and fit representative of the Victorian gentleman's lost childhood.

Chapter 3 deals solely with John Ruskin, the first of the two notorious girl-lovers of this project. Here the angle of approach alters significantly: rather than relate Ruskin's literary representations of the self and of juvenile femininity to broad historical movements and public discourses, I present the economic, social, religious, educational, and familial circumstances of his immediate personal background. The following paradox is thereby highlighted: although Ruskin's autobiography *Praeterita* supplies a strong example of the paradigm that has general currency in the Victorian era, his existence is certainly not paradigmatic for his class and gender in this period.

I study the self-feminizing tropes of the autobiography and describe the ways in which Ruskin's "school-girl" text of the 1860s, *The Ethics of the Dust*, reproduces the essential elements of the myth of the little girl's antiquity. In Ruskin's schema, young femininity is connected to the unsullied and vital purity of long-lost origins, and placed in opposition to the defiled world of the present day and a miserably compromised and decrepit male maturity. Ruskin's principal mode of representing the little girl within this myth is to view her in terms of the ancient and precious stones of the earth, to depict her as a brilliantly hard gem, jewel, or crystal: an erotics of aesthetic impenetrability appears again and again in his prose. This beautiful unyielding crystalline girl is not only an object of desire, however, but ultimately *Praeterita*'s figure for both the lost self of childhood and the continuing true self.

The study of Lewis Carroll in chapter 4 makes a virtue out of the fact that this particular worshipper of juvenile femininity left behind no autobiographical reconstructions of his own early years. In the absence of a textual narrative setting forth a fantasy of original femininity, I focus on Carroll's passion for the new phenomenon of photography and ask whether the images produced by this Victorian invention offered him an alternative means of substantiating a lost past.

The photograph, simply through the mechanics of its technological process, coincides with the nineteenth century's dominant mode of viewing children: Carroll's studies of little girls evince an uncanny ability to confound oppositions, most notably that between adult and child. In stark contrast, tableaux or "photographic moments" from *Through the Looking Glass* and *Sylvie and Bruno* send quite different messages: without photography's inherent ability to combine past and present in a single image, Carroll's textual fancies paint only the most sentimental of portraits of the little girl, her signifying potential radically reduced by the inclusion of adult figures, usually the nostalgic old man, within the scene.

Seen from this perspective, Carroll's decision to avoid the genre of autobiography is to be applauded: this is an artist who is much more likely to find a successful form for his fantasies of the little girl when he is able to efface the traces of his own presence. The fifth and final chapter charts the destruction of the fantasy of the ideal girl. Anxieties about girls and sexual activity begin to move into mainstream discourses in the last quarter of the nineteenth century, finding their high-water mark in the *Pall Mall Gazette* of July 1885. The luridly titled "Maiden Tribute of Modern Babylon," W. T. Stead's sensational exposé of what he claimed was the regular and widespread debauching of virgins in London, led to the raising of the age of consent in the Criminal Law Amendment Act of that year. The furor is a continuation of the unresolved conflicts examined in chapter 2: still at issue is the glaring disparity between the construct of idealized girlhood, and the depiction of girlhood as a lived experience for the working class.

The worries aroused by the working-class girl, implicitly sexual in the 1840s, are now explicitly sexual, and the archetypal exploited child is no longer a collier or millworker, but a prostitute. Moral concern, whipped to a frenzy by Stead's tactics, elides the real issue of the economic basis of prostitution and delivers a blanket ruling on sexual activity for all girls under the age of sixteen. To satisfy the desire to establish an all-inclusive realm of protected girlhood, all girlhood, paradoxically, has to be viewed through the lens of sexuality. Cast in this light, girls could no longer play their former role for the Victorian psyche.

The book concludes with a brief glimpse of three prime girl-lovers in the wake of that turbulent summer of 1885. For Ruskin, immersed by turns in madness or idealized reconstructions of the past, there can be no response to the sexualization of his favourite human figure. Carroll, formerly the nineteenth century's closest observer of juvenile femininity, now advises that we all simply turn away.

The final glance falls upon Rhymers' Club poet Ernest Dowson, whose brand of little-girl adoration most strikingly demonstrates the change in tenor of the late eighties and nineties. Analysis of his sonnet sequence "Of a Little Girl," reveals that Dowson's child is a potentially sexual receptacle for emotion, rather than the guarantor of the sealed perfection of the man's lost girlhood. Her innocence discussed and legislated out of existence, the little girl tumbles from grace at the end of the nineteenth century, leaving the way clear for a new star to rise. The boy, neglected for almost three generations, returns to embody a new image of childhood for a new age.

Chapter 9

On The Cause of The Break

Charles Lutwidge Dodgson, known to the world as Lewis Carroll, died on January 14 1898 at the age of sixty-five. For almost 100 years now his life has been the subject of speculation and controversy, which shows no sign of dying away. The broad facts are well enough known. He studied at Christ Church, Oxford and later taught mathematics there. He wrote Alice's Adventures in Wonderland for the three daughters of Henry Liddell, Dean of the College.

Their names - Ina, Alice and Edith - are almost legend, the golden afternoon on the river that gave rise to the story immortalised in Dodgson's own verse. He never married. He liked the company of female children. But beyond this much is unknown, contradictory and curious. Was his love for girl children a suppressed sexual passion? Or was it as innocent as he always maintained? What happened to the four volumes of his diary 'lost' after his death? Who cut certain pages from the remaining volumes? And why?

While researching a screenplay for a forthcoming film, quite by chance I came across a small piece of paper, tucked away among a mass of Dodgson family records in the archive at Guildford. About five inches by three, torn rather inaccurately from what appears to be an account book, at first glance it hardly looked sensational or revelatory. And yet written on this tatty scrap was, apparently, an answer to one of the most haunting of literary mysteries - the cause of Lewis Carroll's break with the family of Alice Liddell in the summer of 1863.

This event, supposedly a turning-point in his life, has

always been shrouded in silence and secrecy. The scruffy little bit of scribble-pad that has lain in the public record unnoticed for seventeen years contains the only surviving account of what actually occurred during those few vital days in late June. Pneumonia killed Lewis Carroll suddenly and unexpectedly in the January of 1898. He left behind a mass of papers that it fell to his family to sort out. A vast amount they consigned immediately to the fireplace. One notable exception to this was his diary, which ran to thirteen volumes and covered the years from 1855 until his death. It is known to have survived intact and to have been taken into the care of the Dodgson family, where it remained until 1969. Some time between 1898 and 1932 four volumes 'disappeared'. According to the family they were kept in a shoe-box in a cellar and were accidentally lost when someone moved house.

In 1969, the nine surviving volumes were given over to the British Museum, but not before they had been carefully and delicately pruned. Someone, no-one knows who or when, cut out four, possibly five pages from the various volumes, some of the ragged ends remaining testimony to the mutilation. One of these pages contains the vital dates, June 27-29 1863, which cover an important period of change in his relations with the Liddell family. It is nearly twelve months since the legendary day when he first told the Alice story.

The book is still in preparation and his friendship with Alice and her sisters is central to his life. His diary records 'continuous' meetings with them, river-trips, and visits to their home at the Deanery. On June 25 there is a big expedition on the river involving the three girls, the Dean and Mrs Liddell, Dodgson and two other young men.

IT is apparently a happy day. On June 27, Dodgson records writing to Mrs Liddell, 'urging her either to send the children to be photographed...' The sentence remains unfinished, because it comes at the end of a page and the following page is missing, cut out by an unknown hand. The word 'either' has also been crossed out, in a different ink, in a rather hopeless attempt to disguise the omission.

The record begins again on June 30. Dodgson notes that

the Liddells are leaving for their summer holiday. They are not mentioned again until December 5, when he records meeting Mrs Liddell and the children at some theatricals, 'but I held aloof from them, as I have done all this term'. Obviously the missing page recorded some kind of crisis in his relationship with Alice's family. Before he is seeing the children all the time; afterwards he makes no mention of them for nearly six months and then records merely that he is keeping his distance.

It is the beginning of the end of his friendship with Alice and her sisters. No-one has ever known what lay behind this change. The Liddel family has shed no light on it; neither have the Dodgsons. That it was a sensitive, possibly scandalous issue seems implicit in the jagged stump where page 91 ought to be. For the past twenty years it has been assumed almost beyond question that this crisis concerned the nature of Dodgson's relationship with Alice Liddell.

It is taken for granted that he was in some sense in love with her, that she was his irreplaceable muse, the love of his life. The 'lost page' has been assumed to contain details of some indiscretion that made his feelings apparent to her outraged parents. In his careful and scholarly recent biography Morton Cohen goes even further and suggests that on one of those late June days Dodgson went so far as to propose marriage to his eleven-year-old inamorata, thus precipitating the displeasure of the Dean and incurring a ban on further contact with the family. The fragment in the Guildford Muniment Room suggests that all this is untrue.

The paper is written on two sides in several different hands. It has obviously been referred to and updated by the Dodgsons over a period of some twenty years at least. One side is full of biographical notes about the Liddell daughters and Alice's descendants. the other is headed 'Cut Pages in Diary' and contains summaries of the contents of three pages, two from Volume Eight and one from Volume Eleven. The second summary from Volume Eight is of the missing page. June 27-29, 1863. It reads:

'L.C. learns from Mrs Liddell that he is supposed to be

using the children as a means of paying court to the governess - he is also supposed [unreadable] to be courting Ina'. It is written in the hand of Lewis Carroll's niece Violet Dodgson, who was co- guardian of the diaries with her sister Menella from the early 1940s to the late 1960s. The unreadable portion may possibly say 'by some'. That this summary is not a guess about an already missing page is shown by the fact that the first of the pages listed is still in the diary. In other words the notes were made before the pages were removed. Violet must have gone through the diary noting the pages to be cut and summarising their most important contents. Later she changed her mind about one and allowed it to remain. The above, then, is the only known account of what happened between June 27 and 29, 1863. What does it mean?

We can assume that as a result of Dodgson's letter to Mrs Liddell on June 27 she either wrote to him or asked him to the Deanery. In either case she told him there were rumours circulating about him and 'the governess' and 'Ina'. As a result he was either told to stay away, or they agreed that it would be safest for him to do so for a while. No mention of Alice, nothing to suggest the business had anything to do with her at all. The governess was Miss Prickett, an unprepossessing female employed by the Liddells to educate their daughters. There had been vague gossip circulating about her and Dodgson back in 1857. He recorded it himself in his diary at the Time, (May 17) with some astonishment, adding that he wasn't bothered by 'so groundless a rumour'. the governess we can probably dismiss as old news, unlikely to trouble the proud Mrs Liddell. The significant individual is 'Ina'.

Ina was Alice's older sister, Lorina Charlotte Liddell. In June 1863 she was fourteen years old and highly developed for her age; a young woman, not a child. By that summer she had already been allowed into Dodgson's company for a good deal longer than Victorian convention would have considered proper. He was young, handsome and unmarried. She was tall and strikingly attractive. Girls were legally marriageable at twelve. By thirteen she would have been considered to have left her childhood behind. Yet this bright, 'imperious' creature was still accompanying her younger sisters on long unchaperoned river trips with the thirty-one-year-old Mr Dodgson throughout her fourteenth summer and beyond.

She is mentioned in his journal at this time in ways that set her apart from Alice or Edith and may be significant. On August 6 1862 Dodgson observes that Ina will probably not be allowed to go out with him and her sisters for much longer, noting that the day's excursion was 'her fourteenth time'. It is Ina who invites him to visit at her grandparents' house in April 1863, Ina again who writes and asks him to come and help out at a charity bazaar where she and her sisters are running a stall. On April 17 1863 Dodgson comments on her precocious development (she is growing 'so tall'), and notes for the first time that Mrs Liddell has insisted on a chaperone.

Is this a sign that the mother was becoming suspicious of the exact nature of the relationship between this man and her daughter? Did she watch them together a few weeks later, during the happy outing of June 25, and draw her own conclusions? Is this why, two or three days afterwards, she warned him off?

The paper in the Dodgson archive means that we must recognise how much of Dodgson's life remains a mystery, and that a great deal of the current biographical 'truth' is no more than supposition dignified by repetition. Is this true of his relationship with Alice Liddell? Has the fact that her name is immortalised in his two works of genius beguiled us into believing that she was far more important to him than she really was? In truth, was he 'courting' her older sister on those 'golden afternoons' on the Isis? Are there other possibilities not yet explored? Why, for example, was he allowed such latitude with these girls in the first place? Why, having offended the family in June, is he welcomed back quite happily in late December? Why did Mrs Liddell forbid her husband's biographer to mention Dodgson's name? Dodgson's relationship with the Liddell family is crucial, curious and - this newly discovered paper emphasises - little understood. With the centenary of his death approaching it is perhaps time to start looking for answers to these questions.

Chapter 10

Secrecy and Autonomy in Lewis Carroll

Victorian novels quiver with morbid secrets and threatening discoveries. Unseen rooms, concealed doors, hidden boxes, masked faces, buried letters, all appear (and disappear) with striking regularity in the fiction of Victorian England. So many of these secret spaces contain children, and especially little girls, little girls in hidden spaces.

The young Jane Eyre sits behind a curtain in the hidden window seat, escaping the vindictive wrath of John Reed. Repulsed by her angry brother, Maggie Tulliver flees to the house attic, fantasizing that her family will fear that she has died. Little Dorrit withdraws from the common space of the Marshalsea into her private room above the prison, and Little Nell hides behind trees and walls, silently observing clandestine meetings. Finally the seven-year-old Alice falls down a rabbit-hole into a Wonderland, the dreamspace of her own psyche.

Of these images, none can be more embedded in our cultural imagination than the child Alice dropping into the subterranean well of Wonderland. Indeed, of the many celebrated scenes in the Alice narratives, the most memorable, most potent, most quoted is Alice's initial descent to the bottom of the rabbit-hole. The lastingness of this scene seems even greater when we realise that, although neither Carroll in Alice's Adventures Underground nor Tenniel in the first edition of Wonderland illustrated the moment with a picture, it still became (along with the Mad Hatter's tea party) one of the signature images of the Alice stories. Why, we must ask, did the Victorians retain, with a powerful tenacity, this vision of a little girl moving through a tight space toward the hidden world of Wonderland?

The answer to this question is not—at least not wholly—that the scene simply represents a child's metaphorical progress through the [End Page 1] birth canal and that this, in turn, symbolizes some kind of rite of passage, a movement towards some deeper knowledge. For then how do we explain Alice's conspicuous lack of internal development in both stories? Indeed, for a narrative that thematizes motion, Alice's psychical growth remains disturbingly static. Throughout both narratives, Alice displays little emotional variation, for when she is not frustrated or anxious, she is, for the most part, vapid or expressionless. In fact, one is immediately struck by her coolness and indifference as she drops through the rabbit-hole. Thus, because scene changes in Wonderland and Looking-Glass rarely betoken any emotional or intellectual modulations, Alice's falling into Wonderland signals no internal transition.

But the image does relocate her body and within this fictive world, location is everything. The scene gestures Alice's departure, her separation, her movement towards an autonomy of which every child dreams when, in play, retreating to a hidden space. A child's impulse to hide, to create a secret space, is one of the most compelling of all human wishes, the wish for autonomy and autarchy—"to be cut off from the word and yet owner of the world." Throughout Victorian literature, the fantasy of autonomy sets children dreaming of far-away worlds and hidden gardens.

The young Cathy and Heathcliff flee to the isolated moors, filling the open, empty space with dreams of unrestricted freedom. Little Dorrit envisages the locked garden behind the Marshalsea as an alternative world to the foul prison atmosphere. And what are the Bronts Angria and Gondol but disconnected, self-governing realms imagined from the standpoint of childhood powerlessness? The image, then, of Alice's fall begins to fulfill this powerful wish for autonomy, which culminates, finally, in Alice's self-coronation at the end of Looking-Glass. Yet it is only within the child's willing imagination that a secret space can encroach so closely upon autonomy, for as we shall see, secrecy and autonomy are irreconcilable not only in the demanding world of realism, but even in the more elastic world of Carrollian fantasy.

Alice's descent into Wonderland and her entrance into the Looking-Glass kingdom would seem like ripe metaphors for Carroll to explore the thoughts and fantasies of Alice's psyche. What could be more oneiric than an underground world or a secret realm beyond a mirror? Further, the construction of the dream frame in nineteenth- and twentieth-century literature usually signals an author's undertaking of psychological realism. Much has been written on the Freudian thematics of the Alice stories, but if, as many have argued, Alice falls down into the dreamland of her own unconscious, she meets there not identification and revelation, but rather frustration and deferral. Recall that in both works Alice awakens not as from a wish fulfilled, but as from a desire thwarted.

If Wonderland really represents the underground of her own psyche, it is a psyche not entirely her own, more different than mysterious, more foreign than obscure. This becomes most apparent when we realise that the emotional and cognitive dissonance between Alice and her dream creatures reflects a larger disunion of energies that marks the narratives. Throughout both stories Carroll works hard to illustrate the incongruousness of sensibilities that estranges Alice from the other figures. The scene in Looking-Glass in which the Queen offers Alice a dry biscuit, unfittingly, to quell her thirst is a paradigm of the sharp discordance between characters.

Inappropriate and irrelevant responses such as the Queen's fill both Alice stories and reveal an atmosphere depleted of psychical recognition and sympathetic reaction. To read a text as an exposition of a subject's inner world is to assume that it is through the lens of that subject's psyche that we identify symbols and organize meaning. However, the psychological dissociation between Alice and the Wonderland and Looking-Glass figures disallows this genre of interpretation. The dream frame does open up the possibility for psychological realism, but Carroll closes it off just as quickly. One way of apprehending this is by comparing Wonderland with The Wizard of Oz—a narrative similar in structure and content. Both are stories of a young girl's dream of a passage through, and return from, a kind of fairy-tale land. But the dream frame in Baum's text shapes itself into a psychoanalytic examination of Dorothy's psyche.

The parallels between the waking world and the dream world inform one another, and we begin to see how Dorothy's unconscious translates her lived experience into the metaphors of dreamwork. In Carroll's text, however, the connection between Alice's waking reality and her dreamscape is radically tenuous; the two worlds are almost autonomous. How can we say that Alice's dream is an exposition of her unconscious when Carroll paints her and her world in only the broadest strokes? Further, Alice's desire to reach the garden never equals the pitch and urgency of Dorothy's longing to return to Kansas. In the simplest terms, Alice lacks the passion and commitment to her own destiny that advances Dorothy's journey through Oz. As Alice encounters the creatures of Wonderland and the Looking-Glass world, Carroll creates not a quest for identity, or a solitary journey into the self, but rather a sequence of spectacles for childhood voyeurism.

The inhabitants of her dreamworld are hollow signifiers that repel interpretation, not layered symbols that lure penetration. The Mad Hatter's madness, after all, forms no pattern, generates no repetition. When Alice asks him what happens when he has returned, full circle, to the head of the table, he has no answer and can only redirect the subject of their conversation. The Mad Hatter's inability to answer reflects a larger tendency in the narratives to skim surfaces and deflect inquiry. Throughout both stories Alice continually asks "What will happen next?" but Carroll always accelerates his narrative and whisks us to a new scene before Alice's question can be answered.

In much Victorian fiction the movement into secret enclosures begins as a retreat from the urban world but develops, ultimately, into an act of self-exploration. But this is not true of Carroll's fiction. Indeed, the many instances in the Alice stories of characters positioned with their heads facing downwards betokens repellence, not introspection.

The spatial imagery and objects that fill Wonderland and the Looking-Glass world are similarly misleading. Hidden doors, dark tunnels, ungraspable keys and dense woods all create an architecture crowded with secret spaces and hence suggest an atmosphere of concealment and discovery. Upon closer inspection, however, we see that Alice's dreamworlds and secrecy are strangely incompatible. This is a crucial insight, for as we shall see, the Alice narratives lack precisely what other narratives must have in order to hatch a fictive world that contains secrets. In apprehending the reasons for this absence of secrecy in Carroll, we will establish a grammar of terms that can aid us in the project of exploring hidden spaces in other fiction.

Let us first examine the terms of Wonderland's complex spatial dynamics. One notices immediately the fantastic elasticity of space and size that Alice experiences as she travels to the garden. Space is created as she moves through it and closes up behind her as she exits. It is as if space does not exist unless she inhabits it; the hole deepens as she falls through it; doors, keys, and corridors materialize as she needs them.

Suddenly she came upon a little three-legged table, all made of solid glass; there was nothing on it except a tiny golden key. . . . However on the second time round, she came upon a low curtain she had not noticed before, and behind it was a little door. . . . There seemed to be no use in waiting by the little door, so she went back to the table . . . this time she found a little bottle on it. . . . This kind of ad-hoc spatiality differs radically from the spatial imperatives that we find in, say, Hardy, who continually reminds us that physical structures outlive their human makers. For instance, the amphitheater in The Mayor of Casterbridge has existed for centuries past and will remain long after Henchard dies. Similarly Tess's fate at Stonehenge is but one moment in the long history of the ancient structure. Thus Hardy establishes a setting and then animates it with characters and events. In Carroll, however, place and character cannot be detached, for one immediately generates the other.

That space dissolves as Alice departs from it explains why there is no backward motion in Wonderland, no possibility to return to an established place. Thus Alice must never climb back up the rabbit-hole in order to escape. If we say that there is no reverse motion or return in Wonderland then we have made a crucial discovery: There can be no secrecy or secret spaces in Wonderland for such secrecy demands stability, a constancy that permits return. To hide an object, a person, a story, a memory, implies that there is a constant, an unwavering signifier that can be hidden, which is to say, a floating signifier eludes concealment. Conversely, if there is only backward motion (as in most of Through the Looking-Glass), then there can be no secret places either, for secrecy also requires the forward motion of a sequacious, progressive logic: A must exist before B can hide it.

But location is not the only instability that disallows secrecy in Wonderland and Looking-Glass. If space and motion are irregular, so then is time. Carroll at once creates and undermines the continuous narrative trajectory of traditional fiction. True, both narratives advance in sequent linearity, one scene following logically from another, with Alice's progress to the garden (and the eighth square in Looking-Glass) as the shaping structure and her dream as the outermost frame. But there is a kind of fragmentation—an abrupt skittishness that terminates the scenes—that compromises this linearity and that becomes more prominent in Looking-Glass. Although, as we have noted, Alice continually asks, "What will happen next," she is answered with only the most evasive responses or, more commonly, with sudden changes of scene and location, making the narrative more like a series of dashes than an unbroken linear path.

The scenes in both texts are almost autonomous moments, a succession of vignettes, thus preventing the narratives from accumulating a history from which to form secrets and establish locations. Hence we can see that stability—some kind of continuity of time and permanence of location—is requisite for a narrative to produce secret spaces.

What we have been saying, essentially, is that secrecy demands contextualization, a surrounding set of variables towards which it can stand in relation and in which it can find a location. Secrecy and, more specifically, secret spaces are ensconced within a larger sphere—both spatial and temporal—that a narrative must create. This suggests, further, that autonomy deflects secrecy. Its essence, its status as independence, disconnectedness, disallows the incorporation that is requisite for secret spaces.

In Dickens's Little Dorrit, Amy narrates a short story that illustrates exquisitely this point that secrecy requires contextualization. The story goes as follows: A poor tiny woman who lives alone in a cottage is seen through her window by a beautiful princess who has the power of knowing secrets. One day the princess enters the cottage and, without provocation or prelude, asks the tiny woman, "Why do you keep it there?" Her question reveals to the woman that the princess knows of her secret "box of shadows" which she then removes from a "very secret place." She tells the princess that she lives alone in order to protect her secret box which, she claims, will sink into her grave when she dies.

The princess continues to pass the cottage almost every day, whereupon the two would exchange knowing glances. One day the princess learns that the tiny woman has died and, upon inspecting her cottage, realizes that the woman had been correct: her "treasured shadow" has accompanied her to the grave.

The story reveals Dorrit's wish for silence and noninvolvement, and also echoes Dickens's larger narrative in several places. But for our purposes we need only note the details as outlined. To begin, the tale is striking for its absence of conflict; not only is the secret never revealed, but it is, moreover, never threatened with exposure. For this reason, the princess may seem extraneous to the story, for she poses no threat and alters nothing of the fate of the tiny woman or her secret. The princess, at first, seems to be but a narrative object, lacking agency or interest, but she is essential to the story. She is the tale's most indispensable element. Without her, the tiny woman with her box of shadows is an autonomous life, not the site of secrecy. By riding past the cottage every day, the princess locates the secret within a spatial, temporal, and communal field. She is the context without which the box would not be a secret.

Thus secrets cannot, if you will, float around in emptiness. They emerge out of an already existent presence, for they are derivative, ineluctably secondary. Further, a secret, in order to remain a secret, cannot break off from its conceiver; it is always owned, never autonomous.

We can see also that what Carroll and his critics call the nonsense jargon of the Alice stories is a kind of autonomy of signifiers. For nonsense claims autonomy—detachment from any signifieds. How then can there be secrecy where there is no stable meaning and hence nothing to hide? But this interpretation that meaning is absent from the Alice texts relies upon the reader believing Carroll's insistence that the narratives are hollow of meaning, that they house no secrets, only surfaces. As critics, we have developed a vast collection of essays and articles arguing that the so-called nonsense jargon is itself a concealer of meaning and a shunting of our interpreting glances. Indeed, pure nonsense cannot produce a narrative, and, while the narratives are unusual, they are narratives nevertheless.

The Alice stories, then, articulate a double message: on the one hand, they create the illusion of secrecy, they entice us with answerless riddles and imagery of hidden doors, unseen passages and ungraspable objects; on the other hand, however, they avert our scrutiny with the characters' nonsense jargon and absurd logic. It is as if the stories draw us towards them and then teasingly turn away. There may be no secrecy, as we have seen, but there is no straightforwardness either.

Evasiveness governs the semiotic structure of both narratives. Throughout the Alice stories, there is an implicit decorum to speak indirectly, to refer, not address, to allude, not define. We continually hear the characters use the demonstrative that (always italicized), instead of directly describing their subjects:

"Why, because there's nobody with me!" cried Humpty Dumpty. "Did you think I didn't know the answer to that? Ask another."

"Do you call that a whisper?" cried the poor king, jumping up and shaking himself. "If you do such a thing again, I'll have you buttered."

It was all very well to say 'Drink me,' but the wise little Alice was not going to do that in a hurry.

To state unequivocally threatens the fictive spell. In Wonderland, Alice awakens from her dream at the moment when she unambiguously addresses and defines the King and Queen:

"Who cares for you?" said Alice . . ."You're nothing but a pack of cards!" At this the whole pack rose up in the air, and came flying down on her: she gave a little scream . . . and tried to beat them off, and found herself lying on the bank, with her head in the lap of her sister . . . .

Similarly, in Looking-Glass, the fawn darts from Alice's embrace at the moment that it can precisely define her:

"What do you call yourself?" the Fawn said at last . . . . "I wish I knew!" thought poor Alice. She answered rather sadly, "Nothing, just now." . . . So they walked on together through the wood, Alice with her arms clasped lovingly round the soft neck of the Fawn, till they came out into another open field, and here the Fawn gave a sudden bound into the air, and shook itself free from Alice's arm. "I'm a Fawn!" it cried out in a voice of delight. "And, dear me! you're a human child!" A sudden look of alarm came into its beautiful brown eyes, and in another moment it had darted away at full speed.

Speech that defines subverts entrancement, agitates the mesmeric spell. It is essential to see that this endorsing of indirectness is evasion, not secrecy, and dispersal, not definition. The fawn's fear of capture can be seen as a metaphor for the narrative's rejection of definition, of linguistic capture. That is to say that Carroll's text prohibits the articulation of meaning, which it here metaphorizes as a kind of seizure. Just as the fawn detaches from Alice's hold, so too the signified disconnects from the signifier. But secrecy, as we have seen, presumes stable meaning, a secure connection of signifier and signified. Thus by terminating the link between signifier and signified, Carroll terminates the possibility of secrecy. In other words, the autonomy of the signifier precludes secrecy. Autonomy and secrecy, I am suggesting, are rival imperatives.

What, then, is the difference between these two conditions? Clearly both intimate a kind of solitude that is their deepest connection. But secrecy, as I have earlier shown, implies a pocket of solitude within a subsuming sphere; moreover, it implies, as its etymology makes clear, separation which, in turn, implies severed contact. To be secret is to have once been connected; contact, connection is secrecy's most subtle distinction. Autonomy, however, suggests self-containment, not connection.

Secrecy and, now we can add, contact, are almost entirely absent from Carroll's vision. Wonderland and Looking-Glass are worlds of cruel autonomy, symbolized most powerfully by the Cheshire cat's head that can live detached from its body, and still grin. Scenes of failed contact imbue both narratives. Alice follows the White Rabbit down the hole, but she can never fully reach him. In Looking-Glass, objects are similarly unattainable: The goat's beard "seemed to melt away as she touched it", and the rushes also "melted away almost like snow". The absence of physical touch here plainly represents the scarcity of emotional connection, and even love, in Wonderland and Looking-Glass. And whatever else we may say about the humour and sophistication of Carroll's nonsense jargon, the conversations that lead nowhere illustrate, at bottom, the hollowness of relationships in Alice's dreamworlds.

This failure of contact may be a kind of fear of contact deriving from what psychoanalysis has named Alice's oral aggression and what Nina Auerbach has called Alice's "subtly cannibalistic hunger." In both narratives, Alice's presence portends potential danger. Can Alice really be so unwitting of Dinah's threat to the Wonderland animals? And in Looking-

Glass when Alice threatens to pick the daisies, one begins to wonder whether her "curiosity" is not childhood innocence, but rather fallen aggression. One cannot help but notice a schism between Alice's popular image as an artless child of nature and her actual representation as a demure yet fearless little wanderer.

But how, we must ask, did this myth of Alice emerge from Carroll's original portrayal of her as the dark-haired, bewitching-eyed child of Alice's Adventures Underground? The evolution of Carroll's dreamchild is a curious phenomenon indeed and beckons our critical attention. When one reads the text of Underground, one notices a dramatic difference between Carroll's and Tenniel's illustrations. Alice's progression from the dark lady-child of Underground to the saccharine, blonde ingenue of Wonderland is visible to even the most cursory glance and is only one symptom of the larger transformation of the Alice myth. Carroll's representations of her, especially when she changes size, are more offbeat, somewhat surreal and certainly more disturbing.

In a particularly vivid picture, Alice is portrayed as an oversized head, no neck or body, only feet and hands extending from beneath her chin. On the next page, she is depicted as a long neck with a head on top, no body or feet below, like a human lollipop. This kind of eccentricity is muted in Tenniel's drawings, which are, for the most part, flat and insipid. For instance, most of Tenniel's illustrations are single caricatures, departing far from Carroll's more populated and detailed sketches.

Tenniel's illustrations established a tendency, continuing even now, to imagine Alice as a paragon of childhood innocence. Films, cartoons, theater productions and modern illustrations all recreate, in some way, this idea of Alice as a symbol of unwitting purity and wide-eyed curiosity. Clearly Carroll's readers have revealed a desire to read the Alice stories according to Tenniel's illustrations.

Although Tenniel's interpretation diverges from Carroll's representation, there must be in Carroll's texts something, some moment, some scene or theme, to stimulate this popular construction of Alice. Surely our acceptance and affirmation of Tenniel's representation finds some provocation in Carroll's writing. Is there, beneath the texts' portrayal of Alice's predatory nature, a wish for childhood innocence—a longing for Alice to be what she plainly is not—an uncorruptible essence of humanity? Both narratives, as we shall see, emit a subtle message saying just this: that solitude and autonomy are afflictions of the soul; and human contact and love, our most precious remedy. The deepest tension of the works, then, is the lure between perfect autonomy and human contact—a conflict which crystallizes the problem of secrecy in Wonderland and Looking-Glass.

In his introduction to the Modern Critical Interpretations volume on Lewis Carroll, Harold Bloom intimates that Wordsworth is the precursor poet standing behind and shaping much of the Alice narratives. Locating Wordsworth's strongest presence in "The White-Knight's Ballad"—what he calls a "superb and loving parody of Wordsworth's great crisis-poem "Resolution and Independence" —Bloom argues that the White Knight is Alice's/Carroll's Leech Gatherer—"a man from some far region sent, / To give me human strength." The alternative to human contact for Wordsworth, Bloom further suggests, is misery and madness, but for Carroll it is Wonderland, that is, play and nonsense.

Bloom's observation summons our knowledge of Wordsworthian Romanticism and we quickly find ourselves filling out the corners of his evocative suggestion. To begin, the White Knight's constant positioning with his head downwards and his headlong fall into the ditch symbolize his Romantic self-absorption, as do his absurd inventions that make sense only to him. His repeated declaration "It's my own invention" reflects his narcissism and self-deception, his conviction that he has created all that surrounds him. That he is sated by the imagining of pudding, and not the actual tasting of it, further represents his retreat into his own subjectivity.

If the White Knight functions as a Wordsworthian solitary, awakening the dormant well of human sympathy, then Alice's soul must require arousal, inspiriting. And indeed it does, for

Carroll twice reminds us that Alice does not cry in response to the White Knight's song. But her encounter with him does become her "memory recollected in tranquillity," a significant moment, the remembering of which in theory brings her to a deeper sympathy with nature and the outer world. With a Wordsworthian sentimentality, Carroll describes Alice's experience:

Of all the strange things that Alice saw in her journey Through the Looking-Glass, this was the one that she always remembered most clearly. Years afterwards she could bring the whole scene back again, as if it had been only yesterday—the mild blue eyes and kindly smile of the Knight—the setting sun gleaming through his hair, and shining on his armour in a blaze of light that quite dazzled her—the horse quietly moving about, with the reigns hanging loose on his neck, cropping the grass at her feet—and the black shadows of the forest behind—all this she took in like a picture, as, with one hand shading her eyes, she leant against a tree, watching the strange pair, and listening, in a half-dream, to the melancholy music of the song.

The absence of irony in this passage stands in sharp relief to the other scenes in the narrative, which are almost all governed by parody and satire. Carroll's sincerity here is striking, and the scene derives much of its power from this unique earnestness of tone. Indeed, the popular misrepresentation of Alice as an innocent dreamchild issues, in part, from our misremembering the tenor of the whole story to be similar in tone and content to this passage. Like Alice, we remember this scene as a representative moment, not as the anomaly that it is. Thus Carroll masterfully orchestrates layers of revisionary remembering, reconstructive imagining.

This impulse towards revisionary remembering too emanates from a Romantic sensibility. Throughout Wordsworth's poetry, human memory does not simply duplicate in thought the past, but it moreover emendates reality, reconstructs a vision that resembles, but does not perfectly reproduce, the original event. In "I wandered lonely as a cloud," Wordsworth describes the difference between the primary experience and the retrospective contemplation of it. The waves beside them danced, but they outdid the sparkling waves in glee: —

A Poet could not but be gay
In such a laughing company: I gazed—and gazed—but little thought
What wealth the shew to me had brought:
For oft when on my couch I lie
In vacant or in pensive mood.
They flash upon that inward eye
Which is the bliss of solitude,
And then the heart with pleasure fills,
And dances with the Daffodils.

During the actual experience the poet can luxuriate in the vision before him, but he cannot perceive its full purport until the time of retrospection. To remember the daffodils is not to replicate in thought an exact picture, but rather to alter a past moment, to assign emotions, designate associations, reappraise significance, re-edit temporal boundaries. Thus no memory is free of imagination, and no imagining is free of memory. When we remember we reimagine and when we imagine we pluck from our well of memories, for we can create only out of that which we know. Hence memory and imagination each construct the other.

Fittingly, the chapter that contains the interaction between the White Knight and Alice, "It's my own invention," displays beautifully this Romantic bonding of memory with imagination. Just as in this scene Alice acts as a repository of memory, positioning the moment in the foreground of her Wonderland recollections, the Knight, with all his nonsense inventions, represents the agency of imagination that accompanies the act of remembering. I have until now been arguing that Carroll disunites any psychical connection between Alice and her dream creatures, but this scene clearly poses an exception. Here the White Knight and Alice function as concomitant mental processes. Because the two work synchronistically, it follows that the White Knight requires Alice's guidance as he departs from her sight: "I sha'n't be long.

You'll wait and wave your handkerchief when I get to that turn in the road! I think it'll encourage, you see". "Encourage" may seem peculiar at first, but its root meaning "to give heart" expresses accurately the unusual intimacy between them—their psychical integration of one another.

Alice's and the reader's revisionary remembering reflects a Wordsworthian consciousness in still another sense. Like Wordsworth's, Carroll's reconstructive imagination manifests itself primarily as an elision of conflict and tension. If Alice and the reader locate this scene as exemplative of her Wonderland and Looking-Glass experience, then memory has been acutely selective. As we have noted, Alice's primary emotion has been frustration and anxiety, not the love and entrancement she feels as the White Knight's song dreamily lulls her. The scene is an anomaly, not a representative moment. This tendency to delete pain Carroll confesses in the opening poem to Looking-Glass.

And though the shadow of a sigh
May tremble through the story,
For "happy summer days" gone by,
And vanish'd summer glory —
It shall not touch, with breath of bale,
The pleasance of our fairy-tale.

We see this inclination to omit conflict throughout Wordsworth's poetry. In his narrative poem "Michael," for instance, Wordsworth describes Luke's moral descent—the tragic event of the story—in only five and one-half lines (the poem is 491 lines in total). Notice the vagueness with which Wordsworth relates this core episode:

Meantime Luke began
To slacken in his duty, and at length
He in dissolute city gave himself
To evil courses: ignominy and shame
Fell on him, so that he was driven at last
To seek a hiding-place beyond the seas.
(ll. 451-56)

A hurried glance and nothing more for the tragic turn in Michael's life, the very impetus for narration. In a more stunning example of elision, "A slumber did my spirit seal," the poet expresses in two stanzas the shock of Lucy's premature death.

In the first stanza, Lucy still lives and the poet remembers his deluded disbelief of her mortality—the happy ignorance that is past. In the second stanza, Lucy has died and the poet imagines the difficult concept of nonexistence and a world that is absent of her being.

A slumber did my spirit seal;

I had no human fears: She seemed a thing that could not feel

The touch of earthly years.
No motion has she now, no force;
She neither hears nor sees,
Rolled round in earth's diurnal course
With rocks and stones and trees.

Swift and terse to be sure, but no less elegant and eloquent for that. In less than fifty words the lyric speaks profusely and articulates succinctly the human reaction to what always seems the suddenness of death. But between the two stanzas—between his love for her when she lived and his grief in the aftermath of her death—sits a blank space, an elision of the very moment of death itself. This absent stanza seems even more striking when we realise that Wordsworth was writing within an elegiac tradition that almost always recounts a death scene. As in "Michael," Wordsworth excludes the moment of discontinuity, the very event that stimulated the act of writing.

For both Carroll and Wordsworth, then, the imaginative effort of writing is a kind of memory freed from pain. But memory for Wordsworth also heals pain and binds the human community. It is memory in this sense that bears most upon the Alice books and that will deliver us, ultimately, back to the subject of secrecy.

The ending of Wonderland bears an uncanny resemblance to the final fifty lines of Wordsworth's "Tintern Abbey," in which the poet addresses his sister, who has stood by his side during his meditation that comprises the body of the poem. At the close of both texts, the authors momentarily rechannel the narratives through the consciousness of the protagonist's sister, and thus unfold an alternative vision on the scene—one that perceives from the vista of a different standpoint in time. Just as Wordsworth envisages his sister's impression of the landscape, Carroll imagines Alice's dreamscape as seen through the eyes of her older sister.

In Wordsworth's poem, Dorothy's presence binds the rift between the poet's original visit to Tintern Abbey and that of his present one. Robert Langbaum explains: "Now he sees in her what he once was, and sees in the difference between them what she shall be. He has a transforming vision of her as a child of nature blessed in all stages of her life; and by identifying her future memory of this visit with his own and his present memory of his last visit, he sees in the different stages of their development along the same line the rhythm and harmony of things."

> *For thou art with me, here, upon the banks*
> *Of this fair river; thou, my dearest Friend,*
> *My dear, dear Friend, and in thy voice I catch*
> *The language of my former heart, and read*
> *My former pleasures in the shooting lights*
> *Of thy wild eyes. Oh! yet a little while*
> *May I behold in thee what I was once . . .*

This gesture of uniting fragments of time into a coherent formulation is, among other things, part of the process of narrativization, of transforming experience into story. Its position at the end affirms its formal significance. Further, Dorothy's function of uniting disparate moments of time diverges from the autonomous vignettes that construct the Alice books.

But time is not all that Wordsworth joins. By linking past, present, and future, he also bonds himself to Dorothy, whose presence in "Tintern Abbey" has been criticized as unnecessary, an autonomous fragment dangling from the core of the poem. Contrarily, as Wordsworth weaves her into the thread of his experience the message becomes clear: the memory of the abbey means little without its significance to another. In other words, memory is meaningful only insofar as it weds us to the experience of others and hence integrates us into the human landscape. The psychological desideratum of the poem is not a heightened perception of the abbey, but rather a deeper union with his sister. Memory, Wordsworth implies, releases sympathetic communion.

Similarly, at the conclusion of Wonderland, Alice recalls her dream to her older sister, who functions much like Dorothy in "Tintern Abbey," mediating the central action of the poem—the fall down the rabbit-hole and the journey to the garden—through the lens of an alternate perspective, one that differs in age from the protagonist's. Like Wordsworth, Carroll stages layers of temporal perspectives:

But her sister sat still just as she left her, leaning her head on her hand, watching the setting sun, and thinking of little Alice and all her wonderful Adventures, till she too began dreaming after a fashion, and this was her dream:—First she dreamed of little Alice herself, and once again the tiny hands were clasped upon her knee, and the bright eager eyes were looking up into hers—she could hear the very tones of her voice . . . and as she listened, the whole place around her became alive with the strange creatures of her little sister's dream . . . Lastly, she pictured to herself how this same little sister of hers would, in the after-time be herself a grown woman; and how she would keep, through all her riper years, the simple and loving heart of her childhood; and how she would gather about her other little children, and make their eyes bright and eager with many a strange tale, perhaps even with the dream of Wonderland of long ago: and how she would feel with all their simple sorrows, and find a pleasure in all their simple joys, remembering her own child-life, and the happy summer days.

Alice's memory of her dream generates a psychical intimacy between her and her sister that is expressly absent in the book's opening, where her attention quickly recedes from her sister's voice. The recollection of her dream, then, yokes Alice's and her sister's hitherto disconnected psyches.

If we say that memory cultivates human contact, then we begin to see shades of our subject rising back into view, for contact, as we have seen, is secrecy's most subtle distinction. To remember a person, an experience, a place, a moment in the past is to reject autonomy, to reconnect to what once was. Memory thus merges autonomous subjects and also knits fragments of time into narrative.

That is to say that memory repels dissociation, or in Carrollian terms, nonsense. As memory contextualizes, meaning emerges and nonsense dissolves into abstraction. Finally, secrecy takes shape out of the continuity and contextualization created by memory. Hence, where there is memory, there is secrecy. The closing scene in Wonderland, as well as the White Knight scene in Looking-Glass, then, by celebrating memory, advances the possibility of secrecy, which we have seen to be strangely absent in Alice's dreamworlds.

Because remembering broods a secrecy that Carroll disallows, we see in Wonderland and Looking-Glass, fittingly, the precarious status of memory.

> Let me think: was I the same when I got up this morning? I almost think I can remember feeling a little different. But if I'm not the same, the next question is, Who in the world am I? . . . . I'll try if I know all the things I used to. Let me see: four times five is twelve, and four times six is thirteen, and four times seven is—oh dear! I shall never get to twenty at this rate! However, the Multiplication Table doesn't signify: let's try Geography. London is the capitol of Paris, and Paris is the capitol of Rome—no, that's all wrong . . . .

Indeed, Alice is by no means amnestic, but her faculty of recollection is clearly compromised. After this scene, Alice almost never considers, even in passing, her waking life, her reflections on Dinah posing the only exception. Memory's deficiency signifies, again, autonomy's supremacy and hence secrecy's absence.

Let us now return to the White Knight scene in Looking-Glass—the scene that most overtly figures memory as a mode of human connection. The scene moves on several planes: The knight's poem about his encounter with the "aged-aged man" alludes to Wordsworth's confrontation with the Leechgatherer which, in turn, parallels the White Knight's meeting with Alice, which finally represents Dodgeson's relationship with Alice Liddell. By staging these multiple gestures of interaction, Carroll rejects, and reveals a disgust for, the autonomy and solitude he has thematized all along.

It is as if Carroll here renounces his philosophy of nonsense in favour of a Wordsworthian faith in the human spirit. Like Wordsworth, Carroll affirms the redemptive force of love and sympathy.

Carroll's optimism, however, is a fleeting, momentary indulgence—an intellectual slip. The scene, like all of Carroll's, is a self-contained imaginative flash. Thus Alice's interaction with the White Knight does not alter her or bring her any deeper knowledge.

Although the scene does initiate her movement to the eighth square and hence her queening, Alice's internality hardly even flutters. Her crowning, like so many of Carroll's metaphors, seems hollow of meaning, a symbol without a referent, a facade that conceals nothing.

The pull between the desire for memory and the compulsion towards autonomy represents the deepest tension of the Alice narratives—a tension neither resolved nor cathartically worked through, but rather left taut and unchanged. The drive to suppress memory and contact, meaning and context, however, necessarily subverts secrecy. For secrecy presupposes an existence of meaning, a renunciation of nonsense and jabberwocky. To hide something is to affirm that some truth, some signified, exists. But there is, finally, only nonsense in Wonderland and Looking-Glass, nothing, and therefore nothing to hide. Secrecy can find no place within a created world such as Carroll's, for it is, in its naked essence, a confirmation of truth, an admission of faith.

Chapter 11

The Defamation of the Restatement (Second) of Conflict of Laws in Cyberspace

The defamation of choice-of-law in cyberspace: countering the view that the restatement of conflict of laws is inadequate to navigate the borderless reaches of the intangible frontier

So she sat on, with closed eyes, and half believed herself in Wonderland, though she knew she had but to open them again and all would change to dull reality....

The new information age has caused scholars to consider the adequacy of traditional jurisdictional regimes where interstate disputes arise in cyberspace. Personal jurisdiction has been one of the first of these regimes to undergo criticism and, for the most part, has come out relatively unscathed, despite its opponents' arguments that traditional notions of personal jurisdiction have no place in cyberspace. While the assault on personal jurisdiction in cyberspace has lessened in recent years, in its wake has come yet another attack on conventional jurisdictional notions: a criticism of traditional choice-of-law regimes in cyber-disputes.

Much in the same vein as their assault on personal jurisdiction, many scholars argue that traditional choice-of-law doctrines are inadequate to determine which state law to apply in interstate cyber-disputes. While these critics assert many arguments in support of their view that traditional choice-of-law approaches are inadequate for cyberspace, the overwhelming criticism is that "old choice-of-law doctrines fail to provide any meaningful guidance in the virtual world because these doctrines depend on notions of physical location." Essentially, the argument is that "because there is no `there' in the virtual world, [traditional choice-of-law] doctrines are virtually useless." In the same breath, many scholars are eager to propose offending alternative regimes to these perceived problems with choice of law in cyberspace, most of which deal with choice of law by ignoring it.

While many opponents criticize traditional choice-of-law regimes in cyber-disputes arising out of contracts, trademark infringement, and other areas of law, much of the criticism focuses on the law of defamation in cyberspace, or "cyber-defamation". The brunt of this scholarly attack on traditional choice-of-law regimes almost certainly falls on cyber-defamation actions. This is because of the unique aspect the law of defamation brings to cyberspace: publishing on the Internet is publishing instantaneously all over the world.

Thus, in a multistate cyber-defamation action, a defendant could conceivably collect for damages in any state where the defamatory material was published. As one scholar notes, "[t]he Internet allows anyone connected to it to disseminate information, statements, gossip, and so on, to millions of people with a few strokes on a computer keyboard. Thus millions of people now have their own electronic printing presses—capable of inexpensively communicating with millions of others worldwide." Clearly, the law of defamation represents the perfect lens through which to examine the adequacy of traditional choice-of-law regimes in cyberspace.

Despite the various choice-of-law doctrines available, the focus of this Note is almost entirely on the Restatement (Second) of Conflict of Laws ("Restatement (Second)") for two reasons. First, the Restatement (Second) is an eclectic mix of dominant policies and principles taken from traditional choice-of-law doctrines. Second, of those states turning away from the original Restatement of Conflicts of Laws, most are adopting the Restatement (Second).

This Note examines the adequacy of the traditional choice-of-law rules, including the Restatement (Second), in interstate cyber-defamation disputes, and argues that there is nothing different or unique about cyberspace which warrants the modification or abandonment of traditional choice-of-law regimes for cyber-defamation disputes. A distinction must be made, however.

This Note does not attempt to argue the adequacy of traditional choice-of-law approaches in and of themselves; the disparaging of traditional choice-of-law doctrines in the real world has been and continues to be a pastime among practitioners and scholars alike. Further, this Note does not argue which choice-of-law approach would be most effective in dealing with cyber-defamation. The only goal of this Note is to demonstrate that traditional choice-of-law rules are not confounded by defamation disputes arising in cyberspace.

THE LAW OF DEFAMATION AND THE RESTATEMENT (SECOND) OF CONFLICT OF LAWS

Cyberspace is a breeding ground for defamation. Several factors contribute to this. As one commentator suggests, "[T]he low cost of cyberspace communications makes wide-scale distribution of wrongful communications possible." Therefore, "the caution ordinarily exercised in face-to-face real space tends to recede in the world of anonymity and solitude that one finds in front of computer terminals.

The temptation to engage in otherwise reckless behaviour increases the probability of [cyber-defamation]." Further, messages in cyberspace "transmit few social cues, so people communicating electronically tend to talk more freely than they would in person." Moreover, cyberspace provides numerous forms by which people can engage in cyber-defamation, whether via an e-mail message, a message posted to a newsgroup or bulletin board, or an available file via file transport protocol or database.

More than ever before, people are linked to one another across the country by engaging in various forms of communication. The more people communicate with one another, the greater the potential for defamation suits.

Due to the ease with which one can publish defamatory

material via cyberspace, the potential for global publication of the material instantaneously, and the varying defamation laws among states, choice-of-law plays an even more crucial role in interstate defamation actions.

A. The Law of Defamation

In general, defamation refers to a "false written [or spoken] statement that exposes a person to public ridicule, hatred, or contempt, or injures [their] reputation." The basic elements of a defamation action commonly include: (1) a statement of fact was published by showing or saying it to a third party; (2) the statement was false at the time it was made; (3) the statement was defamatory; (4) the statement reasonably refers to the plaintiff; (5) the statement was made with the requisite degree of fault; and (6) the statement caused actual injury.

Despite the common elements of defamation shared among states, many key variations in defamation law exist. For example, state defamation laws may vary on the requisite degree of fault required in defamation cases, the requirement of falsity, distinctions between fact and opinion, the defamatory nature of the statement, the requisite reference to the plaintiff, the availability of defenses and privileges, and special procedural rules. These differences among state defamation laws "reflect deliberate state policy choices, stemming from a balance of free speech values against interests in compensating injured plaintiffs." Such state policy choices are what choice-of-law doctrines, like the Restatement (Second), serve to protect.

In a defamation action, a plaintiff may sue (i.e., personal jurisdiction is proper) in any state in which the plaintiff can prove that someone received the defamatory message. "However, that forum's law will not necessarily govern the suit. It is that forum's choice of law rules that direct the court to the applicable law." As is evident, choice of law is a critical tool for the sophisticated attorney in interstate defamation actions; it is one tool that could easily determine the ultimate outcome of the case.

B. THE RESTATEMENT (SECOND) OF CONFLICT OF LAWS APPROACH FOR DEFAMATION

Whether the case ends up in the federal court system by way of diversity jurisdiction or in the state court system, a judge must always apply the forum state's choice-of-law rules. In addition, in order for a state law to be selected in a constitutionally permissible manner, a state must have a significant contact or contacts creating a state interest such that the choice of its law is neither arbitrary, nor fundamentally unfair.

Under the Restatement (Second), the first step is to determine whether the alleged defamatory material was published in one state, or two or more states. Where alleged defamatory material is published in only one state, there is a presumption that the law to be applied is "the ... law of the state where the publication occurr[ed]." This presumption can only be rebutted by demonstrating that "some other state has a more significant relationship, to the occurrence and the parties, in which event the ... law of the other state will be applied." Thus, all relationships being equal, the law where the defamed party is domiciled controls by default.

In multistate defamation actions, where the defamatory statement is contained "in any one edition of a book or newspaper, or any one broadcast over radio or television, exhibition of a motion picture, or similar aggregate communication" there is a strong presumption that the state with the most significant relationship will be "the state where the person was domiciled at the time, if the matter complained of was published in that state." In multistate defamation actions involving corporations or other legal persons, "the state of most significant relationship will usually be the state where the corporation, or other legal person, had its principal place of business at the time, if the matter complained of was published in that state."

Again, in order to overcome all presumptions stated above, one must demonstrate that another state has a more significant relationship to the dispute. Judges make this determination by applying the choice-of-law principles listed in section 6 of the Restatement (Second). The seven factors relevant to the determination of the applicable law include: (1) the needs of the interstate and international system, (2) the relevant policies of the forum, (3) the relevant policies of the interested states, (4) the protection of justified expectations, (5) the basic policies underlying the particular field of law, (6) certainty and uniformity of result, and ease in determining and applying the law.

The Restatement (Second) also provides a list of relevant contacts to be taken into account when applying the factors listed in section 6, which include: "(a) the place where the injury occurred, (b) the place where the conduct causing the injury occurred, (c) the domicil, residence, nationality, place of incorporation and place of business of the parties, and (d) the place where the relationship, if any, between the parties is centered." As far as the law of defamation is concerned, "[t]he place of the plaintiff's domicil, or on occasion his principal place of business, is the single most important contact for determining the state of the applicable law." These considerations serve to ensure that a court will not apply the law of a state with little interest in the case.

Comments to the Restatement (Second) clearly establish that the section 6 and 150 lists are not meant to be exclusive. "[A] court will on occasion give consideration to other factors in deciding a question of choice of law." Further, the factors listed in both lists are not arranged in any order of relative importance. "Varying weight will be given to a particular factor, or to a group of factors, in different areas of choice of law." In sum, the approach in the Restatement (Second) seeks to preserve state policies by requiring courts to apply the law of the state with the most significant relationship with the dispute.

DEMYSTIFYING CYBERSPACE

As is the case with most breakthroughs in technology, people are eager to denigrate the efficiency of traditional legal rules, including choice of law. Early in the 1990s, as the Internet spread throughout the world like a forest fire, people became enamored with it. Poetic sentimentalities in the face of a brave new era gave rise to phrases such as "surfing the Web," "visiting a Web site," "netizens," "entering chat rooms," and the "virtual world." Indeed, the term "cyberspace" itself denotes some other "place" outside of traditional space and time; a place where anything and everything is possible at the touch of a button. In short, cyberspace established itself in the American psyche as a world of its own.

In line with this cliched ideology, some people assert themselves as "residents of Cyberspace, [resistant] to law emanating from outside of Cyberspace." One "netizen" of cyberspace went so far as to declare a "Declaration of Independence of Cyberspace," which states, "Governments of the Industrial World, you weary giants of flesh and steel, I come from Cyberspace, the new home of Mind. On behalf of the future, I ask you of the past to leave us alone. You are not welcome among us. You have no sovereignty where we garner." This self-styled "declaration" epitomizes netizen dogma.

Cyberspace is no longer a "new frontier," but a fixed communication device that is commonplace and woven into the fabric of American society. The fixation with cyberspace as another world is rapidly losing its poetic luster and becoming just another exhausted metaphor used for the amusement of the sci-fi generation. As one commentator eloquently stated, "As we master and understand [cyberspace], we demystify it."

Cyberspace, contrary to netizen dogma, is not a "world." Cyberspace is another source of information, not a new state of being. A person does not sleep, eat, or play "there" anymore than they sleep, eat, or play in the pages of Time magazine. A person's reputation, whether defamed by a hard copy of USA Today or by the USA Today Web site, is still injured in the real world. It is conceivable, even though most likely unachievable, that—in the far distant future—humans might conceive of a way to physically place their bodies in the cyber-ether, thus truly becoming "netizens." In such a world, cyberspace could conceivably be their sovereign. Until that dream comes to fruition, however, the term "netizen" denotes no more than a person in real-space, under the law of real sovereign states, gazing into the dull reality of a real-space computer screen (most likely playing FreeCell or shopping on Ebay).

COUNTERING THE ARGUMENTS AGAINST TRADITIONAL CHOICE-OF-LAW DOCTRINES IN CYBERSPACE

Thus far, criticisms of the traditional choice-of-law regimes for cyber-defamation can be classified into two groups, which may occasionally overlap. Within the first group rests those arguments based on a perceived premise that something is uniquely different about cyberspace. Within the second group rests cloaked arguments that are asserted as "because of the uniqueness of Cyberspace," but ultimately are deep-rooted arguments routinely used to disparage traditional choice-of-law regimes, as well as other areas of law, in "real" space.

These proposals for changing choice-of-law principles for cyber-defamation rely on the perceived notion that defamation in cyberspace is somehow different and, therefore, cyber-defamation needs different choice-of-law rules. This perception is false. By demystifying cyberspace, it becomes all too clear that there is nothing about cyber-defamation that in any way challenges the adequacy of traditional choice-of-law regimes, including the Restatement (Second).

A. Criticisms Based on a Lack of Boundaries in Cyberspace

The most cited argument by far for why traditional choice-of-law rules are inadequate for cyber-defamation actions is the "boundless medium" argument. "[M]ost traditional [choice-of-law] rules are based on the locations where activities take place[,]" including the Restatement (Second). The argument is that these choice-of-law rules are inadequate for cyber-defamation actions because cyberspace is boundless; it defies national boundaries, and therefore, undermines the viability and validity of laws based on geographic borders. These critics argue that cyberspace activities differ from real-space activities in that "they are free from any concept of locality or distance."

Critics argue that "like most post-Restatement authorities ... the Restatement (Second) offers courts little substantive guidance concerning choice-of-law decisions." Regarding the Restatement (Second), critics argue that the geographical principles listed in section 145(2) are confounded by cyberspace. Critics wonder how these relevant contacts and principles are to be considered in cyberspace. For example, how is "place of injury, place of conduct causing injury, principle place of business, and nationality" determined in cyberspace? Some dismiss a user's ambivalence to political border crossing in exchange for the claim that "[f]requently, users are unaware that they have even `crossed' a political border in the course of their virtual travels." Some critics use "boundless medium" arguments to support the proposition that the choice-of-law principles in section 6 of the Restatement (Second) are vague and offer little direction because of cyberspace.

Critics fail to support their proposition that the boundless medium of cyberspace makes traditional choice-of-law doctrines inapposite. The way in which most arguments against traditional choice-of-law approaches are laid out is that an author creates a hypothetical cyber-defamation dispute, and then applies a choice-of-law doctrine. Ultimately, without ever explaining why cyberspace is somehow different or unique in their analysis, they conclude by holding that traditional choice-of-law regimes are inadequate or useless in cyberspace. Consider the following variation by John D. Faucher used to demonstrate the inadequacy of the Restatement (Second) for dealing with cyber-defamation disputes:

A offers hundreds of bulletin boards from a mainframe computer in State A. A contracts with B, a movie critic from State B, to disseminate B's weekly movie review column. A publishes B's reviews over its Movie Line bulletin board. The Movie Line bulletin board has readers in all fifty states. In a review of a certain movie, B makes a false assertion. Specifically, B writes that C, the movie's star and a resident of the state of C, belongs to the Ku Klux Klan. After reading the review, African-American, Jewish, and Catholic computer users boycott the movie and its studio, Studio C.

Studio C also resides in State C. C and Studio C sue B and A in federal court in the Western District of State C. They allege defamatory publication in State C, and seek compensatory and punitive damages.

Defamation laws in State A, B, and C vastly differ.

In Faucher's Restatement (Second) analysis to this cyber-hypothetical, Faucher skips entirely the initial presumption that, unless another state has a more significant relationship to the dispute, the law of State C is to be applied in the dispute because the defamatory material was published in State C and the Plaintiffs' domicile and principal place of business are in State C. Instead, Faucher sets out to determine which state has the most significant relationship with the dispute, and asserts that it could just as easily be any one of the hypothetical states.

Without difficulty, Faucher first breezes through the section 145 "physical" contacts list of the Restatement (Second), easily identifying that injury to reputation occurred in State C, conduct causing the injury took place in State B (the place from where the review was sent) and in State A (from where the review was disseminated), Plaintiff's are domiciled in State C, and Defendants are domiciled in States A and B. Based on the face of these contacts, Faucher argues that it is not immediately apparent which state has the "most significant contacts."

Therefore, Faucher turns to the seven choice-of-law principles listed in section 6 of the Restatement (Second) in order to aid in the determination of which state has the most significant relationship to the dispute. Without going through any section 6 analysis, however, Faucher states that "[t]hese criteria are vague and offer little direction." As a result of his cyber-hypothetical, Faucher summarizes by stating that "[b]ecause [the Restatement (Second)] process is long, difficult, and murky, the Restatement (Second) offers little help in [cyberdefamation] cases." As is typical in most critics' analyses, Faucher's analysis of the Restatement (Second) as applied to his cyber-hypothetical identifies nothing unique about the medium of cyberspace that makes the Restatement (Second) any more "long, difficult, and murky" to apply when compared to defamation in real-space. Faucher simply runs through the Restatement (Second) analysis, and then at the end suggests that because it is cyberspace, it is somehow different, and therefore traditional choice-of-law regimes are inadequate for cyber-defamation disputes.

In the end, Faucher fails to address the crucial questions. How Faucher's analysis is applied any differently in real-space? What does cyberspace uniquely offer that makes section 6 principles "vague and of little direction" when compared to the application of section 6 principles in the real world? These questions, and more, are left unanswered by the critics because cyberspace poses nothing unique to traditional choice-of-law regimes in the real world. Consider the following variation on Faucher's cyber-hypothetical involving a defamation dispute in real-space:

A is the publisher of America Today, a nationally read newspaper located in State A. A contracts with B, a movie critic from State B, to disseminate B's weekly movie review column. A publishes B's reviews in the entertainment section of America Today, which has readers in all fifty states. In a review of a certain movie, B makes a false assertion.

Specifically, B writes that C, the movie's star and a resident of State C, belongs to the Ku Klux Klan. After reading the review, African-American,

Jewish, and Catholic America Today readers boycott the movie and its studio, Studio C. Studio C also resides in State C. C and Studio C sue B and A in federal court in State C. They allege defamatory publication in State C, and seek compensatory and punitive damages. Defamation laws in State A, B, and C vastly differ.

The only thing different from Faucher's cyber-hypothetical and this real-space hypothetical is that in Faucher's cyber-hypothetical the defamatory material was published in cyberspace on a computer bulletin board available nationwide, whereas in this real-space hypothetical the defamatory material is published in real-space in a newspaper available nationwide. According to Faucher and other critics, traditional choice-of-law approaches, like the Restatement (Second), are inadequate choice-of-law approaches for cyber-defamation disputes; for choice-of-law purposes, however, there is absolutely no difference between Faucher's cyber-hypothetical and this real-space hypothetical.

An application of the Restatement (Second) to this hypothetical will present identical results as Faucher's cyber-hypothetical. Although Faucher did not provide the initial Restatement (Second) presumption in his cyber-hypothetical analysis, this critical presumption, if performed, remains the same in real-space. Specifically, unless another state has a more significant relationship to the dispute, the law of State C is to be applied in the dispute because the defamatory material was published in State C and Plaintiffs' domicile and principal place of business are in State C. Again, whether the defamatory review is published nationwide in cyberspace or real-space, the presumption in both hypotheticals remains unsurprisingly identical.

Further, section 145 contacts equally remain identical and just as easily identifiable. Injury to reputation still occurs in State C. Conduct causing the injury still takes place in State B (the place from where the review was sent) and in State A (the place from where the review was disseminated). Plaintiffs are still domiciled in State C, and Defendants are still domiciled in States A and B. Incidentally, critics argue that section 145 contacts are confounded by boundless cyberspace, yet Faucher, in his hypothetical used to prove inadequate traditional choice-of-law regimes for cyberspace, has no difficulty identifying these real-world physical contacts. Just as section 145 contacts remain identical in the real-space hypothetical, so too do such contacts remain just as easily identifiable.

Without going through any Restatement (Second) section 6 analysis, Faucher argues that section 6 principles are "vague and offer little direction" when applied in the context of his cyber-hypothetical. Nevertheless, critics of the Restatement (Second) have always asserted that section 6 principles are somewhat difficult to apply, whether in real-space or cyberspace. Policy analysis is a difficult business; that is why lawyering is a profession. Regardless, however "difficult, vague, or of little direction" these section 6 principles are in real-space, and are no more "difficult, vague, or of little direction" in cyberspace.

In order to answer whether cyberspace offers something unique to choice-of-law doctrines for defamation, making section 6 principles "vague and of little direction" as Faucher suggests, it is imperative to analyse section 6 principles in cyberspace versus section 6 principles in real-space. The following focuses on a few relevant principles listed in section 6 of the Restatement (Second) in order to demonstrate that these principles are in no way confounded by cyberspace.

Principles (2) and (3) of section 6 combine to determine the interests of each state by gauging "the purposes, policies, aims and objectives of each of the competing local law rules urged to govern" the controversy. The Restatement (Second) makes no attempt to weigh the relative competing interests. It simply seeks to identify these interests as another factor to determine the appropriate choice of law. At a bare minimum, State C has a legitimate interest in protecting its citizens from fraudulent misrepresentation, but States A and B also have an interest in discouraging fraudulent conduct by persons operating from within its territory. These competing interests are neither confounded nor altered by cyberspace. State C's interest in protecting the reputation of its citizens is not changed simply because someone decides to defame State C's citizen in cyberspace instead of real-space. Likewise, State A and B's interest in discouraging fraudulent conduct by persons operating from within their borders is just as real, regardless of what medium those individuals use to effectuate such slanderous conduct.

Principles (4) and (6) of section 6 can be combined to determine the parties' "justified expectations and certainty and predictability of result." These considerations deal with the proposition that "it would be unfair and improper to hold a person liable under the local law of one state when he had justifiably molded his conduct to conform to the requirements of another state." Specifically, these factors are "of great importance in areas where the parties are likely to give advance thought to the legal consequences of their transactions," such as in the area of contract law." Predictability and party expectations are not significantly relevant in the area of tort law because persons that cause injury usually act without giving much thought (i.e., expectation) to the legal consequences of their actions. Such principles may be of greater importance in the tort law area of defamation, however.

In addition, some commentators argue that the Restatement (Second) approach to cyber-defamation disputes, in its "case-by-case search for fairness ... sacrifices certainty and simplicity." Regardless of its cyber-premise, this argument is merely a traditional real-space criticism of the Restatement (Second). Whether the Restatement (Second) does "sacrifice certainty and simplicity," such a sacrifice is no greater because of cyberspace.

For example, newspapers, conscious of the legal consequences of their actions, will often structure their behaviour around the availability of defenses and privileges to potential actions brought against them for defamation. As sensitive as a newspaper may be to the potential of publishing defamatory material in an article, they also know the potential consequence when they do. That consequence is the inevitability that the state law of where the defamed party is domiciled will most likely govern the dispute. Therefore, a newspaper publisher in no way can argue that it did not have any expectation that the law of the defamed party's domicile could apply. Whether defamatory material is published on the newspaper's Web site makes no difference to the newspaper's expectation. The defamed party's reputation is still injured in real-space, and real-space rules apply. Conversely, in those situations where someone publishes defamatory material without thought of the legal ramifications of his or her conduct, then justified expectations will play an insignificant role in the choice-of-law decision. An individual's reputation is injured regardless of whether someone carelessly defames that person in cyberspace, as opposed to realspace. Clearly, cyberspace otters nothing unique to these principles of expectation and predictability embodied in the Restatement (Second).

Finally, principle (7) recognizes that "[i]deally, choice-of-law rules should be simple and easy to apply" cyberspace does not make ascertaining the applicable law by traditional choice-of-law rules any more difficult. As discussed previously in both hypotheticals presented, the initial presumption of the Restatement (Second) remained exactly the same. Further, the identification of contacts listed in section 145 remained exactly the same. Also, the analysis of section 6 principles was not confounded by cyberspace. However difficult critics may think the Restatement (Second) is to apply to defamation disputes in real-space, this perceived difficulty is in no way more or less difficult to apply in cyber-defamation disputes.

Indeed, much criticism of choice of law in cyber-defamation disputes has been geared toward the Restatement (Second). Despite criticisms, cyberspace is not conducive to the paradigm that sovereignty is traditionally a function of territoriality. Cyberspace in no way challenges the world to reconcile geographical real-space with a nongeographical cyberspace. And why should it? Albeit extremely exciting, cyberspace is simply another medium for the communication of information. Regardless of whether someone defames a party over a broadcast, by fax, in print, or in cyberspace, the defamed party's reputation is still injured in a sovereign state where that state has a real-space interest in protecting its citizens' reputation from injury.

B. Real-Space Traditional Choice-of-Law Criticisms Disguised

The following represents those cloaked arguments that are asserted as "because of the uniqueness of cyberspace," but ultimately, are well-established arguments traditionally used to criticize traditional choice-of-law regimes, as well as other areas of law in real-space. While critics serve these arguments up as novel because of cyberspace, all of the following arguments exist not because of cyberspace, but because of a much broader dissatisfaction with traditional choice-of-law regimes as a whole. Regardless of the dissatisfaction that some may feel toward traditional choice-of-law approaches, that dissatisfaction is in no way amplified because of cyberspace.

One argument is that "[t]he physical acts of copying and distributing take time, during which [an individual] can obtain an injunction before suffering extensive damage." However, in cyberspace the defamatory material can be distributed nationwide at a keystroke. Thus, "[b]y the time the court hears the case, the damage has been done or the advantage has been exploited." Although asserted to support the idea that traditional choice-of-law doctrines are inadequate for cyber-defamation disputes, the fact that humankind has created a medium of communication capable of speeding up the publishing process in no way is related to choice-of-law doctrine. Whether or not this argument presents a problem should be dealt with by the defamation law of states. Choice-of-law rules cut across various areas of state law (i.e., torts and contracts) without modifying them.

A similar argument presented to support the inadequacy of traditional choice-of-law rules for cyber-defamation is that under the single publication rule, a defamed plaintiff can recover for all harm to his or her reputation in or outside the forum state. Thus, in any given cyber-defamation action, it is conceivable that such harm to reputation could occur nationwide. Nationwide defamation actions are just as common in real-space, however, through nationwide newspaper circulations, as they may be in cyberspace. Again, the problem is not with choice-of-law doctrine. Whether or not the single publication rule should be re-examined as it relates to cyberspace may be a question for state legislatures to address in their defamation law. As for choice of law in cyberspace, the single publication rule offers nothing different than what it offers in real-space.

Another argument used to support the notion that choice of law is confounded by cyberspace stems from the fact that defamation law draws a distinction between "private persons who may be unavailable to access the media to respond to the defamation and public persons who have greater access to mass media." The argument is that current law does not account for the fact that private individuals may now respond to defamatory statements via cyberspace bý posting a message to any number of Internet newsgroups. "In effect, the defamed person can very quickly and easily become the mass media himself by using the Internet." Nevertheless, whether cyberspace provides private individuals with an opportunity to respond to defamatory statements they previously did not have bares no relation to choice-of-law doctrine.

A state legislature or court may or may not wish to re-examine and/or possibly alter the requisite degree of fault that private plaintiffs must prove in cyber-defamation disputes. However, choice of law in cyber-defamation disputes is not affected by or concerned with this new opportunity afforded by cyberspace for private individuals to respond to defamatory statements.

Lastly, some critics argue that cyber-defamation is confounded by traditional choice-of-law approaches because the opportunity for forum shopping in cyber-disputes is intensified. For example, in a defamation action, a plaintiff may bring suit in any state in which the plaintiff can prove that someone received the defamatory message. Thus, in any given multistate cyber-defamation action, a plaintiff may conceivably forum shop around fifty states for the most beneficial choice-of-law rules. A plaintiff could initiate an action in a state with an insignificant interest in the dispute only to take advantage of that state's choice-of-law rules, thus controlling to a degree what substantive law governs the dispute. Critics argue that "[t]his type of `forum shopping' may not only adversely affect the defendant; it may also undermine the policies and laws of [states] which have substantially greater interest in the cause of action."

It is somewhat ironic that states, in order to deal with the laws differing among them, created choice-of-law rules that themselves differ among states. Indeed, forum shopping is a problem. This Author is of the opinion that states should come to a consensus on one choice-of-law rule to not only decrease the opportunity for forum shopping that undermines the interests and polices of a given state, but also accord even greater comity among states. Regardless, forum shopping is no greater because of cyberspace. A nationwide cyber-defamation action poses no greater opportunity for forum shopping than a nationwide real-space defamation action. If USA Today contains defamatory material about an individual and it is read in all fifty states, the defamed party may forum shop in all fifty states for a beneficial choice-of-law approach. Likewise, if USA Today decides to publish the defamatory material on its Web site as opposed to its hard copy newspaper, and that material is read in all fifty states, the defamed party may still forum shop in all fifty states.

The only unique aspect of cyberspace is the heightened potential for a defamatory statement to have an effect nationwide. Once a defamatory cyber-statement does have an effect on a national level, however, that statement is no different than a real-space statement published in a nationally recognized magazine. Again, the problem of forum shopping exists with equal force in cyberspace and in real-space. Although now asserted as existing because of cyberspace, the forum shopping argument is nothing more than a classic criticism of the fact that traditional choice-of-law regimes differ among states.

This argument is not novel because of cyberspace, but has always been a criticism grounded in real-space. This heightened potential for cyber-statements to gain national attention may call for states to rethink the potential severity of their defamation laws. Alternatively, this heightened potential may call for states to utilize the same choice-of-law approach for defamation. However, there is no reason to make new or modified choice-of-law rules for cyber-defamation disputes because, for choice-of-law purposes, such disputes in no way differ from real-space disputes.

C. Problems with Proposed Alternative Approaches

In response to the perceived inadequacy of traditional

choice-of-law regimes for cyber-defamation disputes, scholars propose various alternatives in the law. Among these numerous alternatives, the main proposals are: (1) creating a federal common law for the Internet that would effectively eliminate the choice-of-law process, and (2) simply making cyberspace a sovereign of its own. No courts apply these novel regimes.

In the rush to be the first to establish new choice-of-law regimes for cyberspace, some scholars seem to have forgotten the reason behind choice-of-law regimes: to respect state sovereignty. Despite the overarching argument that cyberspace offers nothing novel for traditional choice-of-law regimes in cyber-defamations, an analysis of these cyberspace approaches will also reveal that they offer little as alternatives to traditional choice-of-law approaches.

Faucher argues that to bring order and predictability to cyber-defamation cases, judges should create a federal common law to govern cyber-defamation. According to Faucher: "Such an approach would allow judges to fashion a defamation law that is relevant to electronic communication" as well as "avoid the conceptual difficulties of applying choice-of-law rules to torts that have little relation to a single geographical area." Faucher states: "If the law is uniform across all states ... choice-of-law problems disappear." Faucher's federal common law approach changes the law of cyber-defamation itself, as opposed to modifying traditional choice-of-law regimes for cyberspace. Assuming, arguendo, that the creation of a federal common law does not violate the Erie and Klaxon doctrines as Faucher suggests, a federal common law for cyber-defamation would fundamentally violate the principles and policies of state sovereignty.

Faucher's solution to the perceived problem of choice of law in cyberspace is, essentially, to bypass the choice-of-law question entirely. Faucher argues that "the federal law would advance the forum's interest best because, under a federal common law, the forum is the United States rather than an individual state." This argument is circular and loses sight of one crucial factor; the federal forum's minimal interest exists at the expense of a state's interest in a cyber-defamation action involving its citizens. The entire point of choice-of-law rules is ultimately to respect state sovereignty. A common law federal approach does not respect the sovereignty of any state's law. In fact, it would rob states of such sovereignty. Where choice-of-law rules exist to respect state sovereignty, a federal common law would exist to deny it. Faucher argues for an easy way out of perceived tough choice-of-law issues at the expense of everything choice of law exists to protect. Thus, Faucher's approach offends state sovereignty.

As well as offending state sovereignty, a federal common law for defamation seems difficult and unreasonable. As one commentator states: "When is the choice of law question for a particular cyber-dispute appropriately determined by this new model?" "Simply `touching and concerning' cyberspace, however, is not a sufficient reason to invoke an entirely new choice of law methodology." For example, suppose USA Today publishes defamatory material in its newspaper distributed nationwide. Clearly, a defamation action arising out of these events would be governed by sovereign states, and the law applicable would be decided by traditional choice-of-law rules.

Conversely, if USA Today, instead of publishing the material in its newspaper, publishes the defamatory material on its Web site, then, under Faucher's approach, this dispute would be covered by federal common law. However, what law governs—federal or state—when USA Today publishes the same defamatory material at the same time in both real-space (in a newspaper) and in cyberspace (on a Web site) as is predominantly the case? Does a plaintiff recover for Web site damages under federal law and newspaper damages under state law?

Regardless of these quandaries, it is entirely unreasonable that a state should lose its interest in protecting its citizens involved in a defamation dispute merely because a different medium was chosen to publish the defamatory material. There cannot reasonably be said to exist a federal interest in defamation via cyberspace that justifies stripping states of their principal interest, that of protecting their citizens. Indeed, a federal common law is not only difficult to apply, but also completely offensive to notions of state sovereignty. These are the primary interests choice-of-law rules exist to protect.

Alternatives proposing that cyberspace should be recognized as a sovereign within itself suffer from the same failing as Faucher's federal common law alternative. One such alternative similar to Faucher's approach is to make choice-of-law issues virtually irrelevant by having courts recognize a new law of cyberspace, called lex cyberalty. The argument is that courts heating cyber-disputes should look to lex cyberalty in order to determine the applicable "substantive standard of behaviour." Besides suffering from the same faults as Faucher's federal common law approach, it is unrealistic that this unwarranted approach would ever emerge because, for such a system to work, the states would have to relinquish their sovereign control over cyberspace.

Choice of law is a difficult subject area because of what is at stake not only in an interstate system, but also in a unique federal system. Choice-of-law rules serve to facilitate comity between the states. Comity between states is of extreme importance, but so too is comity between the federal system and the state system. Of equal importance in a federal system, however, are the states' rights to reign supreme over the areas of law rightfully reserved to them. It is imperative for the functioning of both the interstate and federal systems that jurisdictional doctrines do not lose sight of the vital principles embodied in state sovereignty.

Despite the view of some, choice-of-law issues arising in cyberspace are only sui generis in substance, not form. Instead of creating new regimes for cyber-defamation disputes, most courts apply traditional choice-of-law doctrines—usually sub silentio—and utilize old analogies to deal with the substance of cyberspace. Stated another way: "Instead of following a virtual path for these Internet cases, most courts travel the well-worn path of traditional choice-of-law principles." As cyberspace becomes more grounded and less mystifying, it becomes much clearer that cyberspace does not offer any unique problems for choice of law in defamation disputes.

The desire to criticize traditional jurisdictional rules is misplaced. The effects of cyber-defamation remain the same in real-space, and traditional choice-of-law regimes are in no way confounded by cyberspace. cyberspace is neither unique nor special for choice-of-law purposes, and as a result, there exists no reason to single out cyber-defamation as something in need of reformulated choice-of-law rules. Nor is there a need to abandon traditional choice-of-law rules. Besides, proposed alternatives are difficult to apply, unreasonable, and serve only to strip states of their sovereignty over cyber-defamation disputes.

As for whether traditional choice-of-law regimes are confounded by cyber-disputes arising out of other areas of law, it would seem that the answer would be no. Just as cyber-defamation poses no difficulty for traditional choice-of-law regimes, cyber-contracts, for example, should also pose no difficulty. Similarly, other traditional choice-of-law methods should fare just as well in cyberspace as the Restatement (Second) does. Nevertheless, as far as the application of the Restatement (Second) to cyber-defamation disputes is concerned, there is nothing different or unique about cyberspace warranting the modification and/or abandonment of traditional choice-of-law regimes for cyber-defamation disputes. In the end, the constant slandering of traditional choice-of-law regimes for cyber-defamation disputes must give way to the dull reality of real-space.

Chapter 12

Chasing Alice Down the Rabbit Hole

Imagine this: I'm sitting at my computer and I've just typed the above words. I sit back, read the words, and feel the momentary contentment that usually accompanies that first attempt to get started. Suddenly I have a feeling that I'm not alone. Charles Lutwidge Dodgson (aka Lewis Carroll), dead for over one hundred years, is looking over my right shoulder. He reads my opening heading and sighs, 'Not another reference to poor Alice. Why don't they just let the old girl rest in peace?' I try to resist the temptation to recall Alice and her famous words — 'What is the use of a book without pictures and conversations?' — but I can't.

Rabbits and other creatures that live beneath the surface will emerge later in the discussion when I'll look closely at three recent texts. Through various literary and illustrative devices, these texts demonstrate the complex interplay between two symbolic mediums. By my reading of the content and form of these books, I want to draw attention to the need to engage students in a critical discourse which attends not only to the aesthetic and literary properties of these texts, but also considers their social and political implications.

As a way of framing my discussion of the three picture books, I shall consider the uneasy relations which exist between the affective and the cognitive. By considering this 'hearts-and-minds' dilemma, I wish to emphasise that in our quest to develop critical readers we do not lose sight of the pleasure that can be gained from these books. Rather than see pleasure as something that is taken for granted in a discussion of picture books, I want to foreground it by looking at the aesthetic properties of the genre and argue that aesthetics and critical literacy can comfortably cohabit the student body. With a climate which is increasingly scrutinising the teaching profession from all angles, we need to resist the temptation to return to a skills-driven curriculum in a user-pays educational world. If we fail to do so, we run the risk of confirming Foucault's observation about teachers:

It's quite an achievement the way teachers manage to make learning unpleasant, depressingly grey, unerotic! We need to understand how that serves the needs of society.

PICTURE BOOK AS AESTHETIC OBJECT/EXPERIENCE

The pleasures that can be gained from reading picture books invariably stem from their aesthetic properties. In particular, it is the visual component which first arrests the reader's attention and becomes the focus of critical review. Lewis argues that this emphasis on the illustrations rather than the words is a direct result of an 'over-riding concern with the aesthetically fine'. As a theory of art, aesthetics seems to court considerable debates about the nature of beauty, whether it is an objective product or a subjective response on the part of the viewer. Picture books are an object of beauty and at the same time provide readers with an aesthetic, multi-sensory experience: eyes scan each illustration drawn to the elements of colour, shape, line; hands touch the surface feeling the texture of the pages, moving parts that lift up, slide and rotate.

However, to conceive of picture books only in sensory terms fails to take into account the ways they, like other forms of literature, provide a surface on which a diverse range of events, commentaries, and experiences are made available to readers. In this sense, picture books offer readers the opportunity to understand themselves and their world. Students will not become 'readers' and more rounded individuals with a heightened sense of social responsibility and awareness simply because well-intentioned teachers 'immerse' them in picture books. However, picture books have the potential to stimulate inquiry into their content and form which may result in the reader making a series of intellectual, emotional and perceptual shifts. Picture books embody a range of 'virtual' aesthetic forms in that artistic representation gives a sense of the real.

Such virtualities can recast experience in a different light, thus providing means for discussion, reflection and action. Consequently, picture books not only exemplify the classical doctrine that literature for children is both a source of delight and a vehicle of (moral) instruction, but they also create spaces for imagination and reason, thought and emotion, morality and sensuousness. It is by invoking these aesthetic polarities within us that we are afforded opportunities to see ourselves as subjects of aesthetic experience, and not disinterested objective viewers/readers.

The question which needs to be asked is: In the current educational climate of critical literacies, is there a place for aesthetics? If so, then how can students be assisted in reaping the benefits Of the two approaches by becoming critically aesthetic readers/subjects? In looking to answer these questions, the following discussion considers some of the theoretical and pragmatic issues which inform a critical aesthetics.

TOWARDS A CRITICAL AESTHETICS

Historically, aesthetic theory was once preoccupied with questions of worth — what constitutes good art, good literature? In its attention to 'high art', the aesthetic experience was one which was rarefied, separated from everyday social life, and available to a privileged few. Furthermore, access to the discourse of art/literature was further limited by one's knowledge and experience.

Approaches to English teaching, and, in particular, literature study, have followed a similar path. The student has been pathologised as always being in need or lacking in some way (McWilliam, 1997). Awareness in the student of his/her own lack of knowledge becomes patently clear when questions of form and content are unable to be answered. Twenty years ago, with the advent of reader response theories, teachers were encouraged to elicit students' 'personal' responses to a text. This pedagogical approach created a healthy market for writers of teacher-texts, with the result that the 'personal' response became somewhat 'standardised' as the array of strategies for eliciting response took on a familiar ring.

While response theories broke the stranglehold of literary criticism held by the modernists with their preoccupation with form and structure, there is nevertheless a similarity in the two approaches in that the text remains the object of attention and the range of responses becomes limited by the practicalities of acceptable classroom protocols. And though reader response approaches are still in vogue, the influences of critical literary/literacy theories influenced by poststructuralism are becoming more apparent in the textual practices in which students engage in the classroom.

Teachers encourage students to deconstruct texts, resist their inherent ideologies, identify the gaps, and give voice to their silences. Postmodernism's refusal, among many things, to separate aesthetic judgement from its social context has helped redirect the teaching of English and the reading of literature. Whereas English teaching was once enamoured of the classical notion of developing a cultivated, sensitive individual, current practices are more likely to be concerned with developing critical readers who are alert to the social injustices and inequities in the world.

THE NATURE OF THE AESTHETIC READER/SUBJECT

Critical theorists have taught us that texts are never innocent; even seemingly 'innocent' picture books for young children have an implicit and sometimes explicit ideology. In this sense, picture books communicate a view of the world, albeit a constructed view, which at once discloses and obscures political and social viewpoints. The extent to which readers are able to discern or critique these viewpoints will depend largely on their personal histories, and 'experiential and symbolic reference points'(Beyer, 1996: p. 265). Access to the aesthetic properties of a text, including its embedded symbolism and allusions, depends on readers and texts sharing a degree of familiarity about the ways words and visuals function as culturally coded systems. In the case of children, their experiential and symbolic reference points may be limited, yet their natural inquisitiveness and capacity for imagination and invention mean that they are open to the challenges of the unconventional and unfamiliar.

Schools are sites where students become aware of their own aesthetic capabilities and limitations. When students either respond to or write literature, their efforts are judged in ways which call attention to their aesthetic in/adequacies. Furthermore, students' aesthetic selves are shaped not only by their participation in a culture which bombards their senses daily with a plethora of visual and aural stimuli, but also by curricula and pedagogical approaches which embody particular Western ways of seeing.

The confusion this causes in the non-Western student is understandable. Rizvi (1994: p. 55) supports this view by noting that 'much of what goes on in schools is based on a set of cultural assumptions that are antagonistic to diversity'. It seems then that it is impossible to speak of the individual without considering the social: while art and literature are experienced at a personal level, they are also produced and consumed in a social context.

THE SOCIAL IMPLICATIONS OF A CRITICAL AESTHETICS

As the earlier discussion indicated, aesthetic experience is both affective and cognitive; that is, it has as much to do with experiencing through the senses as it does with mentally engaging in that experience or sensation. In the case of picture books, their content and form have the ability to affect readers emotionally and to impact on their perceptions of the subject it addresses. Even the most basic or unsophisticated picture book has this potential for certain readers. However, the aesthetic experience, while always individualistic, can also be developed so that the reader is able to examine and reconsider the experience and come to an awareness and critical understanding of its social implications. Such awareness and understanding are necessary if a critical aesthetic with its possibilities of social action and new knowledge and understanding is to be realised. I am not advocating a 'call to arms' by young children: such radicalism lies outside both the genre and its readers. Nor I am seeing all picture books as having a social message or didactic intent.

I am proposing the idea that picture books, through their 'virtual' representations of social life, environment, history and personal triumphs and tragedies, offer readers the opportunity to reconsider what is taken-for-granted, unseen or unspoken and to gain 'a sense of possibilities that are unrealised and that might be realised' (Dewey, in Young, 1995: p. 7). These elements of social justice and critical self-reflection sit comfortably within the parameters of critical literacy theories.

In developing a critical aesthetics, many of the same strategies teachers use for developing students' critical literacies will be useful, e.g., using open-ended questioning, encouraging diverse viewpoints, problematising issues and assumptions, and envisioning alternatives. Art, like literature, has its own set of conventions and devices which provides the experiential and symbolic reference points mentioned previously. Students need to develop an understanding of both literary and artistic elements in order to be able to participate in discussions which arise from these texts, and as a means for developing their own aesthetic subjectivities.

In the case of picture books, attention, therefore, needs to be given to both visuals and print text. The teacher's role in providing students with a language for talking about literature and art continues to be important. Ultimately, it is the fusion, rather than the separation of, knowledge and feeling, intellect and senses, that is needed in order to develop the critically aesthetic reader/subject who is able to act upon the outer world of experience by drawing upon the inner world of the body.

In the discussion that follows, I want to put into practice the critical aesthetics for which I have been arguing. The three texts can be termed 'picture books' even though two of them do not fall into the category of fiction. I chose these three texts for the following reasons. First, they are recent examples of innovative picture book texts which offer readers multiple narratives and viewpoints. The second reason relates to the aesthetic quality of the illustrations. All three texts experiment with media, design and technique to develop illustrations which are visually pleasing as well as demanding, provoking readers to make symbolic associations beyond the literal surface appearances.

The third reason is one which is purely coincidental; and, that is, the three books deal with creatures that live beneath the surface — sand swimmers, rabbits, and fish. I found the metaphorical association between their natural habitats and the nature of reading beyond the surface structure irresistible.

SAND SWIMMERS: THE SECRET LIFE OF AUSTRALIA'S DEAD HEART

This stunningly illustrated information book by Oliver (1999) cleverly explores the notion of the seen and unseen which coexist in the same environment. The centre of Australia was called 'the dead heart' by those white explorers who could see only the apparent lifelessness of its hot, red surface: 'not a living thing to be seen, not an ant, not a cricket, or a grasshopper'. However, as Oliver explains, 'some Aboriginal tribal groups' have lived in the desert for thousands of years, knowing where to find creatures that hide beneath its surface and plants which yield nutritious desert fruits and vegetables. She encourages the reader to see with new eyes, a lesson which the early explorers such as Sturt were unable to learn.

Oliver traverses time — back and forth — as she leads the reader on a journey to discover the secrets of this desert land. This is a land whose appearance is deceiving, offering surprises for the uninitiated: 'But, like much of the Australian desert, the salt lakes have their surprises. Disguised as a ripple of salt, the salt-lake ground-dragon slips from its winter hide-out beneath the salt crust.' The book begins in the present; the initial hand-coloured linoprint sprawls across the opening double page. The vivid contrasts of the expansive blue

Australian sky and the orange-red expanse of the central desert immediately hold the reader's eye. The past is revealed in the following doublespread where the bright dual colours of the opening pages disappear and in their place are the soft, muted greens of the same environment during the middle Miocene epoch: a time when there was 'plenty of rain' and 'Diprotodontids as big as cows roamed the forests. And dolphins played in lakes that were never dry.' While the lushness of this period has long gone, traces of its former self can still be found today for those with a keen eye.

Despite the fact that the central narrative in this book is about Sturt's unsuccessful attempt to find the inland sea he dreamed of discovering, there are other parallel and subterranean stories accompanying it. The contrasting accounts between the explorers and the desert life provide subtle juxtapositions between what the explorers endured, their blindness to the life of this alien land, and the survival and adaptability of the desert creatures and plants which thrive in this seemingly inhospitable environment. These contradictory viewpoints encourage the reader to see the ways texts are always partial; for every account offered there is another that is equally valid. The account of the explorers' journey and the account of the desert life are both relative to one another as the impact of one is best felt in terms of the other.

This book offers readers multiple ways of reading and seeing. The writing style draws on different language patterns and structures (vivid imagery, zoological terminology, exposition and narrative). In a similar way, the illustrations offer different kinds of interpretations: generously sized, colourful linocuts dominate the pages while smaller ones, the size of postage stamps, provide closeups of small animals and plants; sepia-toned rubbings of linocuts suggest both the hazy account of the past and the heat of the desert; maps track Sturt's tortuous journey. Although irony pervades the hapless journey of Sturt and his party, there is another kind of irony in that the illustrations, unlike the text's theme of secrecy and the unseen, hold no secrets as Oliver has gone to great lengths to include keys to the names of animals which may at first seem invisible as they blend into the colour and textures of their environment.

THE RABBITS

Whereas illustrations of Sand Swimmers are in a representational style, Shaun Tan's illustrations for The Rabbits by John Marsden (1998) are surrealistic. Surrealism, as a modernist style, was an attempt to break away from the popular view that art needed to depict 'reality'. Nodelman (1992: p. 140), however, notes that in their depictions of unrealistic situations, surrealists often were able to make 'the impossible seem strangely possible'. The text and illustrations of this allegorical tale have created a surrealistic world where past, present and future merge, where the 'impossible' has already happened. The literal surface story is ostensibly about the invasion of 'rabbits' into a strange and foreign land. However, this serves to make a thinly concealed account of the politics and consequences of colonisation. This story of imperialism needs to be read within the social and historical contexts in which it is situated — both past and present.

The design of the book cleverly and successfully integrates the words into the illustrations so that the two work as one. Initially, the style of telling is languid yet ominous: 'The rabbits came many grandparents ago'. Both illustration and text signal that things are about to change. Goannas lie on the boulders staring out to the horizon where a distant black funnel belching smoke serves as the visual omen. While the illustrations are colourful, symbolic and varied, the text remains sparse. The simple, unadorned text serves to underscore, rather than detract from, the illustrations which tell elusive and multiple visual narratives.

The tone of the book is sombre, detached and cold. At the textual level, the story resembles an oral tale, one that has been passed down from generation to generation. The telling is precise, matter of fact, yet its surface simplicity resonates with feelings of anger, hurt and grief: 'They ate our grass. They chopped down our trees and scared away our friends ... and stole our children.' In the illustrations, colour conveys emotions and feelings and, in some instances, serves an ironic function. For example, when the 'rabbits' arrive in their big ship it is painted in colours of gold and its size is enormous, signs suggestive of the wealth and might of the Empire.

The naval officers, carrying a musket and flag, are similarly resplendent in grand uniforms of blue, red and black with gold braid and trims. However, the effect is one of hyperbole as the exaggerated size and colour of the ship and its occupants look strangely ridiculous and incongruous, especially in relation to the two, small original inhabitants who, spear in hand, stand on a nearby cliff watching the spectacle unfolding before their eyes. The bright, rich colours of the land and sky, dominant in the introductory illustrations, soon give way to a low-colour scheme of greys and browns, symbolic of the havoc and destruction the invaders wreak on the land and its inhabitants.

Tan's semi-abstract shapes, organic and inorganic forms suggest additional layers of symbolic meaning. The organic lines which delineate the natural environment are soon replaced by the inorganic shapes of the material symbols of progress and colonial power — factories, buildings, furnaces, machines, weapons. Lines are harsh, straight, repetitive, suggestive of the drive for mass production, conformity and sameness. The impact of technology is a recurring and embedded element. Time is measured by multiple clocks, land is surveyed and assessed using mathematical formulae, machines operate on and scar the land, guns and other weaponry exert superior powers for destruction against the spears of the inhabitants.

The two groups represented in this story — the colonisers and the colonised — are also represented in abstract forms. The colonisers or 'rabbits' are depicted in a strange hybrid form suggesting that they are a blend of both animal and human, while the colonised group are more animal-like though an indefinable mix of different animal species — kangaroo, possum, and, perversely, rabbit. The penultimate illustration depicts a single member of each group facing each other from opposing pages. The final illustration brings the two together sitting under a starlit sky staring at (contemplating?) the reflection of the night sky in a pool of water. The text asks: 'Who will save us from the rabbits?'. This is a rather ambiguous conclusion as, despite the book's post-colonial sentiments, the final question suggests that survival will depend on the heroics of an, as yet unknown, 'other'. This interpretation appears at odds with the image which suggests a sense of reconciliation between the two groups.

ONE LESS FISH

Like the previous ones, this book (by Toft & Sheather, 1998) can be read at different levels. It is a counting book, but one where the significance of the count-down from 12 to 0 goes beyond simply assisting a young reader with mastering a decreasing number sequence. A cautionary tale about endangered fish species, its explicit message is conveyed through different textual and visual means.

One Less Fish is a book which demands that the reader take notice. There are two kinds of pictures — large, colourful, eye-catching silk-screen images of the various fish, and small pen and ink drawings, both of which are attention seekers but in different ways. The colourful images are almost breathtaking in their beauty. The richness of their colours, the shape and patterns of the fish depicted, capture a reader's attention and hold it almost spellbound, such is the force of the image. While this force is necessary to draw the reader's attention to the plight of the fish, whose lives are literally numbered, it also works against the book's intent to some extent, as the reader can become so seduced by the dazzling colours and forms that they may fail to see that one by one the fish population is declining.

The pen and ink drawings, on the other hand, appear as delicate thumb-prints and as such are a subtle contrast to the bold extravagance of the colourful images. Whereas the colourful images are explicit in depicting the subject, there is, nevertheless, a subtlety in the removal of a fish on every other page. The pen drawings have no such subtlety: aeroplanes spraying pesticides, oil spilling tankers, and deadly boat anchors make it clear that these are the enemies which threaten the fish world.

Size acts as a metaphor in this book. The opening double-spread of twelve angelfish, resplendent in their colours of gold and green, swim in their underwater world which is conveyed in blues and purples. Page by page, as the fish numbers decline, the framed picture on the left side of the page also diminishes in size.

This is not only a metaphoric reference to the book's theme, but also serves as a visual interpretation of the number system. By the time the count-down has reached one, the left-hand page shows a small framed surgeonfish (its partner having met its fate) while the righthand page introduces 'one lonely lionfish' swimming in its ocean home; the drawing of this fish is somewhat personified as it looks down at the mouth and utterly miserable.

When zero is reached there are no fish left to be seen in the full double-spread illustration of the oceanic underworld. However, unlike the opening doublespread illustration, this one is bereft of fish and has only minimal plant life. The final page is somewhat of a resurrection as all the species of fish mentioned in the book appear in all their colourful glory. This scene offers readers an opportunity to re-envision their world and consider what could be, rather than the dismal reality of what is, or is likely to be.

At the textual level, this book employs rhyming verse, exposition, and numerals. The rhyming verse is obviously targeted at young readers as it attributes human characteristics and emotions to the fish, thus making the message even more powerful for a younger readership: 'Eight weary wrasses fed by naughty Kevin. Shouldn't feed the fish – now there are ...'. The reader's guess at the missing word is confirmed when the page is turned. This playful cloze activity is reinforced in the accompanying illustration where the reader can count the number of fish to see if the illustrator might have got it wrong.

As in all aspects of visual culture, pictures seem to take on a life of their own, as their desires (in terms of what they demand of the viewer) may not simply be reducible to what their producers and readers project on them. In the case of this book, the pictures offer additional information about underwater plants, colours and shapes which is not contained in the text. It is this surplus exceeding any intention that makes the aesthetic experience limitless and indeterminate.

Reading picture books is akin to Alice's journey down the rabbit hole. There is a sense of adventure as the familiar is often rendered strange. Just when you think you have found the little golden key to unlock the mysteries of the text, you are left to reconsider, to question, perhaps change your viewpoint. The act of interpreting and making meaning of a text, let alone one which employs both words and visuals, is not a simple, straightforward matter.

The process is made all the more complicated by the knowledge that any academic interpretation needs to be strong enough to withstand the buffeting gales of opinion that emanate from different theoretical perspectives. Meanings do not simply reside in the words or illustrations waiting to be revealed by the clever reader. Just as Alice was to discover as she travelled down the rabbit hole, things are not always as they appear on the surface. A text such as a picture book often has meanings which are multiple, elusive and complex. Meaning is not something which can be definitively determined one way or another.

In one sense, the three books discussed here can be seen as instructive tales about the Australian environment and how history has affected, and continues to affect, its human and animal inhabitants. However, to read them in this narrow sense of information processing means we are missing out on the affective impact they can have on readers. These books are essentially aesthetic texts whereby words and visuals combine to offer readers particular kinds of intellectual, emotional and pleasurable experiences.

In this broader sense, they illustrate how we can come to see things differently, to perceive human actions, history and nature through different lenses when we are given opportunities to reconsider and re-experience what we may have come to take for granted or failed to apprehend. As vehicles of aesthetic experiences, picture books require different 'literacies' which implicate the senses and intellect in the act of reading.

In the case of the examples discussed here, picture books are also ideological texts whose meanings can be powerfully conveyed through words and visuals which demand close attention.

In recognising the aesthetic, political and social potential of picture books, teachers and students might develop a critical aesthetics necessary for considering Dewey's unrealised possibilities discussed earlier and for seeing and reading beneath the surface.

Chapter 13

The Myth of Two Coases

"When I use a word, it means just what I choose it to mean—either more nor less."

—Humpty-Dumpty in Lewis Carroll's Through the Looking Glass.

In the December 1992 issue of this journal, E. Ray Canterbery and A. Marvasti take issue with the Coase theorem, claiming that it has "generated a negative externality for economists" |1992, 1188~. The literature on the theorem is enormous, running the gamut from criticisms and defenses to real-world illustrations to experimental tests. The Coase theorem (if one can use this term, given the numerous variants floating around in the literature, not to mention the fact that this "theorem" has never been proved) has certainly generated more heat than light. Nonetheless, it remains at the core of much of main stream law and economics.

While Canterbery and Marvasti's critique of the Coase theorem is largely on the mark, I wish to deal with another issue: their treatment of Ronald Coase and his relation to the world of zero transaction costs and the Coase theorem. As Canterbery and Marvasti correctly point out |1992, 1179 at note 1~, the ideas underlying the Coase theorem were first elucidated in Coase's 1959 article "The Federal Communications Commission" and were subsequently more fully developed in "The Problem of Social Cost". The first precise formulation of the Coase theorem comes from George Stigler in his book The Theory of Price. Over the years, the zero transaction costs world of the Coase theorem has become so closely identified with Coase that it is often referred to as a

"Coasian world." Those who support this view, as well as the attendant view that the Coase theorem is at the heart of Coase's message, have gone astray, as a close examination of "The Problem of Social Cost" and many of Coase's other writings clearly illustrates. In fact, Coase's writings reveal a view that has some important elements in common with certain aspects of the institutional tradition.

"THE PROBLEM OF SOCIAL COST"

"The Problem of Social Cost" and the subsequent literature that it has generated offer an interesting study in the interpretation of texts. The message of "The Problem of Social Cost," if judged by the professional response, is what has come to be known as the Coase theorem—that if rights are fully specified and transaction costs are zero, voluntary bargaining between agents will lead to an efficient (and according to Coase at the time, an invariant) outcome, regardless of how rights are initially assigned. However, this chapter makes at least three other major contributions, and even the argument relating to the Coase theorem has been misunderstood.

The zero transaction costs world of the Coase theorem is merely one of the means to an end for Coase, that end being the goal of focusing economists' attention on what he sees as the wrong-headed nature of the Pigouvian approach and, specifically, Pigou's claim that externality problems should be resolved (and can only be resolved) through taxes, subsidies, or regulations. The zero transaction costs world is a world without frictions, a world where markets function perfectly.

It is the world of mainstream economic theory, the body of theory that has so whole-heartedly embraced the work of Pigou. What Coase intended with his analysis of the zero transaction costs world was to show that in such a world, Pigouvian remedies (e.g., taxes, subsidies, and regulations) are not necessary to resolve externality problems: "The significance to me of the Coase theorem is that it undermines the Pigouvian system. Since standard economic theory assumes transaction costs to be zero, the Coase theorem demonstrates that Pigouvian solutions are unnecessary in those circumstances".

As noted above, the world of zero transaction costs has often been called a "Coasian world." This is a label that Coase himself explicitly rejects, saying that "nothing could be further from the truth". Rather, he says, "It is the world of modern economic theory, one which I was hoping to persuade economists to leave". For Coase, the real world is the world of positive transaction costs, as a few quotations will illustrate:

The argument has proceeded up to this point on the assumption ... that there were no costs involved in carrying out market transactions. This is, of course, a very unrealistic assumption, emphasis added.

... while consideration of what would happen in a world of zero transaction costs can give us valuable insights, these insights are, in my view, without value except as steps on the way to the analysis of the real world of positive transaction costs. We do not do well to devote ourselves to a detailed study of the world of zero transaction costs, like augers divining the future by the minute inspection of the entrails of a goose.

It would not seem worthwhile to spend much time investigating the properties of such a |i.e., a zero transaction costs~ world. What my argument does suggest is the need to introduce positive transaction costs explicitly into economic analysis so that we can study the world that exists. This has not been the effect of my chapter.

In fact, a close reading of "The Problem of Social Cost" reveals that only pages 2-15 deal with (or assume) a world of zero transaction costs. The remainder of the paper deals with the world as it actually exists-where positive transaction costs abound.

Canterbery and Marvasti, observing Coase's 1988 statement that economists have neglected to take account of the role of transaction costs, seem to accuse Coase of a late-in-life transformation: "Coase has shifted his argument," they say, "from the assumption of zero transactions costs to the effect of various legal arrangements on the allocation of resources when transactions costs are non-zero". As laid out above, however, the importance of transaction costs and the effect of various legal arrangements on economic performance in such a world has been Coase's point all along. Indeed, Coase was making this point as early as the 1930s, where, in "The Nature of the Firm", he says that ". . . there is a cost of using the price mechanism" (i.e., transaction costs) in devising a rationale for the existence of firms. Coase has not in any way "shifted his argument," and there are not, as Canterbery and Marvasti would have us believe, two Coases. There is only one Coase and a legion of people who have misinterpreted (or failed to read) Coase's message.

COASE AND GOVERNMENT

There is little doubt that the allure of the Coase theorem in certain quarters of the legal and economic professions comes from the perception that the Coase theorem takes government out of the picture. This, of course, is a false perception because government is present in the creation and assignment of rights, just as it is in policies of taxation or regulation of externalities. This is a fact that Coase plainly recognizes. For Coase, the point is that when transaction costs are zero (and let us, for a minute, grants the extreme assumption of no income effects), law (or government) is irrelevant because the parties involved will always bargain to the socially optimal outcome once rights have been assigned. But regardless of whether alternative assignments of rights generate identical, or merely fairly similar, outcomes in the zero transaction costs case, it is quite apparent that the character of the situation is very different in the presence of transaction costs that are of sufficient magnitude to preclude bargaining.

Here, we have what might be called a "legal flypaper effect," with no reallocation of rights consequent to the court's decision. This is the sort of situation that Coase is drawing us toward. Recognizing that the court's decision will in fact determine the final assignment of rights, how should this decision be made? For Coase, the solution involves assigning the right where the value of output will be maximized.

Given that the government is the ultimate arbiter of rights, and hence of externality questions (either through the courts or through the tax/regulatory apparatus), the bigger question, and indeed Coase's central question in "The Problem of Social Cost," is: What is the appropriate mechanism for dealing with externality problems? Contrary to the implications of Canterbery and Marvasti, Coase is not against the use of tax or regulatory mechanisms in correcting externality problems. This, too, appears time and time again in his various writings. Coase's point is that economists and others see regulatory remedies as the obvious (and indeed the only) solution to externality problems, but in doing so they fail to take into account the costs of these remedies.

Recalling that Coase's objective function is to maximize the value of output in society, the decision regarding the appropriate remedy (e.g., tax, regulate, or do nothing, or, in the case of courts, assign the right to A or B) becomes an issue of benefit-cost analysis: "It is all a question," he says, "of weighing up the gains that would accrue from eliminating these harmful effects |i.e., externalities~ against the gains that accrue from allowing them to continue".

There is no question that Coase is of the opinion that the costs of regulation often outweigh the gains, and that the optimal solution to many externality problems is to do nothing at all. However, he is also of the mind that ". . . there is no reason why, on occasion, . . . governmental administrative regulation should not lead to an improvement in efficiency", and he cites pollution externalities in large numbers situations as an example of where regulation may well be efficiency-enhancing. More generally, Coase says that "I can't object to any expenditure by the government which makes the total situation better off. . . . I say: Let's set up government departments when they do more good than harm".

However, the crux of the matter, for Coase, is that of approach. Coase contends that the usual approach of economists is to compare the regulatory outcome with the optimal conditions of economic theory to illustrate how neatly and cleanly Pigouvian remedies can generate the socially optimal outcome. In the process, they neglect to fully (or even partially, in Coase's view) examine the costs of these remedies or to assess the effect of these remedies in the real world, as compared to the existing real-world situation. Because of this faulty approach, says Coase,

It is my belief that economists, and policy-makers generally, have tended to over-estimate the advantages which come from governmental regulation. But this belief, even if justified, does not do more than suggest that government regulation should be curtailed. It does not tell us where the boundary line should be drawn. This, it seems to me, has to come from a detailed investigation of the actual results of handling the problem in different ways. But it would be unfortunate if this investigation were undertaken with the aid of faulty economic analysis. The aim of this chapter is to indicate what the economic approach to the problem should be.

The approach that Coase is advocating is very different from the usual approach of economists and other policymakers:

A better approach would seem to be to start our analysis with a situation approximating that which actually exists, to examine the effects of a proposed policy change and to attempt to decide whether the new situation would be, in total, better or worse than the original one. In this way, conclusions for policy would have some relevance to the actual situation.

In order to carry out such analysis, it is necessary for economists to make detailed studies of those areas at which economic policy is targeted. Only then, says Coase, can we obtain an understanding that is sufficient to allow us to properly evaluate the effects of various potential government policies (including doing nothing at all). Without such detailed studies, our equations, graphs, and verbiage tell us very little and may well lead us astray, as Coase showed with his study of the British lighthouse system.

Canterbery and Marvasti are quite correct in their assertion that, owing to the costs that have accompanied the effort put into the Coase theorem literature, "the Coase theorem has generated a negative externality for economists".

They are wrong, however, to lay the responsibility for this at the feet of Coase. The true source of this externality lies in the failure of economists to pay attention to what Coase is really saying, both in "The Problem of Social Cost" and elsewhere. If nothing else, this illustrates the pervasiveness of the traditional way of doing economics, where transaction costs are nonexistent and institutions lurk in the background as exogenous and unexamined components of the economic system.

Coase's most important contributions to economic theory are his recognition of the importance of transaction costs and of economic institutions in structuring economic performance. The former calls us to analyse the world as it actually exists, where markets do not function costlessly and smoothly. The latter calls us to recognize that different institutional structures (e.g., different mechanisms for resolving externality problems) may lead to very different outcomes and that the choice of the appropriate institutional framework necessitates an analysis of the outcomes engendered by each—that is, comparative institutional analysis.

The fact that these messages have been a part of Coase's work throughout his career explicitly contradicts both the traditional view of Coase and Canterbery and Marvasti's claim that there are two Coases. If there really are two Coases, they are the "popular Coase" who is perceived by the profession and the Coase who is actually revealed by his writings. The "popular Coase" is a fiction. Unfortunately, fiction is often more alluring than reality.

Chapter 14

Paranoia, Trauma and Melancholy

Mood was always romantic matter—Wordsworth's "sweet mood when pleasant thoughts / Bring sad thoughts to the mind" is representative of the self-absorption of the later poetry of sensibility. But what mood does he mean? Melancholy is the period term for such undertow; Wordsworth employs it memorably in "Resolution and Independence," in a voice that swings from dejection to elation. This antic turn was famously satirized by Lewis Carroll as terminal self-referentiality.

The mood swing lies at the heart of the poem, but our critical condition is hardly equipped to grasp or respond to it. Latter-day, rehistoricizing critics have not been very helpful in making the mood matter again for reading such texts despite suggestive work by Kay Redfield Jamison on manic depression, Peter M. Logan on hysteria, and Rei Terada on emotion in theory. The construction of romantic ideology has upstaged the affective intensity of the best writing of this period, as characteristic as the minor key in Beethoven.

Thomas Pfau's new book is concerned to demonstrate why mood matters in ways that would reintegrate it with social and intellectual history, and with reading of the disciplinary, institutional kind that he practices. Working off an extensive range of sources in the period, as disparate as scripts of the treason trials of 1794 and Adam Muller's conservatively romantic Staatswissenschaft, Pfau restores a cast of German informants to the picture while remaining within the orbit of the familiar English story beginning from Burke. He makes an original and compelling case for the bearing of German philosophy on Gefuhl, Kant's equivalent term for feeling or emotion, peculiar synonyms perpetuated in this form by Martha Nussbaum, among others.

But the vocation of this book is larger, for it would draw attention to the social circulation of affect, and of affective disorders such as paranoia, trauma, and melancholia, far beyond the romantic horizon, in politics and public life and of course in the arts of the Age of Prozac, so typically afflicted with psychic disruption. The Berlin films of Wire Wenders and the desolate canvases of Anselm Kiefer and Cy Twombly come to mind in this connection, but the consuming paranoia of popular film is perhaps Exhibit A, as Pfau suggests in passing. What is it, exactly, that is stalking us? Was soll all der Schmerz und Lust?

Situational anxiety is the nominal source of the grand funk endemic to modernity, in the author's reckoning with its romantic affiliations. His synthesis adds up to a quest for the origin of modern affect in the romantic element, with references all over the map of theory. Modern Angst flows from the "utter lack of any transcendent point of reference or 'ground'" and it drives the lonely, autonomous subject of modernity to seek restlessly for its sources. Pfau's quest for integrated historical understanding rehearses this anaclitic trajectory, exemplifying the anxious interiority that he is conjuring with. L'Angoisse ne trompe pas, in the apt phrase of Jacques Lacan, who turns up occasionally in the book.

Anxiety is for real because it is bred in the bone, a reflex of animal instinct and human mortality. But it is polymorphous, culturally and historically specific in expression, latent as well as manifest. Logan's very interesting cultural history of nerves settled on hysteria as the key concept, but Pfau disputes this, along with the diagnostic ethic involved.

In Logan's account, what period readers recognized as the nervous body is represented by Caleb Williams, the first-person narrator of his own persecution at the hands of the gentry. Godwin's sensational novel associates the nervous body with the revolutionary impulse of the early 1790s in provocative ways. Pfau opens a long second chapter from this exemplary text, undermining the affective essentialism involved in Logan's important study because it would reduce the integrity of Godwin's text by referring its voice's fits and starts to an identifiable pathological condition.

Such an interpretive strategy is associated with Freudian reading, of course; it is typically modern, and Pfau's resistance to it suggests that we are off the analyst's couch here. Yet he would substitute paranoia for Logan's diagnosis of hysteria, even as he insists that "the following readings most certainly do not posit paranoia as a self-evidently or even covertly 'pathological' condition.

Rather, 'paranoia' in my account names a situation of extreme interpretive agitation and urgency whose specific historical tensions are legible in the (narrative) way in which it dreams their solution in specific literary-aesthetic forms". His readers will recognize the hermeneutic bind that Godwin dramatizes and duplicitously reifies in the end. Does it really have nothing to do with the code of the nervous body as Godwin plainly represents it in Caleb's theater of calamity?

The questions raised by so imperious a turn against Logan's thoughtful historical recovery work are worth pursuing a little because they are indicative of the critical blind side of Pfau's reckoning with romantic interiority.

This he treats as a textual condition, plain and simple—a case of affect in the library, though he never recognizes affect as such, only Stimmung, mood, refined from Heidegger's employment of it, banishing the organic life (in Coleridgean parlance) from consideration. If Caleb is a case of paranoid agitation, surely the back story begins with the "epidemic of nerves" that Logan documents in the England of the period. If such pathology is suspect as some odiously positivist residuum, why sublate paranoia as Pfau would like to, smuggling it into critical parlance stripped of its historical association with psychosomatic illness?

Is it beside the point that Coleridge coined the word psychosomatic in this nervous moment? Do paranoids have real enemies? These are irrelevant questions for his construction of early romantic interiority under pressure. Pfau's dogged pursuit of literary-aesthetic autonomy is buttressed by reference to The Political Unconscious. Godwin's text is a perfect specimen of political dreamwork of the Jameson variety because of the way that it identifies the narrator's contrarian turn with nervous affliction. Things as They Are, its first title, would tell the inside story of English society from this special point of view within it.

What are readers to make of the story if the narrator's politics can be seen as linked to affective disorder? The problem is hardly resolved by Pfau's reference to a paradigmatic "transition involv[ing] the paranoiac's recognition that the very transformation he had sought to defend against by indicting it as someone else's as yet unconsummated design has already succeeded and, consequently, has also shaped his anxious outlook on it, perhaps even made him an unwitting co-conspirator in it".

For while Caleb does take some responsibility for his personal tragedy, his unwitting complicity in things as they are only complicates Godwin s attack on the character of a class-bound society and its institution of justice. Caleb's nervous condition and its consequences must qualify the social critique involved, but they cannot resolve the messenger's story into paranoid megalomania tout court.

Pfau's pursuant readings of 'radical knowledge' in key texts of the period confirm his determination to treat affectively charged political interventions such as Reflections on the Revolution in France as delusional. At least this line of attack is supported by its opponents' animadversions in the period.

Thus, "it will not do to read the conspiratorial designs that Burke and Paine impute to one another as the mere symptoms of an underlying subjective and pathological disposition. Rather, we ought to approach their views as literary devices—advanced in the guise of a deeply held belief [emphasis in original]—that seek to conjure up and sustain conspiratorial fears among a gullible audience. Far from being the cause for the overwrought representations of the text, conspiratorial anxiety emerges as the effect of the text's transferential designs on the affective economy of its audience". The psychological tack is appealing, yet limited by the working conception of that audience. For what it knew as the nervous body came into readers' calculations by design. Call it what you will, this recognizable type added more than rhetorical strategy to the story. Godwin's political dreamwork had something to tell its audience about the special character of the contrarian personality. Such is the work of the political unconscious in a text that still speaks to our condition.

Dwelling on this primal scene of Pfau's argument is a way of adumbrating the special stresses of his demonstration for informed readers. Constantly provocative, even brilliant, his running commentary on textual romanticism is as disoriented as Caleb's psyche. Nowhere is this truer than in his construction of an historical succession of affective moments, the architecture of an episodic display of real erudition.

The ambition of this panorama of romantic interiority is breathtaking, but so schematic that it cannot command anything like whole assent. Pfau envisions "a paradigmatic, loosely chronological sequence for British and German romanticism—paranoia (1689-1800), trauma (1800-1815), and melancholy (1815-1840)", to be attempted by "redrawing the extended, insecure borderline between literary, historical, and psycho-analytic modes of explanation".

It is plain enough how this relates to the political and social history of the period. There really is something like historical mood and literature does reproduce it, though experience suggests that it's hardly a straightforward translation. Zeitgeist is recognized by Hazlitt's employment of the idiomatic "spirit of the age" and again by Carlyle's "signs of the times." But what does it mean to quantify Zeitgeist under affective headings? Here it means something like a history of romantic interiority, stripped of positivist illusions.The reintegration of social and historical understanding to the idea of a specifically romantic idiom has been the work of newer historicists with whom Pfau's book is deeply at odds. He takes on Jerome McGann in discussions of Keats and Byron, but the bearing of his case lies uncertainly between this orientation and others. If he would like to replace McGann's rear-view mirror portrait of the period with something more sensitive to romantic Stimmung, open conflict with the disciplinary assumptions of such interested critical work is unavoidable. His opening shot at Logan on hysteria is perhaps meant to represent his disaffection with historical reconstruction work of the kind.

But the diagnostic approach is his immediate object here, and his rejection of it is a shot across the bow of interdisciplinary work that would presume to consider the writing of the period pathologically. So objective an attitude is offensive to the feelings of the romanticists, as their willful ignorance of Jamison's diagnosis of Byron's condition showed.

Mood as Pfau employs the concept is a virtual object that would deflect attention from the disabling affective disorders of Holderlin and Heine, resolving their lyrics into a toxic Zeitgeist. So we are not obliged to notice Coleridge's depression, announced in so many words in a letter of 1796 and brilliantly thematized in "Dejection," his most accomplished lyric, here treated under the heading of the logic of trauma instead of melancholy—an interesting twist. Nor should we take as matter for reflection Byron's manic binges and their vital relation to his compositional habits.

Considering the liabilities of such idealism, there is plenty to like in Pfau's readings of the romantic lyric from Wordsworth to Heine. These he performs with rare application, informed by the ground-breaking work of Cathy Caruth on trauma in particular. He considers the lyrical ballad in connection with Freud's repetition compulsion, a terrifically suggestive way of thinking about literary form and its relation to content, as a moment's reflection on "The Rime of the Ancient Mariner" intimates.

His textual prototype is "Michael," which "completes and reflexively sublates (in the Hegelian sense) the project of Lyrical Ballads". As an epitome of that experimental venture, the poem "takes as its proper object the limitations of the ballad form by dramatizing, at the level of action, its protagonist's precarious transition from the self-enclosed world of local (balladic) knowledge into the unbounded world of agrarian capitalism and its myriad connections with urban commerce and speculation".

His sensitive reckoning with the trace of history in Michael takes aim at the new historical accusation of its "evasion of history" by Marjorie Levinson, among others.

The poem is no nostalgic pastoral, as Pfau reads it; rather it registers the traumatic force of history via Michael's repetition compulsion, his reversion to the diurnal rituals of his smallholding.

Such an understanding should involve our recognizing the aging shepherd as a figuration of trauma, an affective disorder with characteristic symptoms and behavioral features.

For his is not an ethical choice in an existential snake-pit. It is an organic destiny like that of victims of ethnic cleansing. The sequence of "lyric awakenings" pursued by Pfau in the wake of his discussion of "Michael" and Lyrical Ballads is proof of the value of his way of construing the romantic as always already postmodern.

This is the most accomplished moment of his display, negotiating carefully between English and German examples of the writing of the period. Professional readers should not miss these; global romanticism must mean returning to the continent first, as an older generation of readers knew instinctively.

Such a turn should not be considered a detour on the road to the Lake District, like the escape to Ratzeburg and Gottingen in 1799. Brentano and von Arnim, Eichendorff, Gorres and Heine are essential sources for making sense of the eventful transition from older to modern writing.

Romantic readers were once the cosmopolitans of the literary-critical canon. Too many have become provincial, a cast of Lancashire Irregulars, turning their backs on everything outside the little ken of their Grasmere local.

Returning to Rousseau, Baudelaire and Nietzsche means recognizing the romantic agony outside such homely contexts, useful as they might be for teaching romantic ideology.

Romantic Moods marks the way back to the continent,

providing larger ideas for constructing the significance of the romantic moment, and also of our own.

MAJOR WORKS

Carroll's best-known works, all produced under the pseudonym Lewis Carroll, were his fantasy novels, Alice's Adventures in Wonderland and Through the Looking-Glass. Famously innovative for their unconventional use of language, the stories were also among the first non-didactic, non-moralizing texts aimed at children. Carroll's nonsense verse, most notably The Hunting of the Snark (1876) and "Jabberwocky" (from Alice's Adventures in Wonderland) are usually considered related to his prose works by virtue of the similarity of language.

His serious verse, published in several collections, is considered uninspired and is largely forgotten today. The later novels Sylvie and Bruno (1889) and Sylvie and Bruno Concluded (1893) were his only fictional works aimed at an adult reading audience. Far more serious and didactic than the Alice stories, the two texts have often been treated by critics as a single, two-volume work, and occasionally as a fairly conventional Victorian novel.

Far less famous than his fictional works are Carroll's writings on mathematics and symbolic logic. They include A Syllabus of Plane Algebraical Geometry, Part I (1860), An Elementary Treatise on Determinants (1867), Euclid and His Modern Rivals (1879), and Symbolic Logic, Part I: Elementary (1896).

CRITICAL RECEPTION

Carroll's publications as Lewis Carroll, particularly the Alice stories, were enormously popular with juvenile readers at the time of their publication and have since attained an assured place in the canon of children's literature. They have been reprinted countless times in a wide variety of editions and have been translated into virtually every modern language. The two books were originally considered nonsense for the amusement of children and were considered unworthy of analysis by serious scholars. Beginning in the 1930s, however, the Alice stories and the nonsense poem The Hunting of the Snark have attracted increasing attention from literary critics and philosophers. Psychoanalytic critics in particular have for many years been preoccupied with the details of Carroll's life, particularly his sex life. In addition to the much-documented phallic and womb imagery of his fiction, his extreme fondness for pre-adolescent girls—he often took them on overnight outings and photographed many of them nude—made Carroll a suspicious character in his own time and even more so today.

Morton N. Cohen confronts speculation about Carroll's relationship with his young friends, claiming that the author was a "model Victorian" who never acted on whatever erotic impulses he may have harbored for the young. As Cohen puts it, "Carroll knew that, given his preference for the friendship of children, if he once succumbed to any temptation, he would never be able to befriend them again.

His own uncompromising standards, his forthright, pious nature would not permit it. Besides he loved innocence so, how could he ever violate it?" Robert M. Polhemus seems to agree: "Freudians have had grand times analyzing the kinks in Charles Dodgson's personality, but the striking irony is that psychoanalysis and its theories ... seem to flow right out of Carroll's wonderland."

Michael Irwin also acknowledges that "the Alice books, of course, are a gift to the Freudian, proliferating as they do in holes, tunnels, doors, locks, keys, fluids and size-changes." Nonetheless, Irwin claims, "that game is all too easy." Daniel Bivona reads Alice's Adventures in Wonderland in the context of nineteenth-century imperialism, referring to Alice as ethnocentric because she assumes that the language and behaviour of the creatures in Wonderland operate according to no rules simply because they fail to conform to English rules.

"Alice's 'imperialism,' such as it is," contends Bivona, "is a semiotic imperialism: she is incapable of constructing, on a model radically different from her own, the 'system' or 'systems' that give meaning to the behaviour of the creatures."

Several critics maintain that Carroll's fictional work anticipates modernism and even postmodernism, and his name has been linked with many of the literary figures of those movements. Polhemus reports: "From out of his rabbit-hole and looking-glass world we can see coming not only such figures as Joyce, Freud, Oscar Wilde, Henry James, Virginia Woolf, Kafka, Proust, Artaud, Nabokov, Beckett, Waugh, Lacan, Borges, Bakhtin, and García Márquez, but also much of the character and mood of twentieth-century popular culture."

Michael Holquist has examined The Hunting of the Snark as a modernist text and concluded that the poem "is the most perfect nonsense which Carroll created in that it best exemplifies what all his career and all his books sought to do: achieve pure order." Carroll's work does not consist of meaningless gibberish, according to Holquist, but is rather "its own system of signs which gain their meaning by constantly dramatizing their differences from signs in other systems."

Peter Heath also rejects the idea that Carroll was a nonsense writer and claims that the author should be more properly categorized as an absurdist. Heath maintains that the Alice books are rational works "whose frolics are governed throughout, not by a formal theory of any kind, but by close attention to logical principles, and by a sometimes surprising insight into abstract questions of philosophy."

Carroll's two later novels, Sylvie and Bruno and Sylvie and Bruno Concluded, have generally been considered far inferior to the author's earlier works. Edmund Miller, however, believes that the two books should be treated as a whole and suggests that the resulting two-volume work has much in common with the early Victorian novel, particularly Emily Brontë's Wuthering Heights. "Both works are infused with the sentiments of the age and yet combine traditional materials in completely original ways," claims Miller.

Carroll never married and had no children of his own, but he was devoted to a succession of little girls he had befriended. The most famous of these was Alice Liddell, the daughter of the Dean of Christ Church, who provided the model for the fictional Alice and for whom Carroll wrote

Alice's Adventures Under Ground, which he illustrated himself and never published, presenting it instead as a gift to Alice Liddell. It provided the basis for Alice's Adventures in Wonderland and its sequel Through the Looking-Glass.

Both works were published under the name Lewis Carroll, a pseudonym Carroll adopted in 1856. He published all of his poetry and fiction under that name, although he continued to produce scholarly texts under his own name. At the same time, he became fascinated with the emerging field of photography and earned a considerable reputation as one of the first art photographers and the nineteenth-century's most celebrated photographer of children. Carroll died at the age of sixty-five in Guildford.

Chapter 15

Sylvie and Bruno

The novel has two main plots; one set in the real world at the time the book was published (the Victorian era), the other in the fantasy world of Fairyland. While the latter plot is a fairytale with many nonsense elements and poems, similar to Carroll's *Alice* books, the story set in Victorian Britain is a social novel, with its characters discussing various concepts and aspects of religion, society, philosophy and morality.

Two chapters from the first volume, "Fairy Sylvie" and "Bruno's Revenge", originally appeared as short stories in *Aunt Judy's Magazine* in 1867. Some years later, in 1873, Carroll had the idea to use these as the core for a longer story. Much of the rest of the novel was compiled from notes of ideas and dialogue collected by Carroll over the years (which he called "*litter*ature" in the introduction to the first volume).

Carroll initially intended for the novel to be published in one volume. However, due to its length, it was divided into two volumes. The novel is not nearly as well-known as the *Alice* books. The poem *The Mad Gardener's Song*, widely reprinted elsewhere, is the best-known part of the book.

There are two strands:

- The conspiracy against the Warden of Outland, instigated by the Sub-Warden and Chancellor, and
- The love of a young doctor, Arthur, for Lady Muriel

CONSPIRACY IN OUTLAND; ARTHUR AND LADY MURIEL

The narrator finds himself in a high room overlooking a public square filled with people. The room is the Warden's breakfast-saloon. The Chancellor has organised a "spontaneous" demonstration. Bruno enters briefly, looking for Sylvie. The Chancellor delivers a speech. The narrator follows Bruno into the study, where he climbs on to the Warden's knee, next to Sylvie. The Warden tells them that the Professor has finally returned from his long wanderings in search of health. They set off for the Library, where the Professor tells them about his concerns with the barometer and with "horizontal weather". The Professor then leads the children back to the saloon.

The narrator finds himself in a train compartment, which a veiled young lady has just entered. He is on his way to see Arthur, a doctor friend, for a consultation; he rereads Arthur's letter, and absent-mindedly repeats out loud its last line, "Do you believe in Fate?" The lady laughs, and a conversation ensues. The scene changes abruptly to the breakfast-saloon, in which the Professor is explaining his plunge-bath invention to the Sub-Warden, his wife, her son, the Chancellor, Warden, Sylvie, and Bruno.

The Chancellor tries to persuade the Warden to elevate the Sub-Warden to Vice-Warden. The Warden asks the Sub-Warden for a private talk. The Sub-Warden's wife asks the Professor about his Lecture, suggesting a Fancy Dress Ball. He gives Sylvie a birthday present: a pincushion. Uggug throws butter over Sylvie. The Sub-Warden distracts his wife by saying a pig is in the garden; the Chancellor drags Uggug out by his ear.

The Warden agrees to the changes. After he has signed the Agreement and left (to become Monarch of Fairyland), the Chancellor, Vice-Warden and his wife laugh about how they have deceived him, the document having been altered at the last minute to give the Vice-Warden dictatorial powers. A beggar appears beneath the window; Uggug and his mother throw water over him. Bruno try to throw him some food, but he has gone.

The narrator wakes up, and he and the lady discuss ghosts. They change trains at Fayfield Junction; he notices her name on her luggage: Lady Muriel Orme. An old tramp is sent on his way. The narrator falls asleep again, and hears the first stanza of the Mad Gardener's Song. The Gardener directs Sylvie and Bruno after the beggar. They give him cake, and he leads them to an underground octagonal room lined with creepers bearing fruit and flowers. His clothes transform, and they find it is their father.

He says they are in Elfland. Bruno tries to eat the fruit (Phlizz) but it has no taste. Their father shows Sylvie two lockets, one blue ("All will love Sylvie") and one red ("Sylvie will love all"). She chooses the red. The narrator finds himself at the railway station of his destination, Elveston. On arriving at Arthur's house, he tells him of Lady Muriel Orme, and it turns out that Arthur knows her and is in love with her. The narrator falls asleep again, and hears the Chancellor warn the Vice-Warden that the Ambassador of Elfland has arrived and that they will need to convince him that Uggug is Bruno, or as able as Bruno.

The Ambassador, Baron Doppelgeist, is given demonstrations of Uggug's abilities which always happen when he is looking the other way. Finding his guestroom full of frogs, he leaves in anger.

The narrator visits Lady Muriel and her father, the Earl, in the company of Arthur. They discuss weightlessness. Later, Arthur and the narrator visit the beach. Arthur goes home. Sylvie and Bruno go in search of the Beggar, their father. She rubs the red amulet, and a mouse is transformed into a lion, which they ride. Their father listens to their account of the Ambassador's visit; he cannot rectify the situation, but casts a spell.

Uggug refuses to learn his lessons. The Vice-Warden and his wife try on disguises: jester and dancing bear. Uggug sees them and runs off to fetch the Professor. When he arrives, they are dressed normally, and they tell him that the people wish to elect an Emperor — the Vice-Warden.

INTERMEZZO

The Professor takes Sylvie and Bruno to see the Other Professor. The Professor asks him about the Pig-Tale, which he promised to give after the Professor's Lecture. Bruno asks what "inconvenient" means. By way of illustration, the Other Professor recites *Peter and Paul*, 208 lines of verse. After a discussion, the Other Professor vanishes. Sylvie and Bruno complain to the Professor about their treatment, and ask him to tell the Gardener to open the garden door for them, so they can go to Fairyland to see their father.

They walk a long way, stopping briefly to visit the King of Dogland, before entering the gate of Fairyland. Arthur tells the narrator that he has discovered that he has more wealth than he thought, and that marriage with Lady Muriel is at least possible. The narrator spends a month at London; when he returns, he finds that Arthur has still not yet declared his intentions. The narrator sets off to speak to the Earl; on the way he encounters first Sylvie (who is helping a Beetle) and then Bruno (who is spoiling Sylvie's garden). He persuades Bruno to help weed it instead. Bruno weeds the garden with the narrator's help.

ERIC

The Earl invites Arthur to a picnic in ten days' time. On the day, walking to their house, the narrator encounters Sylvie and Bruno again. The party leave the Earl's Hall and travel to a ruined castle, the site of the picnic. Muriel sings, but the narrator falls asleep, and her song becomes that of Bruno. Muriel introduces Captain Eric Lindon, a highly presentable young man. Arthur is in despair, and declines to return with the party in the same carriage. The narrator falls asleep again, and there is a meeting between Lindon, Sylvie, Bruno, and the Professor.

A week later, Arthur and the narrator go to church. They discuss religion with Muriel, condemning High Church affectations, and moralising which relies on Pascal's Wager. The narrator helps carry a lame little girl upstairs at the railway station, and buys a posy in the street. The girl turns out to be Sylvie.

He brings Sylvie and Bruno to the Earl's Hall. The Earl is astonished by the flowers, none of which are English. Muriel sings a new song. A couple of days later, the flowers have vanished. The narrator, Muriel, and the Earl idly sketch an alternative scheme for the animal kingdom.

Sylvie asks the Professor for advice. He unlocks the Ivory Door for the two of them, and they meet Bruno. The Professor boasts of having devised the Emperor's new Money Act, doubling the value of every coin to make everyone twice as rich, and shows the narrator an "Outlandish" watch (essentially a kind of time machine). Sylvie finds a dead hare, and is horrified to learn that human beings hunt them.

Arthur is even more discouraged. Muriel is surprised to discover that Eric has met Sylvie and Bruno. Eric saves Bruno from being run down by a train. The narrator tries to use the Outlandish watch to prevent an accident, but fails. He then uses it to witness, in reverse, some scenes of family life. Later, the narrator is talking to the Earl when he learns, and Arthur overhears, that Muriel is engaged to Eric.

Sylvie and Bruno present a variety show to an audience of frogs, including "Bits of Shakespeare", and Bruno tells them a long rambling story. A week after discovering that Muriel is engaged, Arthur and the narrator go for the "last" time to the Earl's Hall. They discuss with Muriel how the Sabbath should best be kept, and the nature of free will. Arthur informs the narrator that he is leaving for India.

A CLEAN SLATE

Several weeks pass in London. The narrator sees Eric Lindon at a club, and learns that Eric's engagement to Muriel is over, and that Arthur is still at Elveston. The narrator meets Bruno in a park; Sylvie gives Bruno his lessons. A thunderstorm drives the narrator home, where he finds a telegram from Arthur, asking him to come. As before, the narrator meets Lady Muriel while changing trains at Fayfield Junction. She is giving money to the old tramp. On their way to Elveston she says that Eric broke off their engagement because of her evident discomfort with Eric's lukewarm faith. Arthur does not know this.

The next morning, on a walk, Arthur discusses his anti-socialist views, and condemns charity bazaars as "half charity, half self-pleasing". Sylvie and Bruno contrive that he should meet Muriel, who is also out walking. The narrator presses on without him to Hunter's farm to order milk. On his way he meets the farmer, who is talking to a woman about her hard-drinking husband, Willie. At the farm, the dog Nero catches a boy who is stealing apples.

The three of them meet the farmer's wife, daughter Bessie, and Bessie's doll, Matilda-Jane. On their way back to Elveston they pass the Golden Lion, a new public house. Willie comes walking down the road; Sylvie and Bruno invisibly drag him away from the pub.

He delivers his wages to his wife, and swears off drink. The narrator walks back to the house, and learns that Arthur is now engaged to Muriel. At the Hall, the narrator finds Muriel with a man called "Mein Herr," who has a beard and a German accent. He bears a remarkable resemblance to the Professor.

He shows them Fortunatus's Purse, and describes a gravity-powered train, a method of storing up extra time so that nobody ever gets bored, a carriage with oval wheels (with the end of one wheel corresponding to the side of the wheel opposite it, so that the carraige rises, falls, rolls, and pitches, and so anybody in the carriage gets vomitingly sick) He also describes a carriage designed to prevent runaway horses from getting anywhere. Oddly enough, nobody seems to remember where they first met "Mein Herr", or what his real name is, or where he lives, or where he's from.

Lady Muriel admits that she never realized what a mysterious man he is until she met the narrator. A party is planned. Ten days pass. The day before the party, Arthur, Muriel and the narrator have tea at the Hall. Arthur argues that the gravity of a sin must be judged by the temptation preceding it. The Earl returns from the harbour-town with news of the spread of a fever.

A BRIEF MARRIAGE

At the party, conversation ranges over sanity and insanity,

cheating at croquet versus cheating at whist, rational honeymoons, teetotalism, and keeping dinner parties interesting. An interlude, with the arrival of Sylvie and Bruno, the discussion of wine (which is transformed into a discussion of jam) and an unsatisfying musical performance.

Another interlude, with "Mein Herr" telling tall tales about his country. He describes how nobody in his kingdom ever drowns, because they have been eugenically bred for dozens of generations to weigh less and less until everybody is lighter than water. He also hears about how the largest map ever made on Earth was six inches to the mile; as his country is older, it has gone through maps that are six feet to the mile, then six yards to the mile, next a hundred yards to the mile—finally, a mile to the mile (the farmers said that if such a map was to be spread out, it would block out the sun and crops would fail, so the project was abandoned). He goes on to portray some devices similar to modern planetary engineering or terraforming, and paint-balls. Finally, he describes a system of government where there are thousands of kings and one subject, instead of the other way around.

Sylvie plays the piano for the assembled company. Mein Herr discusses incomprehensibility, competitive examinations, and scholarships. Mein Herr condemns the idea of a "loyal Opposition" in politics. His speech is interrupted for the narrator by stanzas of *What Tottles Meant.*

Sylvie tells the story "Bruno's Picnic".

Sylvie and Bruno have vanished. The guests, after a brief search, go home; Muriel, Arthur and the Earl discuss what pursuits might be followed in the Afterlife.

Muriel sings *To a Lark* (which is replaced, for the dreaming narrator, by a different song). Arthur is called away to the harbour to treat cases of the deadly fever, and he leaves immediately after his wedding the next morning.

An item in the *Fayfield Chronicle* reports the death of Arthur Forester.

THE RETURN

In December of the same year, the narrator returns to

Elveston, and visits Arthur's grave in the company of Muriel. They have tea with the Earl, and discuss whether animals have souls. Lady Muriel walks the narrator part of the way home, and they meet Sylvie and Bruno, who are singing *A Song of Love*. Back in Outland, the Professor welcomes Sylvie and Bruno back to the palace in time for Uggug's birthday celebrations. They hear the last verse of the Gardener's Song, then hurry to the Saloon.

The Professor delivers his Lecture. It includes Axioms, Specimens, and Experiments. The Banquet takes place. The Other Professor recites *The Pig-Tale*. The Emperor is in the process of making a speech when a mysterious "hurricane" causes him and his wife to regret all of their previous intrigues against the Warden. (No attempt is made to justify this in the terms of the story.) The Beggar returns to the palace, and is revealed to be the Warden. Uggug, who has turned into a giant porcupine, is put into a cage. Sylvie and Bruno visit the ill Professor in the company of the Empress. In the "real" world, the narrator is called urgently to the Hall. Eric Lindon has found Arthur Forester still living — he had been unconscious or delirious for several months, and went unrecognised as the doctor. On returning to his own lodgings, the narrator witnesses his last scene from Outland: Bruno and Sylvie discover that the two Jewels are in fact one.

CHARACTERS

Lead characters

An ill Londoner who visits Elveston to consult his friend about his illness (possibly narcolepsy). While never given a name, (although he is occasionally called "Mister Sir" by Bruno) this character serves a supporting role in every plotline in the novel, and the story is told through his eyes. At first, he serves principally as an omniscient observer in Fairyland, although his part in the real-world story is somewhat more substantial. However, towards the middle of the novel, he begins to take on a more active role in both dimensions of the story.

Sylvie

A young Sprite at the beginning of the novel, and later a true Fairy. Sylvie is the princess of Fairyland, daughter of the Warden, and sister of Bruno. While exhibiting very innocent traits, she seems far more mature than her younger brother, and often becomes exasperated with his illogical statements.

Bruno

Bruno is a very young fairy child, who uses broken grammar and who seems to have a somewhat twisted view of logic. He abhors his lessons, which his sister makes him take on a daily basis.

CHARACTERS IN THE FAIRY WORLD

Later the King of Fairyland. The father of Sylvie and Bruno, and the rightful ruler of Outland. He is the intended victim of the plots of the Emperor, Empress and Lord Chancellor, but is actually in full control of events.

The Emperor (Sibimet)

Originally the Sub-Warden, the Emperor conspires along with his wife and the Chancellor to steal the rule of Outland from the Warden. He is a rather ridiculous character, but not unintelligent.

The Empress (Tabikat)

The wife of the Emperor, she is an entirely stupid woman, and is unknowingly the butt of many jokes. She is content to spend all her time doting over her hideous son, Uggug.

The Lord Chancellor

The chief underling of the Emperor and Empress, he frequently is willing conspirator in their dirty work.

Uggug

An ugly and stupid child who is doted upon and spoiled by his mother, and behaves in an obnoxious manner toward everyone. He changes into a porcupine near the end.

The Professor

A delightfully ridiculous old man, he invents many ridiculous items, and then proceeds to have no purpose for them.

The most wonderful item in his possession is the Outlandish Watch (so-called because it comes from Outland). It has the ability to turn back time, although it cannot allow its holder to truly alter events of the past. It can also play any one hour backwards.

The Other Professor

A Professor friend of the Professor's. He is frequently asleep, and wakes up to recite poetry. In Furniss's illustrations, his face is never shown.

CHARACTERS IN THE REAL WORLD

An intelligent, thoughtful, curious young doctor. He often stimulates the storyline — and the other characters — by introducing questions of morality and religion. He is in love with Lady Muriel. He is an extremely moral person, and eventually sacrifices himself to save a village dying of fever.

Lady Muriel Orme

Another intelligent person, she is the object of Arthur's affection, and often helps to engage in intelligent conversation with many of the other real-world characters, especially the Narrator and the Earl. She endures a failed engagement with Eric Lindon, before marrying Arthur.

The Earl of Ainslie

The father of Lady Muriel, he is both a father figure to the younger characters, and a comrade to the aging Narrator.

Eric Lindon

Lady Muriel's cousin, and one-time fiance. He breaks their engagement upon realizing that she believes that they are religiously incompatible, but will not break it herself. An ex-soldier, he exhibits great self-sacrifice and courage.

Mein Herr (German for "My Lord")

Seemingly a traveller from a distant planet, Mein Herr is the catalyst for both satire and several puns. His planet has already experienced much of what earth is currently dealing with, and he gladly shares the end results of some of our more ridiculous customs.

WHAT THE TORTOISE SAID TO ACHILLES

"What the Tortoise Said to Achilles" (1895) is a brief dialogue by Lewis Carroll which playfully problematises the foundations of logic. The title alludes to one of Zeno's paradoxes of motion, in which Achilles could never overtake the tortoise in a race. In Carroll's dialogue, the tortoise challenges Achilles to use the force of logic to make him accept the conclusion of a simple deductive argument. Ultimately, Achilles fails, because the clever tortoise leads him into an infinite regression.

SUMMARY OF THE DIALOGUE

The discussion begins by considering the following logical argument:

- *A*: "Things that are equal to the same are equal to each other" (transitive property)
- *B*: "The two sides of this triangle are things that are equal to the same"
- Therefore *Z*: "The two sides of this triangle are equal to each other"

The Tortoise asks Achilles whether the conclusion logically follows from the premises, and Achilles grants that it obviously does. The Tortoise then asks Achilles whether there might be a reader of Euclid who grants that the argument is *logically valid*, as a *sequence*, while denying that *A* and *B* are true. Achilles accepts that such a reader might exist, and that he would hold that *if A* and *B* are true, *then Z* must be true, while not yet accepting that *A* and *B are* true.

The Tortoise then asks Achilles whether a second kind of reader might exist, who accepts that *A* and *B are* true, but who does *not* yet accept the principle that *if A* and *B* are both true, *then* Z must be true. Achilles grants the Tortoise that this second kind of reader might also exist. The Tortoise, then, asks Achilles to treat him as a reader of this second kind, and then to logically compel him to accept that Z must be true.

After writing down *A*, *B* and *Z* in his notebook, Achilles asks the Tortoise to accept the hypothetical:

- C: "If *A* and *B* are true, Z must be true"

The Tortoise agrees to accept C, if Achilles will write down what he has to accept in his note-book, making the new argument:

- *A*: "Things that are equal to the same are equal to each other"
- *B*: "The two sides of this triangle are things that are equal to the same"
- C: "If *A* and *B* are true, Z must be true"
- Therefore Z: "The two sides of this triangle are equal to each other"

But now that the Tortoise accepts premise C, he still refuses to accept the expanded argument. When Achilles demands that "If you accept *A* and *B* and C, you must accept Z," the Tortoise remarks that that's *another* hypothetical proposition, and suggests even if he accepts C, he could still fail to conclude Z if he did not see the truth of:

- *D*: "If *A* and *B* and C are true, Z must be true"

The Tortoise continues to accept each hypothetical premise once Achilles writes it down, but denies that the conclusion necessarily follows, since each time he denies the hypothetical that if all the premises written down so far are true, Z must be true:

"And at last we've got to the end of this ideal race-course! Now that you accept *A* and *B* and C and *D*, *of course* you accept Z."

"Do I?" said the Tortoise innocently. "Let's make that quite clear. I accept *A* and *B* and C and *D*. Suppose I *still* refused to accept Z?"

"Then Logic would take you by the throat, and *force* you to do it!" Achilles triumphantly replied. "Logic would tell you, 'You can't help yourself. Now that you've accepted *A* and *B* and *C* and *D*, you must accept *Z*!' So you've no choice, you see."

"Whatever Logic is good enough to tell me is worth *writing down*," said the Tortoise. "So enter it in your note-book, please. We will call it

(*E*) If *A* and *B* and *C* and *D* are true, *Z* must be true.

Until I've granted that, of course I needn't grant Z. So it's quite a necessary step, you see?"

"I see," said Achilles; and there was a touch of sadness in his tone.

Thus, the list of premises continues to grow without end, leaving the argument always in the form:

- (1): "Things that are equal to the same are equal to each other"
- (2): "The two sides of this triangle are things that are equal to the same"
- (3): (1) and (2) Ò! (Z)
- (4): (1) and (2) and (3) Ò! (Z)
- ...
- (*n*): (1) and (2) and (3) and (4) and ... and (*n* – 1) Ò! (Z)
- Therefore (Z): "The two sides of this triangle are equal to each other"

At each step, the Tortoise argues that even though he accepts all the premises that have been written down, there is some further premise (that if all of (1)–(*n*) are true, then (Z) must be true) that he still needs to accept before he is compelled to accept that (Z) is true.

DISCUSSION

Several philosophers have tried to resolve the Carroll paradox. Bertrand Russell discussed the paradox briefly in P. 38 of *The Principles of Mathematics* (1903), distinguishing between *implication* (associated with the form "if *p*, then *q*"), which he held to be a relation between *unasserted* propositions, and *inference* (associated with the form "*p*, therefore *q*"), which he held to be a relation between *asserted* propositions; having made this distinction, Russell could deny that the Tortoise's attempt to treat *inferring* Z from *A* and *B* as equivalent to, or dependent on, agreeing to the *hypothetical* "If *A* and *B* are true, then Z is true".

The Wittgensteinian philosopher Peter Winch discussed the paradox in *The Idea of a Social Science and its Relation to Philosophy* (1958), where he argued that the paradox showed that "the actual process of drawing an inference, which is after all at the heart of logic, is something which cannot be represented as a logical formula ... Learning to infer is not just a matter of being taught about explicit logical relations between propositions; it is learning *to do* something". Winch goes on to suggest that the moral of the dialogue is a particular case of a general lesson, to the effect that the proper *application* of rules governing a form of human activity cannot itself be summed up with a set of *further* rules, and so that "a form of human activity can never be summed up in a set of explicit precepts".

Isashiki Takahiro (1999) summarizes past attempts and concludes they all fail before beginning yet another.

"Which i's his I?": surrealist reflections in Elizabeth Bishop's Mirror.

Chapter 16

To Catch a Bandersnatch

PRELUDE: ALICE IN HERMENEUTICA

In a story called "The Book of Sand", the Argentine writer Jorge Luis Borges tells a story about a meeting between a dealer in rare books and an itinerant Bible salesman, who sells him a very old and worn volume of Holy Writ in an Arabic script. The peddler called it "The Book of Sand" because like the sands it was without beginning and without end and contained an infinite number of pages.

One simply could never turn to the first page or the last and of those pages in the middle, no page which had once been seen could, after turning, ever be found again. While Borges intended this as an allegory for all books, or perhaps more broadly, for the limitlessness of our search for knowledge, I often feel he may have been specifically referring to the *Alice* books2 of Charles Lutwidge Dodgson, *pseud.* Lewis Carroll.

It is doubtful if any two people have ever read quite the same version of these - I certainly never have. They are a constantly shifting, paradoxical mirror of an alien land, one that lays so close to ours as to share a surface (much as the sides of a cube share an edge) whose layers of meaning are revealed as we live, laugh, and grow wise.

Upon every reading, at the very least some hitherto undiscovered phrase will leap from the page, rich in symbolism or suggestion. Sometimes the entire work will be seen in a new light. I should like to enumerate a representative few of the literally hundreds of existing interpretations3 of these works. Shane Leslie, in "Lewis Carroll and the Oxford

Movement" finds the Looking-Glass a thinly disguised history of the religious controversies of Victorian England.

William Empson, in "The Child as Swain", sees the Pool of Tears as a satirical microcosm of Darwin's evolutionary theories. Robert Sutherland's "Language and Lewis Carroll" is full of "signification by morphemic identities" and such. Peter Heath's marvelously annotated *Philosopher's Alice* finds in them "surprising insights into abstract questions of philosophy", and his notes prove these books contain elements of subjective nominalism, Calvinistic predetermination, and somehow the Duck ends up as "illogical positivist". Thomas French, in *Alice in Acidland,* believes she is on a psychedelic trip.

Phyllis Greenacre, among a host of psychoanalytic interpreters, thinks her eating the mushroom was "an act of oral aggression." In Judith Bloomingdale's "Alice as Anima", we learn that her coronation was an "unconscious anticipation of Mary as Queen of Heaven", and that the Duchess was the "Madonna ... in its most grotesque form." However, my favorites so far are Dr. Abraham Ettleson's *Alice In Wonderland: The Secret Language of Lewis Carroll Revealed* and *Through the Looking-Glass Decoded,* wherein he finds the book an elaborate code for the daily and holiday rituals of Orthodox Judaism.

Of course, everyone has a right to *think* about these interpretations, about as much right, as the Duchess reminds us, "as pigs have to fly," but "explanations take such a dreadful amount of time", and there is a fine line to be walked between the assumption that fantasy or myth implies deliberate allegory, and the knowledge that the very stature of these works as immortal splendors is based upon this very quality of enigma, of sand.

Freudians will forever be seeing them through Viennese spectacles, Ecclesiastics through the inverted binoculars of the Church, and all of us will continue, as Joyce put it, to "Wipe your glosses with what you know." In reading these, one is most reminded of the Trial Scene at the end of Wonderland where the King manages to twist the ambiguous poem "They told me you had been to her ..." into a confession. *"Why, look you know, how unworthy a thing you make of me! You would play upon me, you would seem to know my stops, you would pluck out the heart of my mystery ...*

A MEETING OF THE MINDS

So let us ask the question: what makes *these* the Books of Sand? Why are they said to be the most quoted works outside of Shakespeare and the Bible? Simply this, that they are recognizable as exquisitely crafted artifacts of the "shared mind", perhaps the first secular infusion into this world of literature of a certain type: the literature of the "collective unconscious" as Jung lovers would put it.

In current psychological jargon, we have two distinct "minds" which are located as mirror images on the left and right sides of our brains. The "left brain" is the mind of intellect, logic, sanity, Confucianism, social behaviour. It is the coolness of Yin: literal, lineal, and analytic.

The Reverend Charles Lutwidge Dodgson. Its bright daylight surface might be symbolized by a writing desk. The "right brain", contrariwise, is the mind of intuition, insight, myth, dreams, fantasy, the imagination, Taoism. It is the warmth of Yang: metaphorical, simultaneous, and synthetic. Lewis Carroll. Its dark dreamy depths may be symbolized by a raven.

So *why is a raven like a writing desk?* This is a world of paradox, but while the left brain sees irreconcilable opposites the right brain says, with Whitman,

Do I contradict myself?
Very well then, I contradict myself.
I am large, I contain multitudes.

It is the fugal interplay of these two hands of consciousness that determines our thoughts and behaviour. One delineates the printing of musical scores, scales, acoustics, historical notes, instrument manufacture, and performance schedules. The other dreams/composes/plays/hears the *music*. While some like to pretend that only the left bank exists, in the daytime world of lawyers and business, and others live too far up on *Rive Droit* (dreamers, schizophrenics, artists), it is those in touch with *both* sides, drinking from the wellspring of inspiration in the company of an talented (mental) amanuensis, who are the truest contributors to humanity.

What boating up the Isis was for Lewis Carroll, the after-years of patient toil were for Mr. Dodgson. This "conscious" mind then, in the theories of Huxley, Bergson, and others is in the main a filter which conceals far more than it reveals. It is the Porlock of vast and infinite realms of the *Ur*-conscious. It's Magic! So where exactly then is, in Freud's terminology, the "royal road to the subconscious"?

It is not the province of this essay to deal with the plethora of psychological techniques and cults, which proliferate around us which deal with "opening the sixth circuit" (Leary), "getting It" (est™, via Zen Buddhism), "snapping", "finding Jesus", or what have you. I am not particular as to terms, but I find the most convenient for the process "metaphor", and for the destination "magic".

The term "magic" I employ not in its most grotesque sense, that of stage tricks and sleight-of-hand, though they *did* seem to amuse Mr. Carroll no end; nor even in the romantic sense of an inexplicable and wondrous quality of experience, though certainly the *Alice* books contain these elements (and in fact led to his downfall as a writer in his self-styled masterworks, the *Sylvie and Bruno* books); but Magic in its highest sense - the principle of metaphor, of synergy, of illumination, or, simply, that the whole *qualitatively* exceeds the sum of its parts. Language is infinitely richer than the sum of its words, as words are more than the sum of their letters. Subatomic idea-forces and probabilities become atomic; atomic realities molecular; molecular reactions chemical, then elemental; compounds are formed, leading to organic cells, tissues, organs: behold a man.

The whole exceed its parts. These books are twin looking-glasses facing each other, like those in old-time barber shops, in whose pages infinite levels, hidden and secret treasure troves of wisdom, are unveiled on each reading, while the aesthetic surface remains constant. This is *magic,* this is *metaphor.*

"It is the East, and Juliet is the Sun.

Shakespeare, "Romeo and Juliet"

Not that they share sun-like qualities, rather that at this metaphoric level Juliet *is* the sun.

It's not true, but it is Truth.

"Our king holds all the Indies in his arms;
and more, and richer, when he strains that lady.

How I Wonder What You're At

The Walrus and the Carpenter
Were walking close at hand:
They wept like anything to see
Such quantities of sand:
"If this were only cleared away,"
They said, "it would be grand!"

The quality most common to all works of Magic is the quality of sand: elusiveness. *Meanings are dislocated - hidden in unexpected places, multiplied and split, given over to ambiguity, plurality, and uncertainty, the dream represents a decentered universe.* Elusiveness, whose *technique* is ambiguity. *"However, somebody killed something, that's clear at any rate."*

Yes, dear Alice, prosaically clear, but hardly as immortal as what came whiffling through the tulgey wood. And it certainly *did* seem a little provoking ("almost as if it happened on purpose," she thought) that, though she managed to pick plenty of beautiful rushes as the boat glided by, there was always a more lovely one that she couldn't reach.

Vladimir Nabokov, who was among the first translators of *Alice* into Russian (1923) among other things, spent his life collecting butterflies which, as anyone who has tried it knows, is an exquisite combination of pursuit, stealth, and seduction. This applies equally to butterflies of the species *Literatura* as *Lepidoptera*.

Let us turn to **Borges** again: *Music, states of happiness, mythology, faces molded by time, certain twilights and certain places - all these are trying to tell us something, or have told us something: the immanence of a revelation that is not yet produced is, perhaps, the aesthetic reality.* These moments, *epiphanies,* contacts with the magic/metaphoric mind, the awareness of the billion fold potentialities *not* chosen in any moment - this is what is echoed in moments of linguistic ambiguity.

The most magical of all occurrences are these breaks in the form: something that is true at one level of metaphor is suddenly seen in terms of another level. Communicational borders are crossed, context and content enter into the circle of confusion. *"Would you - be good enough - "Alice panted out, after running a little further, "to stop a minute - just to get - one's breath again?" "I'm good enough," the King said, "only I'm not strong enough. You see, a minute goes by so fearfully quick. You might as well try to stop a Bandersnatch."*

There is a feeling then, for both artist and his silent partner, the reader, that despite one's best efforts, there will always be the implication of vast depths of the unwritten, the could-have-been-written. *His answer trickled through my head like water through a sieve.*

This is at the core of most magical writings, and its symbol is most often the young girl. Why is the most popular love story in the Western world, perhaps then by implication our society's archetype of the perfect love, the story of a fourteen year old girl who spends a total of *one evening* with her Romeo? Ah, perfection. Ah, elusiveness.

To have grown old together in a respectable suburban neighborhood in Verona would hardly be the poignant allegory it is. Helen, the abducted bride, was twelve when she launched a thousand ships. Dante's beloved Beatrice was but eight when he met her. Nabokov uses Lolita, also twelve, a nymphet possessed in body but never in soul, as the corporeal symbol of this quest for the ungraspable.

In the sandiest book of all time, the most linguistically playful, ambiguous, and multilevel book ever written, Joyce's *Finnegans Wake* (below), the central story of this centerless book is a father's implied voyeuristic escapades with his young daughter and her twin.

And need we mention Madama Butterfly, fifteen, or even the Virgin Mary, who was fourteen when she bore her child? So what are we "rejoicing" in? Stuff and Nonsense! Works of a powerful humour whose structural foundation is, if you'll excuse the grandiosity, Truth. Freud's discovery of the extent to which our "conscious" life is controlled by the *Ur*-conscious hints at the ineluctable importance of the role of language in this process.

We have entered, by rabbit hole or looking-glass into the realm of magic, *a.k.a.* metaphor, inspiration, genius, imagination, humour. The tradition was brought to the secular world for the first time by Lewis Carroll who invoked, by innovative linguistics, this dark realm of Chaos and Old Night, and of splendors undreamed.

This linguistic tradition was taken up in a series which includes such luminaries as Ezra Pound, Gerard Manley Hopkins, T.S. Eliot, Gertrude Stein, and Mallarmé in France, but above all, James Joyce, and it is to him, and his debt to Carroll, that I would like to turn for a minute.

JOYCE - CARROLL NOATES

These are but wild and whirling words, my lord. Alice's fictional adventures in Wonderland took place on the 4th of May 1859, the corporeal Alice (Liddell)'s seventh birthday. Eighty years later, again on the 4th of May, 1939, a book was published simultaneously in England and America which stands in relation to post-Carrollian English as the "Alice" books to the Victorian.

It was a feverishly overgrown tropical island whose dense oneiric jungle grew out of the winds of Wonderland which had once born aloft a seed called "Jabberwocky". It was written in a language loosely based on English, and was called *Finnegans Wake.* It was immediately received as *glossolalia,* but as the years went by this work, while still enjoying only a tiny and cultish readership, is slowly becoming recognized as the greatest work of the twentieth century's acknowledged master of English prose.

Joyce did not know of Carroll's work until he was halfway through this "Work in Progress" as it was then known, although he had heard bits and pieces from friends. What he *did* read was *Sylvie and Bruno* and finally, years later, the *Alice* books. *It must have astonished Joyce, that avant-garde innovator, proud of his Irish nationality, contemptuous of the Church of England, and confident of his own originality, to find that he had been forestalled in so many of his discoveries by a mid-Victorian Englishman in minor Anglican orders.* James Atherton, in *The Books at the Wake* calls Carroll Joyce's "unforeseen precursor" in an essay from which the above was taken.

The surface of *Finnegans Wake* is a Jabberwock of gargantuan proportions. Its primary linguistic technique is the condensing and interweaving of two or more words into one, which was called the "portmanteau" by Carroll (after a kind of small suitcase). But Carroll's *enfant terrible* consisted of words such as "slithy", which Humpty Dumpty explained was composed of the words "lithe" and "slimy".

If "slithy" could be packed into a portmanteau, it would take a steamer trunk to hold a self-referential construct of Joyce's like "astroglodynamologos". Joyce also discovered in Carroll such things as the attempt to portray the dream state by the drifting and merging of identities and personalities, and the multilayered use of language to reach the *Ur*-conscious: not only to describe it, but to *actively stimulate its use.*

He finds in Alice another incarnation of the inspiration of the young girl Art being pursued by the stammering old Dodgson of its realization. A looking-glass twin as the symbol of self-reflection, self-absorption, self-referentiality. Humpty Dumpty as symbolic of the Cosmic Egg, and the Fall of man, and Isa Bowman, one of Carroll's child friends and the actress who brought Alice to the stage, are found therein, but it is the jabberwocky which is the most conspicuous feature of the *Wake*: at once the most crucial, rewarding, and difficult.

These suitcases must be delicately and carefully packed. *The art of packing is the last lecture of wisdom.* There must be a structural resemblance to ordinary words, for there is little art in simple concatenation. Rather, the meanings must be found in phonetic, morphological, etymological, and rhythmical resemblance.

It is a technique of such power that the entire work can be summed up in a sentence: *...every person, place and thing in the chaosmos of Alle anyway connected with the gobbly dumped* *turkery was moving and changing every part of the time: the travelling inkhorn (possibly pot), the hare and turtle pen and paper, the continually more and less intermisunderstanding minds of the anticollaborators, the as time went on as it will variously inflected, differently pronounced, otherwise spelled, changeable meaning vocable script signs* or a single word "volupkabulary".

Finnegans Wake has (thankfully) thus far found no Humpty Dumpty to translate it into simple English. *"The question is," said Alice, "whether you can make words mean so many different things." "The question is," said Humpty Dumpty, "which is to be master - that's all."* We have all had the experience of taking a perfectly ordinary word and repeating it, *mantram*-like, until it has lost all meaning and become pure sound.

Joyce himself discouraged scholarly exegeses and believed, with the Duchess, that his readers should *"Take care of the sounds and the sense will take care of itself."* The genius of this technique is that it places the reader in contact with the other "ineluctable modality", the *Ur*-conscious, and even the most common of words are festooned with bouquets of associations.

An exercise, by way of example: The original Alice, the girl to whom Carroll told his immortal tale, was the daughter of the Dean of Christ Church, Henry George Liddell, co-editor of the foremost Greek lexicon of his day.

He named his child Alice, a name of unquestionably Greek derivation, although its exact source is unknown. Speculation runs through *alis*, "abundantly"; *aletheia*, "truth"; *alysso*, "to wander in mind" [akin to the Latin *hallucinor*]; *allistos*, inexorable; *allos*, another; *alastos*, unforgettable; *lithos*, "stone"; *lis* or *lisse*, "smooth"; *lussa*, "madness" [or *alussa*, "curing madness"]; or perhaps *alion*, "a land of wandering" (Wanderland?).

We may regard Carroll's setting of *this* girl in these books as an "inexorable, unforgettable, smooth wandering in the mind - another madness - a Wanderland, abundant with the stone truth." Phonetically related is the Latin *lux*, "light", hence *Lucia*, Joyce's young daughter who became quite mad; and *Lewis* himself.

Taking all this into *consideration* (from the Latin *con* - with, *sideris* - stars) and never forgetting the *allure* of *elusive illusions*, rest here a moment, and (*alleluia!*) play the game (L. *lusus*) of *liaisons* and *scions*, mysteries *Eleusinian*, and take a simple commonplace word which, in this case, has the ouraboric quality of reflecting its meaning on itself and say it aloud; you will hear a few allusions:

allure elusive illusions
Eleusinian hallucination
Alice Lucia Lewis

And now, dipped into the storm-tossed seas of the *Ur*-conscious, the retentive and stodgy notions of language are beginning to warp and to crack around the edges, and let a bit of daylight in. We must not set about in the first ecstasy of discovery to blast open all rules, and descend into chaos and gobbledygook. It is the unique genius of men like Carroll and Joyce to restrain, to structure, to contain. Humpty Dumpty always paid his words extra when he made them do a lot of work, and Alice "didn't venture to ask what he paid them with" but the reading of *Finnegans Wake* leaves little doubt: his sight, his reputation, his sanity, and, finally, his life.

But this is the destiny of Icarus, who caught the "air of a different world" and as the sun strikes the feathers which have fallen back to the ground at just the right angle, their iridescence reveals traces of the "fabulous artificers" who inspired the possibility of Flight.

All old Dadgerson's dodges one conning one's copying and that's what wonderland's wanderlad'll flaunt to the fair (374.1) *Though Wonderlawn's lost us for ever. Alis, alas, she broke the glass! Liddell lokker through the leafery, ours is mistery of pain.* (270.19) *Alicious, twinstreams twinestrained, through alluring glass* (528.17) *For always down in Carolinas lovely Dinahs vaunt their view* (226.2) *I am yam ... Dodgfather, Dodgson and Coo* (481.35) *And there many have paused before that exposure of him by old Tom Quad, a flashback in which he sits sated, gowndabout, in clericalease habit, watching bland sol slithe dodgsomely into the nevermore, a globule of maugdleness about to corrugitate his mild dewed cheek and the tata of a tiny victorienne, Alys, pressed by his limper looser.* (57.23)

And here "in the high places of Delude of Isreal" (331.18), we leave Shem the Penman/Shun the Punman in the midst of "jest jibberweek's joke" (565.14) and return to the ...*high white night. Whitest night mortal ever saw ... Lewd's carol* (501.28)

And if you will excuse an abrupt change in narrative, now that our terms have been defined, and all disclaimers as to meaning have been dutifully uttered, I should like to briefly retell, by way of example, how this one gentle reader has seen the various eggs of meanings successively disappearing from every shelf upon closer examination.

Fugue: The Dream-rushes

"It shall be called Bottom's dream, because it hath no bottom" Shakespeare, "A Midsummer Night's Dream" To begin, well, near the beginning anyway, my father is slightly mad. After all, *"I'm mad, you're mad, we're all mad here"* As a student in college he wrote two papers on Carroll comparing Alice's world to those of Henry Ford and Aldous Huxley.

My first contact with Wonderland, therefore, was as they were meant to be first encountered - read out loud, by an Elder, to a child. But let us leave this happy little lad and join a teenager setting out, with all the pharmacology of Western culture at his disposal, to rediscover Wonderland. *"Things flow so about here..."*

Ah, the days spent "drifting down the stream/Lingering in the golden gleam". The Cyril Ritchard records made the perfect companions to an eight hour trip "our wanderings to guide". Each stage24 was so clearly delineated. "Imperious Prima flashing forth ..." *The excursion into the preposterous sends one with renewed pleasure into the actual.*

But those drug references! Man, Mr. C. must have been some crazy head! The hookahsmoking caterpillar, the endless "Eat Me"s and "Drink Me"s among the magic mushrooms. The question had to be asked: could anyone *know so well* and not have indulged? Laudanum was freely available at the time, and of his contemporaries, Coleridge was into opium, Baudelaire and Dumas hashish. Was this really the "unforgettable, inexorably strange smooth wandering in the mind, abundant with the stone truth"? And what *did* happen during those two years missing from his diary? I'm afraid we must leave such speculations up in the Smoky Mountains from which they emanated.

A careful reading of his diaries, and the biographies of *Mssrs.* Collingwood and Green left it difficult to conjure up an image of the Reverend Dodgson "on the loose wig" after a hard day at Christ Church. I (reluctantly at first) concluded that the answer must lie elsewhere. Where was that little golden key? About this time (early 70s now) the woods of Santa Cruz, wherein I was attending the University of California, were fairly teeming with Cosmic Consciousness. Gurus now replaced connections, meditation getting high, and harmonious holistic Insights into the Mysteries abounded.

It was to the Looking-glass I now turned in search of Meaning. It became the Quest Myth, a seven stage Voyage of Illumination to answer the Caterpillar's "Who are you?" Alice (All us /All is) was the virgin soul, the eternal Seeker, and her ever-protean.

Teacher took on many forms but was often found in the Lotus Position *Humpty Dumpty was sitting, with his legs crossed like a Turk ... and, as his eyes were steadily fixed in the opposite direction ... he didn't take the least notice of her ...* echoing in some detail his earlier incarnation as the Caterpillar ... *with its arm folded ... taking not the smallest notice of her or of anything else ...*

Sometimes she was split into the Noble Left Hand Path (the contrary and paradoxical Red Queen) and the Noble Right Hand Path (the gentler White Queen, who traveled backwards in time). My speculations at the time turned, I confess, to such questions as "Could there be any symbolism to the corkscrew?"

"It's more like a corkscrew than a path" I mean, Humpty Dumpty woke the fish with one, and arrived at the Queen's with one in his hand. Was it the Mystic Spiral? DNA's helix? I arranged an elaborate schema for fitting Wonderland into the Tarot deck, from the appearance of the Herald (the White Rabbit) corresponding to 0 - The Fool through the Trial (XX - Judgement), and the reawakening (XXI - The World). After all, didn't she say "You're nothing but a pack of cards!"?

NO MATTER! NEVER MIND! NO MIND! NEVER MATTER!

(It) presents a surface so bizarre and irrational yet so colorful and striking, that some ... who approach it for the first time fail to make sense of it, while others, attracted by this surface, take it up in a purely frivolous and superficial spirit. Either response would be unfortunate. If this seems like a criticism of the Alice books, it is not surprising, but it is actually from an introductory essay to some Zen Buddhist writings by **William Barrett**.

In my first venture into the realm of theses I set out, armed only with my fan and white kid gloves, to prove that Alice was really a derelict Canon of Zen Buddhism, full of *koans*, which are "exactly like a riddle with no answer". Zen is perhaps the most directly experiential form of Buddhism.

It migrated from the humid jungles of Northern India (where it was known as *Dhyana*,26 meditation), through the plains of China (where it was *ch'an*), and through the mountains of Japan (where it became *zazen*), and finally, often in the spirit described above, to the "eggheads", "Beats", and "hippies" in the West.

Dr. D.T. Suzuki the most literate expositor of Zen today, describes it thusly: *Zen in its essence is the art of seeing into the nature on one's own being ... All the treatments, sometimes literary and sometimes physical, which are most liberally and kind-heartedly given by the masters to inquiring souls, are intended to give them back to the original state of freedom ... It is to be effected by meditating on these utterances that are directly poured out from the inner region undimmed by the intellect or the imagination ... When the cloud of ignorance disappears, the infinity of the heavens is manifested.*

These "utterances from the inner regions" are called *koans*, and their aim is to give a sudden understanding, insight, enlightenment or *satori* beyond normal consciousness. The parallels of method and aim between the Zen masters and their disciples, and those of the Wonderland are striking.

Zen's aimless aim is to "open the mind-flower" to become a *Child of the pure unclouded brow and dreaming eyes of wonder* Zen demands insight into the problem of problems, the paradox that paradox exists, by denying *everything*, even itself, as real. Its methods, like those of the Wonderland characters, are apparently illogical, sarcastic, even cruel, and yet the treasure is a thousand times worth the perils of the journey. Suzuki places these *koans* into seven categories, as follows:

Paradox

One day Subhuti, in a mood of sublime emptiness, was sitting under a tree. Flowers began to fall about him. "We are praising you for your discourse on emptiness," the gods whispered to him.

"But I have not spoken of emptiness," said Subhuti. "You have not spoken of emptiness, we have not heard emptiness," responded the gods.

"This is the true emptiness." And blossoms showered upon Subhuti as rain. Alice went timidly up to the door, and knocked.

"There's no sort of use in knocking, said the Footman, "and that for two reasons. First, because I'm on the same side of the door as you are: secondly, because they're making such a noise inside, no one could possibly hear you."

Going beyond the opposites

One day four traveling monks appeared at the temple of Hogen and began to build a fire. While they were building the fire, they began arguing about subjectivity and objectivity. Hogen asked: "There is a big stone. Do you "There are no mice in the air, I'm afraid, but you might catch a bat, and that's very like a mouse, you know. But do cats eat bats, I wonder." And here Alice began to get rather sleepy, and consider it to be inside or outside your mind?"

A monk answered: "From the Buddhist viewpoint everything is an objectification of mind, so I would say that the stone is inside my mind." "Your head must be very heavy," observed Hogen, "if you are carrying around a stone like that in your mind went on saying to herself in a dreamy sort of way, "Do cats eat bats? Do cats eat bats?" and sometimes "Do bats eat cats?" for you see, as she couldn't answer either question, it didn't much matter which way she put it.

Contradiction

A monk asked the sixth patriarch of Zen, "Who has attained to the secrets of Wobai?", Wobai being the mountain where the fifth patriarch resided. The patriarch replied, "One who understands Buddhism has attained to the secrets of Wobai." "Have you attained them?" "No, I have not" "How is it," asked the monk, that you have not?" "I do not understand Buddhism."

"That's just what I complain of! You *should* have meant! Even a joke should have some meaning - and a child's more important than a joke, I hope. You couldn't deny that, even if you tried with both hands." "I don't deny things with my hands," Alice objected. "Nobody said you did," said the Red Queen". I said you couldn't if you tried.

Affirmation

A monk asked Joshu, "When the body crumbles all to pieces and returns to the dust, there eternally abides one thing. Of this I have been told, but where does this one thing abide?" The master replied, "It is windy again this morning."

The Footman seemed to think this a good opportunity for repeating his remark, with variations. "I shall sit here," he said, "on and off, for days and days." "But what am I to do?"asked Alice. "Anything you like," said the Footman and began whistling.

Repetition

Hogen asked one of his disciples, "What do you understand by this: 'Let the difference be "I'm afraid you've not had much practice in riding," she ventured to say, as she was helping even a tenth of an inch, and it will grow as wide as heaven and earth?" The disciple said, "Let the difference be even a tenth of an inch, and it will grow as wide as heaven and earth." Hogen, however, told him that such an answer would never do. Said the disciple, "I cannot do otherwise, how do *you* understand this?"

The master at once replied, "Let the difference be even a tenth of an inch and it will grow as wide as heaven and earth."

him up from his fifth tumble. The knight looked very much surprised and a little offended at the remark. "What makes you say that?" he asked, as he scrambled back into the saddle, keeping hold of Alice's hair with one hand, to save himself from falling over on the other side. "Because people don't fall off quite so often, when they've had much practice." "I've had plenty of practice," the Knight said very gravely: "plenty of practice!"

Exclamation

A monk asked Joshu, a Chinese Zen master: "has a dog Buddha nature or not?" Joshu answered, "Mu!" "How should I know?"said Alice, surprised at her own courage, "It's no business of mine." The Queen turned crimson with fury, and, after glaring at her for a moment like a wild beast, began screaming "Off with her head! Off with -" "Nonsense!" said Alice, very loudly and decidedly, and the Queen was silent.

Silence

A monk came to Shuzan and asked, "Please play me a tune on stringless harp." The master was quiet for some little while, and said, "Do you hear it?" "No, I do not hear it." "Why," said the master, "did you not ask louder?" "Come back!" the Caterpillar called after her. "I've something important to say!" This sounded promising, certainly. Alice turned and came back again.

"Keep your temper," said the Caterpillar. "Is that all?"said Alice, swallowing down her anger as well as she could. "No," said the Caterpillar.

Alice thought she might as well wait, as she had nothing else to do, and perhaps after all it might tell her something worth hearing. For some minutes it puffed away without speaking: but at last it unfolded its arms, took the hookah out of its mouth, and said "So you think you're changed, do you?" The aim of these koans is "understanding" - the realization that beyond the "gateless gate," although everything is as it was (the shared surface again) everything is as different as possible.

There is a saying attributed to **Seigen Ishin**: *Before a man studies Zen to him mountains are mountains, and waters are waters; after he gets an insight into the truth of Zen through the instruction of a good master, mountains to him are not mountains and waters are not waters; but after this when he really attains the abode of rest, mountains are once more mountains and waters are waters.* This, of course, is the frame story of *Through the Looking-Glass*, the kitten becoming the Red Queen and then shaking/waking into the kitten again.

This problem of understanding is nowhere put more perfectly than by the White Knight, who explains *"You see," I said to myself, "the only difficulty is with the feet: the head is high enough already. "Now, first I put my head on top of the gate - then the head's high enough - then I stand on my head - then the feet are high enough, you see - then I'm over, you see."* Under**stand**ing. You see? Perhaps the most succinct summary of Zen in all literature was put into evidence at the Alice's trial.

If I or she should chance to be
Involved in this affair
He trusts to you to set them free.
Exactly as we were.
My notion was that you had been
(Before she had this fit)
An obstacle that came between
Him, and ourselves, and it.

WOOL AND WATER

In my next paper, in a Quixotic jab at Sufi metaphysics, I attempted to prove that Mr. Dodgson, an "enthusiastic member of the Psychical Society" according to his biographers, was deliberately weaving a Sufic tale akin to the teaching stories of the Mullah Nasrudin.

Sufis, who are commonly thought to have arisen from mystical Moslem sects, though they consider themselves as the inner core of every religion, even the ancient, are called the "People of Mystery."

Their name derives from the Arabic word *Suf*, meaning *wool*, a reference perhaps to their dress, or perhaps to the cloud of obscurity in which their doctrines and teachings are transmitted.

Perhaps the most well known of Sufi allegorical verse is the "Rubayat of Omar Khayyam", where he sings of divine, or God-realized intoxication, but, for the sake of the uninitiated, refers only to "*wine*", and the pleasures of being "drunk". They speak of the *ninety nine* names of God. It seems to me then that Carroll left us a pretty direct clue in the verse *Then fill up the glasses with treacle and ink Or anything else that is pleasant to drink Mix sand with the cider and wool with the wine And welcome Queen Alice with ninety-times-nine* Their path is one of the journey back to the Godhead.

Most people begin this journey only out of dissatisfaction, with desperately wanting to believe in the divine on one hand, and seeing nothing but suffering, evil, and unfairness on the other. *One thing was certain: that the white kitten had had nothing to do with it - it was the black kitten's fault entirely.*

The journey back to this primal state of awakened consciousness has *seven* stages. Alice, who in Carroll's curiously evocative phrase "began to remember that she was a pawn", takes a seven stage journey through the Looking-glass from Q2 to Q8 and awakens to find a golden crown on her head *"But how can it have gotten there without my knowing it?"*

Although the Sufis often use wine as a metaphor for this state of grace, Mr. Carroll seems rather fond of soup. They speak of the "pearl of great price," that there is no treasure upon earth that is not mere baubles and trinkets in the awesome and ineffable Reality. *"Who would not give all else for twop- Ennyworth only of beautiful Soup."*

And it is into the soup the White Queen disappears in the final "chaosmos" of the Checkmate. Ah yes, the Checkmate. In those final *gonzo* pages, when "all sorts of things happened in moment" and Alice rips away the veil of her previous realities by seizing the tablecloth, and giving a yank, her successive realizations that she was not a pawn, but a Queen; not a Queen, but a player of the game; not a player but the Dreamer, and to continue, as we close the book, not even the

Dreamer, but really Lewis Carroll, dream of Mr. Dodgson - perhaps a perfect parable of the flowering stages of Enlightenment, the transformation of perspective as one awakens to higher dimensions of experience.

MATHEMAGIC

Dimensions. Let us not forget that Mr. Dodgson was a professional mathematician (as was your humble reporter). That Carroll was interested in dimensionality is borne witness by several books in his library, including Charles Hinton's *The Fourth Dimension.*

In a simple analogy, we have all had the experience of driving past a jumble of trees which suddenly, for one exquisite moment, line up in rows and the orchard is revealed. Even after the reversion to the apparent chaos, the revelation, the higher perspective, is forever ours. To be mathematically precise...

A point has **zero** dimensions, a line **one**, a plane **two**, a volume **three**, a hypervolume **four**, and so on. If you will excuse an anthropomorphism, just as a point realizes it is one end of a line, a line realizes it is the edge of a plane, infinitely and incomprehensibly vaster that its previous perception yet still the same, one has the feeling of *In-sight,* of the solution to the *koan,* of a quantum leap to another level of abstraction.

The game of chess employed in *Looking-glass* provides a perfect example of dimensionality. Chess is essentially a game of **one** dimension (*i.e.* opposing forces). It is played on a **two** dimensional surface, the board.

The forces (called pieces) are either of **one** dimension (the pawn, which moves only forward in a straight line); **two** dimensions (Rooks, Bishops, Kings and Queens) which have two degrees of freedom, or directions of movement; and the piece which gives the game its intricacy and life, the **three** dimensional Knight.

It is three-dimensional in the sense that it can pass over another piece in its move, whereas two-dimensional pieces would be blocked. Carroll chooses *this* piece, the wayward and transcendent Knight as his self-image in the book. I also at that time went into metaphysical questions of relative time (the Mad Hatter, the White Queen), relative motion (the Red Queen), and questions such as who exactly is dreaming whom (the Red King). And surely the Cheshire cat *must* have once belonged to Mr. Shroedinger.

Eleison Wonderland

The Sufis say that all religions, at their heart, contain essentially the same truths and wisdom. I therefore reasoned that, as Mr. Dodgson was an Anglican minister his spirituality may have been purely mystic Christianity, the way of Merton, deChardin, and the Saints. *"Well, perhaps you haven't found it so yet," said Alice, "but when you have to turn into a chrysalis - you will some day, you know - and then after that into a butterfly ...* Turn into a Christ/Alice?

This resulted in a 143 pages entitled "Christ, Myth, and Fantasy - a Study of the Oxford Christians" - the world of C. S. Lewis, J. R. R. Tolkien, Charles Williams, and the seminal George MacDonald. As you can imagine, the books were once again easily reshaped into a Christian mythos.

From the questions of dualism posed by the splitting of the Godhead into Good and Evil (Dinah and the black and white kittens, becoming Humpty Dumpty and the black and red Queens) I went on to "prove" that the quintessential summary of the life and teachings of Jesus of Nazareth, his reception in Judea, and the gathering of the Gospels and the spread of early Christianity were to be found in Humpty's poem "I sent a message to the fish," the fish, of course, being an early Christian ikon.

It also went rather extensively into the realm of *Faerie,* which Carroll's preface to *Sylvie and Bruno* commented on (including the "eerie" state, halfway between that world and this), and where it stood in relation to those other worlds which are so near to our familiar one - the subconscious, the astral, the symbolic. I shall spare you the grisly details, but would like to quote from **J. R. R. Tolkien**'s "On Fairy Stories," as it is relevant:

Fairy stories are not, in normal English usage, stories

about fairies or elves, but about Fairy, that is Faerie, the realm or state in which fairies have their being. Faerie contains many things besides elves and fays, and besides dwarfs, witches, trolls, giants, or dragons: it holds the seas, the sun, the moon, the sky, and the earth, and all things that are in it: tree, and bird, water and stone, wine and bread, and ourselves, mortal men, when we are enchanted. ...

The definition of a fairy story depends upon the nature of Faerie, the Perilous Realm itself, and the air that blows in that country...Faerie cannot be caught in a net of words; for it is one of its qualities to be indescribable, though not imperceptible...

Faerie itself may perhaps be most nearly be translated by Magic - but its magic is of a peculiar power and mood (It) is deep and high and is filled with may things: all manner of birds and beasts are found there; shoreless seas and stars uncounted; beauty that is an enchantment, and an everpresent peril; both sorrow and joy as sharp as swords. In that land a man may count himself fortunate to have wandered, but its very richness and strangeness make dumb the traveller who would report it. And while he is there it is dangerous for him to ask too many questions, lest the gates shut and the key be lost. The fairy gold too often turns to withered leaves when it is brought away. All that I ask is that you, knowing these things, will receive my withered leaves, as a token that my hand at least once held a little of the gold.

Impenetrability! That's What I Say!

"Now you talk like a reasonable child," said Humpty Dumpty, looking very much pleased." I meant by 'impenetrability' that we've had enough of that subject, and it would be just as well if you'd mention what you mean to do next, as I suppose you don't mean to stop here all the rest of your life."

But since those salad days, as I stood deep in uffish thoughts, I have returned to the last refuge of the lover, the collecting of artifacts. In joining my father in this quest for ever more rare and interesting editions, translations, indexes, and memorabilia (ranging from original photography of Carroll to plastic Alice pencil sharpeners), I sometimes wonder for what it is we are really searching. Is it the first handwritten copy of *Alice's Adventures under Ground* to flow from the pen of Mr. Dodgson, or is even that only an *aide-mémoire* of a lovely afternoon on the Isis, and even that but a small point in eternity's bounty of the *Ur*-conscious mind?

I am particularly a collector of illustrators, for what *is* the use of a book without pictures of conversations? We also devote a certain amount of time to the Lewis Carroll Society (and, for a decade, to the West Coast Chapter) in order to meet fellow beachcombers along "such quantities of sand".

But always, faithfully, I return to the "Liddell with no answer," holding a few more withered leaves.

The wind has shifted once too often for me to know a hawk from a handsaw. *Alice* has been analyzed, satirized, inspected, dissected, gleaned, weaned, picked, pocked, rotated, quotated, and made to fit into more square holes than you could shake a spear at. She has been Kinboted now for five generations. I am guilty, too, dear, and will say no more.

Still she haunts me, phantomwise,
Alice moving under skies,
Never seen by waking eyes.

Chapter 17

The Poems in Alice in Wonderland

Fifty years ago the child world was made glad by the appearance of Lewis Carroll's Alice in Wonderland. It is a univeral story and so belongs to all time. It has never gone out of fashion and never will as long as children love wonder-stories and grown-ups have young hearts. But those who read the book when it was first published found in it a delight which the child of today misses.

Fifty years ago certain poems appeared in every reader and were read over and over again until the child was stupid indeed who did not unconciously learn them by heart. Today there is a new fashion in literature. Children are whirled from one supplementary reader to another, conning graceful rhymes and pretty stories all illustrated with artistic pictures, but the old things have passed away.

All the poems in Alice in Wonderland are parodies upon these once familiar rhymes. Scattered lines of the poems cling to the minds of older people; they remember being once familiar with them; they recognize the metre and can sometimes repeat two or three opening lines, but the complete poem eludes them, and the author they probably never did know.

The children of today do not know the verses at all, and as a parody ceases to be a parody without the original poem as a background, the trouble of gathering these originals seems worth while. After Alice had fallen down the rabbit-hole and had passded through her first transformation, when she shut up like a telescope until she was only ten inches high and then grew bigger and bigger until 'her head struck the roof of the hall', she became confused as to her identity.

To make sure of it, she tried to repeat a little poem which everybody in those days knew by heart, and to such children is was very funny when it cam out all wrong and she says,

How Doth The Little Crocodile
Lewis Carroll
How doth the little crocodile
Improve his shining tail,
And pour the waters of the Nile
On every golden scale!
How cheerfully he seems to grin,
How neatly spread his claws,
And welcome little fishes in
With gently smiling jaws!

when she though she was repeating that highly moral poem by Isaac Watts,

Against Idleness And Mischief
Isaac Watts
How doth the little busy bee
Improve each shining hour,
And gather honey all the day
From every opening flower!
How skillfully she builds her cell!
How neat she spreads the wax!
And labours hard to store it well
With the sweet food she makes.
In works of labour or of skill,
I would be busy too;
For Satan finds some mischief still
For idle hands to do.
In books, or work, or healthy play,
Let my first years be passed
That I may give for every day
Some good account at last.

Again, in her conversation with the Caterpillar, Alice told him that being so many different sizes in a day was very confusing, as he would find when he changed into a chrysalis and then into a butterfly.

She confessed that she could not remember things and told her experience with 'How doth the little busy bee'. The Caterpillar, wishing to test the matter, ordered her to say, 'You are old, Father William'. How well she succeeded will appear from comparing what she said with what she though she was going to say.

YOU ARE OLD, FATHER WILLIAM

'You are old, Father William,' the young man said,
'And your hair has become very white;
And yet you incessantly stand on your head -
Do you think, at your age, it is right?'
'In my youth,' Father William replied to his son,
'I feared it might injure the brain;
But, now that I'm perfectly sure I have none,
Why, I do it again and again.'
'You are old,' said the youth, 'as I mentioned before,
And have grown most uncommonly fat;
Yet you turned a back-somersault in at the door -
Pray, what is the reason of that?'
'In my youth,' said the sage, as he shook his grey locks,
'I kept all my limbs very supple
By the use of this ointment - one shilling the box -
Allow me to sell you a couple?'
'You are old,' said the youth, 'and your jaws are too weak
For anything tougher than suet;
Yet you finished the goose, with the bones and the beak -
Pray how did you manage to do it?'
'In my youth,' said his father, 'I took to the law,
And argued each case with my wife;
And the muscular strength, which it gave to my jaw,
Has lasted the rest of my life.'
'You are old,' said the youth, 'one would hardly suppose
That your eye was as steady as ever;
Yet you balanced an eel on the end of your nose -
What made you so awfully clever?'

'I have answered three questions, and that is enough,'
Said his father; 'don't give yourself airs!
Do you think I can listen all day to such stuff?
Be off, or I'll kick you down stairs!'

THE OLD MAN'S COMFORTS AND HOW HE GAINED THEM

'You are old, father William,' the young man cried,
'The few locks which are left you are grey;
You are hale, father William, a hearty old man;
Now tell me the reason, I pray.'
'In the days of my youth,' father William replied,
'I remember'd that youth would fly fast,
And Abus'd not my health and my vigour at first,
That I never might need them at last.'
'You are old, father William,' the young man cried,
'And pleasures with youth pass away.
And yet you lament not the days that are gone;
Now tell me the reason, I pray.'
'In the days of my youth,' father William replied,
'I remember'd that youth could not last;
I thought of the future, whatever I did,
That I never might grieve for the past.'
'You are old, father William,' the young man cried,
'And life must be hast'ning away;
You are cheerful and love to converse upon death;
Now tell me the reason, I pray.'
'I am cheeful, young man,' father William replied,
'Let the cause thy attention engage;
In the days of my youth I remember's my God.
And He hath not forgotten my age.'

The Duchess's song to the pig baby.

SPEAK ROUGHLY

Speak roughly to your little boy,
And beat him when he sneezes:
He only does it to annoy,
Because he knows it teases.

Chorus
Wow! wow! wow!
I speak severely to my boy,
I beat him when he sneezes;
For he can thoroughly enjoy
The pepper when he pleases!

is an absurdity in itself, but a much greater one when contrasted with its serious parallel. There is evidently some uncertainty as to the author of this poem, for it occasionally appears as anonymous, but is generally credited as below.

SPEAK GENTLY

Speak gently! it is better far
To rule by love than fear
Speak gently; let no harsh word mar
The good we may do here!
Speak gently to the little child!
Its love be sure to gain;
Teach it in accents soft and mild;
It may not long remain.
Speak gently to the young, for they
Will have enough to bear;
Pass through this life as best they may,
'Tis full of anxious care!
Speak gently to the aged one,
Grieve not the care-worn heart;
Whose sands of life are nearly run,
Let such in peace depart!
Speak gently, kindly to the poor;
Let no harsh tone be heard;
They have enough they must endure,
Without an unkind word!
Speak gently to the erring; know
The must have toiled in vain;
Pechance unkindness made them so;
Oh, win them back again.
Speak gently; Love doth whisper low
The vows that true hearts bind;

And gently Friendship's accents flow;
Affection's voice is kind.
Speak gently; 'tis a little thing
Dropped in the heart's deep well;
The good, the joy, that it may bring,
Eternity shall tell.

'Twinkle, twinkle, little bat' which the Hatter said that he sang at the concert given by the Queen of Hearts, is the most familiarly suggestive of them all.

THE BAT

Twinkle, twinkle, little bat
How I wonder what you're at!
Up above the world you fly
Like a tea-tray in the sky.

Jane and Ann Taylor were two English sisters who wrote together, publishing their poems under such titles as Original Poems for Infant Minds and Hymns for Infant Minds. Jane was supposed to have written most of them, and this one carries her signature.

THE STAR

Twinkle, twinkle, little star,
How I wonder what you are!
Up above the world so high,
Like a diamond in the sky.
When the blazing sun is gone,
When he nothing shines upon,
Then you show your little light,
Twinkle, twinkle, all the night.
Then the traveller in the dark,
Thanks you for your tiny spark:
He could not see which way to go,
If you did not twinkle so.
In the dark blue sky you keep,
And often through my curtains peep,
For you never shut your eye
Till the sun is in the sky.

As your bright and tiny spark
Lights the traveller in the dark,
Though I know not what you are,
Twinkle, twinkle, little star.

Mary Howitt wrote 'The Spider and the Fly', the first stanza of which originally read,

THE SPIDER AND THE FLY

'Will you walk into my parlour?' said the spider to the fly,
''Tis the prettiest little parlour that ever you did spy,
The way into my parlour is up a winding stair,
And I've got many curious things to show when you are there.'
'Oh, no, no,' said the little fly, 'to ask me is in vain,
For whoever goes up your winding stair can ne'er come down again.'

This poem has suffered various modifications and several versions appear in print, but the quoted stanza is doubtless from the original one. The beat of the metre is very perfectly kept in the Mock Turtle's

A WHITING AND A SNAIL

'Will you walk a little faster?' said a whiting to a snail.
'There's a porpoise close behind us, and he's treading on my tail.
See how eagerly the lobsters and the turtles all advance!
They are waiting on the shingle - will you come and join the dance?
Will you, won't you, will you, won't you, will you join the dance?
Will you, won't you, will you, won't you, won't you join the dance?
'You can really have no notion how delightful it will be
When they take us up and throw us, with the lobsters, out to sea!'
But the snail replied 'Too far, too far!' and gave a look askance-
Said he thanked the whiting kindly, but he would not join the dance.
Would not, could not, would not, could not, would not join the

dance.

Would not, could not, would not, could not, could not join the dance.

'What matters it how far we go?' his scaly friend replied.
'There is another shore, you know, upon the other side.
The further off from England the nearer is to France -
Then turn not pale, beloved snail, but come and join the dance.
Will you, won't you, will you, won't you, will you join the dance?
Will you, won't you, will you, won't you, won't you join the dance?'

''Tis the voice of the lobster', which Alice repeats at the gruff order of the Gryphon, returns to Isaac Watts. Probably no poem in the book is further removed from modern thought and modern literary ideals than this one.

THE LOBSTER

'Tis the voice of the Lobster; I heard him declare,
'You have baked me too brown, I must sugar my hair.'
As a duck with its eyelids, so he with his nose
Trims his belt and his buttons, and turns out his toes.
When the sands are all dry, he is gay as a lark,
And will talk in contemptuous tones of the Shark,
But, when the tide rises and sharks are around,
His voice has a timid and tremulous sound.

THE SLUGGARD

'Tis the voice of the sluggard; I heard him complain,
'You have wak'd me too soon, I must slumber again.'
As the door on its hinges, so he on his bed,
Turns his sides and his shoulders and his heavy head.
'A little more sleep, and a little more slumber;'
Thus he wastes half his days, and his hours without number,
And when he gets up, he sits folding his hands,
Or walks about sauntering, or trifling he stands.
I pass'd by his garden, and saw the wild brier,
The thorn and the thistle grow broader and higher;
The clothes that hang on him are turning to rags;

And his money still wastes thill he starves or he begs.
I made him a visit, still hoping to find
That he took better care for improving his mind;
He told me his dreams, talked of eating and drinking;
But he scarce reads his Bible and never loves thinking.
Said I then to my heart, 'Here's a lesson for me,
This man's but a picture of what I might be;
But thanks to my friends for their care in my breeding,
Who taught be betimes to love working and reading.'

'Beautiful Soup' is a very funny parody upon a popular song of the time that runs as follows:

STAR OF THE EVENING

Beautiful star in heav'n so bright,
Softly falls thy silb'ry light,
As thou movest from earth afar,
Star of the evening, beautiful star.
Chorus
Beautiful star,
Beautiful star,
Star of the evening, beautiful star.
In fancy's eye thou seem'st to say,
Follow me, come from earth away.
Upward thy spirit's pinions try,
To realms of love beyond the sky.
Shine on, oh star of love diving,
And may our soul's affection twine
Around thee as thou movest afar,
Star of the twilight, beautiful star.

The most delightful part of the parody is the division of the words in the refrain in imitation of the approved method of singing the song, with its holds and its sentimental stress on the last word.

SOUP OF THE EVENING

Beautiful Soup, so rich and green,
Waiting in a hot tureen!
Who for such dainties would not stoop?

Soup of the evening, beautiful Soup!
Soup of the evening, beautiful Soup!
Beau - ootiful Soo - oop!
Beau - ootiful Soo - oop!
Soo - oop of the e - e - evening,
Beautiful, beautiful Soup!
Beautiful Soup! Who cares for fish,
Game, or any other dish?
Who would not give all else for two p
ennyworth only of beautiful Soup?
Pennyworth only of beautiful Soup?
Beau - ootiful Soo - oop!
Beau - ootiful Soo - oop!
Soo - oop of the e - e - evening,
Beautiful, beautiful Soup!

The poem upon which the last parody is based is not as well known as most of the other, the first two lines being the only ones often quoted.

ALICE GRAY

She's all my fancy painted her, she's lovely, she's divine,
But her heart it is another's, she never can be mine.
Yet loved I as man never loved, a love without decay,
Oh, my heart, my heart is breaking for the love of Alice Gray.
Her dark brown hair is braided o'er a brow of spotless white,
Her soft blue eye now languishes, now flashes with delight;
Her hair is braided not for me, the eye is turned away,
Yet my heart, my heart is breaking for the love of Alice Gray.
I've sunk beneath the summer's sun, and trembled in the blast.
But my pilgrimage is nearly done, the weary conflict's past;
And when the green sod wraps my grave, may pity haply say,
Oh, his heart, his heart is broken for the love of Alice Gray!

Carroll's first writing followed the wording in the original first version:

She's all my fancy painted him
(I make no idle boast);
If he or you had lost a limb,

Which would have suffered most?
They told me you had been to her,
And mentioned me to him:
She gave me a good character,
But said I could not swim.
He sent them word I had not gone
(We know it to be true):
If she should push the matter on,
What would become of you?
I gave her one, they gave him two,
You gave us three or more;
They all returned from him to you,
Though they were mine before.
If I or she should chance to be
Involved in this affair,
He trusts to you to set them free,
Exactly as we were.
My notion was that you had been
(Before she had this fit)
An obstacle that came between
Him, and ourselves, and it.
Don't let him know she liked them best,
For this must ever be
A secret, kept from all the rest,
Between yourself and me.

But for some unknown reason he dropped the first stanza, beginning with the second, thus obliterating all evident resemblance between parody and original.

The parody is not the highest form of art and not the most skillful form of verse, but Lewis Carroll has done these eight so well that doubtless some of them will live after the originals are forgotten.

Even now, in order to search them out, it has been necessary to beat the dust from many a forgotten volume in a library's unmolested corners, but the nonsense rhymes they suggested are jingling upon the tounges of children the wide world over and mingling with their happy laughter.

ALICE'S ADVENTURE IN WONDERLAND / THROUGH THE LOOKING-GLASS

In Alice's Adventure in Wonderland and Through the Looking-Glass the author uses diluted and ineffectual violence, to better entertain his young readers. For something to be truly violent it needs to have two parts, one part is a physical force and the other is damage or injury. The violent acts committed by characters through out the two stores lack the aspect of damage and injury, making the violence watered down and ineffective.

Some examples of this diluted violence are, the fight between the Red Knight and White Knight, the fight between the Lion and the Unicorn, and the cook's actions towards the Duchess. The ineffectual violence allows the author to preserve the unrealistic appearance of both the Wonderland and the Looking-Glass world, from which the pains and injures of reality are forever exiled.

A distinct example of the author's usage of diluted violence to entertain his young readers is shown in the instance of the fight between the Red and White Knight. It is well known, that little kids love fairy tales with knights and kings. For most children at some point in their childhood have imagined themselves being a knight, fighting others knights and rescuing princesses in distress.

This childish craving to become a knight and to do knightly deeds is all to natural. The author uses this desire for petty violence in the scene with the two Knights. Like the knights of fairy tales these two fighters are dressed in full armor and are eager to fight. They attack one another with full force, yet here the author decided to alter the appearance of their violent actions to the reader. For he does not allow them to fight as normal knights should, but gives them nutty features that children can find amusing and even relate to. In the story Alice describes the knights actions by saying,"if one Knight hit the other, he knocked him off his hours; and , if he misses, he tumbles off himself, they hold their clubs with their arms as if they were Punch and Judy...and they always fell on their heads".

The actions of these knights are so juvenile that it makes one believe that the knights were supposed to represent children fighting. Their use of their clubs does not show a violent intention, but more of a playful one, which is further supported by them constantly falling head first from their horses. It is clear that their seemingly violent actions were not intended to cause harm. This is shown in their actions during the battle as well as by them being totally uninjured and unaffected at the end of the fight.

Alice says when they finished fighting that,"they shook hand and the Red Knight mounted and galloped off". The use of diluted and ineffectual violence in this scene makes the actions of the Knights appear childlike, and being so, they become more appealing to the author's younger audience. The author's desire to appeal to his young audience through the use of diluted violence is shown in the fight between the Lion and the Unicorn. To understand this scene one needs to look at a child's mentality towards lions and unicorns, because the story is meant to be seen by children. To most kids, a lion is a powerful animal that in most of the stores plays a role of king of the jungle.

The unicorn on the other hand is looked upon as a fabled creature, represented as a horse with a single horn on forehead. These two animals are both considered by children to be powerful and capable of violent acts. Being that the lion is large, has claws and teeth, and the unicorn has a large, sharp horn. It should then come as no surprise that the author shows these two powerful animals in a violent setting. The author describes the fight between them by saying,"they came in sight of a great crowd, in the middle of which the Lion and Unicorn were fighting, they were in such a cloud of dust that Alice could not make our which was which". The Hatter then adds that,"each of them has been down eighty-seven times".

Yet, these seemingly violent acts are really ineffective, because the Lion and the Unicorn are not effected by the fighting. They do not show any signs of physical damage and the second the fighting stops their thoughts tern towards food. The author could have made the fighting more violent and effective, but he could not dear to do so, because he had given these two character childlike personalities, and if physical pain was alluded to, it would appear as if children were being hurt. Little children are known for fighting amongst themselves for no particular reason.

The Lion and the Unicorn in the story are also fighting for nothing. In the beginning the readier is told that they are fighting for the crown, but when Alice asks the White King if the one who wins would get the crown the King says, "dear no! what an idea". Another aspect in the behaviour of these two creatures that alludes to them being modeled after children is, the speed with which they alter themselves. Most children are known to become board and easily swayed from any action that they have been doing for a long time. This swaying of emotions and desires also took place in both the Lion and Unicorn.

After fighting for what seemed to be a very long time these two combatants instantaneously just stopped fighting as if it was all just a game and shifted their focus from fighting to planing what food they would want to eat. Yet, the most distinctive action on the part of these two creatures that gives away that they are supposed to represent children is, the Lion calling the Unicorn a "chicken".

Name calling is something that is considered a childrens' speciality, and by name calling the two characters shows themselves truly childlike. By making the Lion and Unicorn so infantile, the author handicapped himself, because of it he is unable to use real violence, but only ineffectual violence.

Yet, the ineffectual violence allows him to combine the childlike aspects of the characters with the seemingly violent actions, making the scene both relatable and interesting to his young readers.

Through both stories the author uses ineffectual violence, especially in the instance of the cook and the Duchess. The actions of the cook towards the Duchess at first glance appear to be very violent.

The the author described her actions by saying,"at once [the cook] set to work throwing everything within her reach at the duchess and the baby the fire-iron came first; then followed a shower of sauce -pans, plates and dishes".

If left as is, this would be considered a scene with real violence. Yet, knowing that he needs to appease a younger audience and does not allow real violence to take place for it would shatter his magical sanctuary from reality.

Pain is one of the most powerful sensations in real life, and by showing pain of any kind the author would have brought a strong sense of unwanted reality into the stories.

His stories were designed to provide an escape for kids from the real world and its hardships. What bigger hardship is there then pain. So to prevent the destruction of his wonderful world, he added this to the scene, "the Duchess took no notice of them even when they hit her".

By telling the reader that the violent actions of the cook did not cause any pain or discomfort, the author is able to preserve his fanciful universe.

By implementing ineffectual violence rather then real violence the author was able to both use violent actions to make the story more interesting for his young readers and still preserve its surreal appearance.

It is clear why Lewis Carroll only used the ineffectual type of violence thorough out his stories.

The books main audience was meant to be children, especially young children. If ever a person is able to look at the daily actions of young kids one would probable see a lot of violent tendencies. Little kids are known to fight amongst themselves, to throw things when they are angry or craving attention, and most of the time they are injured doing these violent activities.

In these acts of childish violence the children only have one true internal fear, the fear of pain and bodily injury. That is of course the only deterrent that checks them in their violent perversions. In making the magical worlds of his stores, Lewis Carroll wanted to bring pleasure to children, and what better way is there of doing so as by taking out the only thing that stands between them and the pleasure of childish violence, pain.

By taking out the aspect of pain from all of the violent actions of the characters, as in the instances of the two Knights, the Unicorn and the Lion, and the Cook and the Duchess, he was able to dilute the violence so that it turned the Wonderland into a childrens' Utopia. A place where their playfully violent actions would not have a painful reaction. This was the underlaying goal of the author when he inserted the ineffectual violence into the stories. He was hoping that by doing so he could in some way create a magical escape from reality for his young readers, and by all means he was very successful in accomplishing that goal with the help of diluted violence.

Chapter 18

Chronology of Works of Lewis Carroll

Containing books and some pamphlets:

1845 - Useful and Instructive Poetry published in 1954
1848 - The Rectory Magazine published 1975
1850-1853 - The Rectory Umbrella published with Mischmasch in 1932
1855-1862 - Mischmasch
1856-1857 - The Train
1858 - The Fifth Book of Euclid Treated Algebraically
1860 - A Syllabus of Plane Algebraic Geometry, Systematically Aranged with Formal Definitions, Postulates, and Axioms
1860 - Notes on the First Two Books of Euclid, Designed for Candidates for Responsions
1864 - Alice's Adventures Under Ground Published in 1886
1865 - Alice's Adventures in Wonderland
1866 - Condensation of Determinants, Being a New and Brief Method for Computing their Arithmetic Values
1867 - Russian Journal published privately in 1928 and commercially in 1935
1867 - An Elementary Treatise on Determinants with their Application to Simultaneous Linear Equations and Algebraic Geometry
1867 - Bruno's Revenge published in 1924
1868 - The Fifth Book of Euclid Treated Algebraically,

so far as it Relates to Commensurable Magnitudes
1869 - Phantasmagoria and Other Poems
1872 - *Through the Looking-Glass, and What Alice Found There*
1873 - *The Enunciations of Euclid I-VI, Together with Questions on the Definitions, Postulates, Axioms, &c.*
1873 - *The Vision of the Three T's*
1876 - *The Hunting of the Snark*
1879 - *Euclid and His Modern Rivals*
1882 - *Euclid, Books I, II*
1883 - *Rhyme? and Reason?*
1885 - *Supplement to Euclid and His Modern Rivals*
1885 - *A Tangled Tale*
1886 - *The Game of Logic privately published. Commercially published in 1887*
1886 - *Alice's Adventures Under Ground*
1889 - *The Nursery Alice*
1889 - *Sylvie and Bruno*
1893 - *Sylvie and Bruno Concluded*
1896 - *Symbolic Logic, Part I*
1898 - *Three Sunsets and Other Poems*

Posthumously Published Works:

1907 - *Feeding the Mind*
1932 - *For the Train*
1932 - *The Rectory Umbrella and Mischmasch*
1935 - *The Russian Journal and Other Selections from the Works*
1954 - *Useful and Instructive Poetry*
1975 - *The Rectory Magazine*
1977 - *The Wasp in a Wig*

Bibliography

Bowman, Isa (1899), The Story of Lewis Carroll, Told by the Real Alice in Wonderland, London: Dent

Cohen, Morton N. (1995), Lewis Carroll: A Biography, London: Macmillan. (ISBN 0-333-62926-4)

Collingwood, Stuart Dodgson (1898), The Life and Letters of Lewis Carroll, London: T. Fisher Unwin

Graham-Smith, Darien (2005), Contextualising Carroll, University of Wales, Bangor: PhD Thesis

Huxley, Francis (1976), The Raven and the Writing Desk. (ISBN 0-06-012113-0).

Kelly, Richard, Lewis Carroll. Boston: Twayne Publishers, 1990.

Kelly, Richard, Alice's Adventures in Wonderland.

Leach, Karoline (1999), In the Shadow of the Dreamchild: A New Understanding of Lewis Carroll, London: Peter Owen Publishers

Lennon, Florence Becker (1947), Lewis Carroll, London: Cassell

Reed, Langford (1932), The Life of Lewis Carroll, London: W. and G. Foyle

Sunghyun Kim, 'Political Unconscious in Fantastic Narrative: Lewis Carroll's Alice's Adventures in Wonderland(Korean)', Yonsei University Graduate School, 2005

Taylor, Alexander L., Knight (1952), The White Knight, Edinburgh: Oliver and Boyd

Taylor, Roger & Wakeling, Edward, Lewis Carroll, Photographer. Princeton University Press, 2002. (ISBN

0691074437). Catalogues nearly every Carroll photograph known to be still in existence.

Wilson, Robin (2008). Lewis Carroll in Numberland: His Fantastical Mathematical Logical Life. London: Allen Lane. ISBN 9780713997576.

Wullschläger, Jackie, Inventing Wonderland, (ISBN 0-7432-2892-8) — also looks at Edward Lear (of the "nonsense" verses), J. M. Barrie (Peter Pan), Kenneth Grahame (The Wind in the Willows), and A. A. Milne (Winnie-the-Pooh).

n.n., Dreaming in Pictures: The Photography of Lewis Carroll. Yale University Press & SFMOMA, 2004. (Places Carroll firmly in the art photography tradition.)